IMAGES
of America

FREEPORT

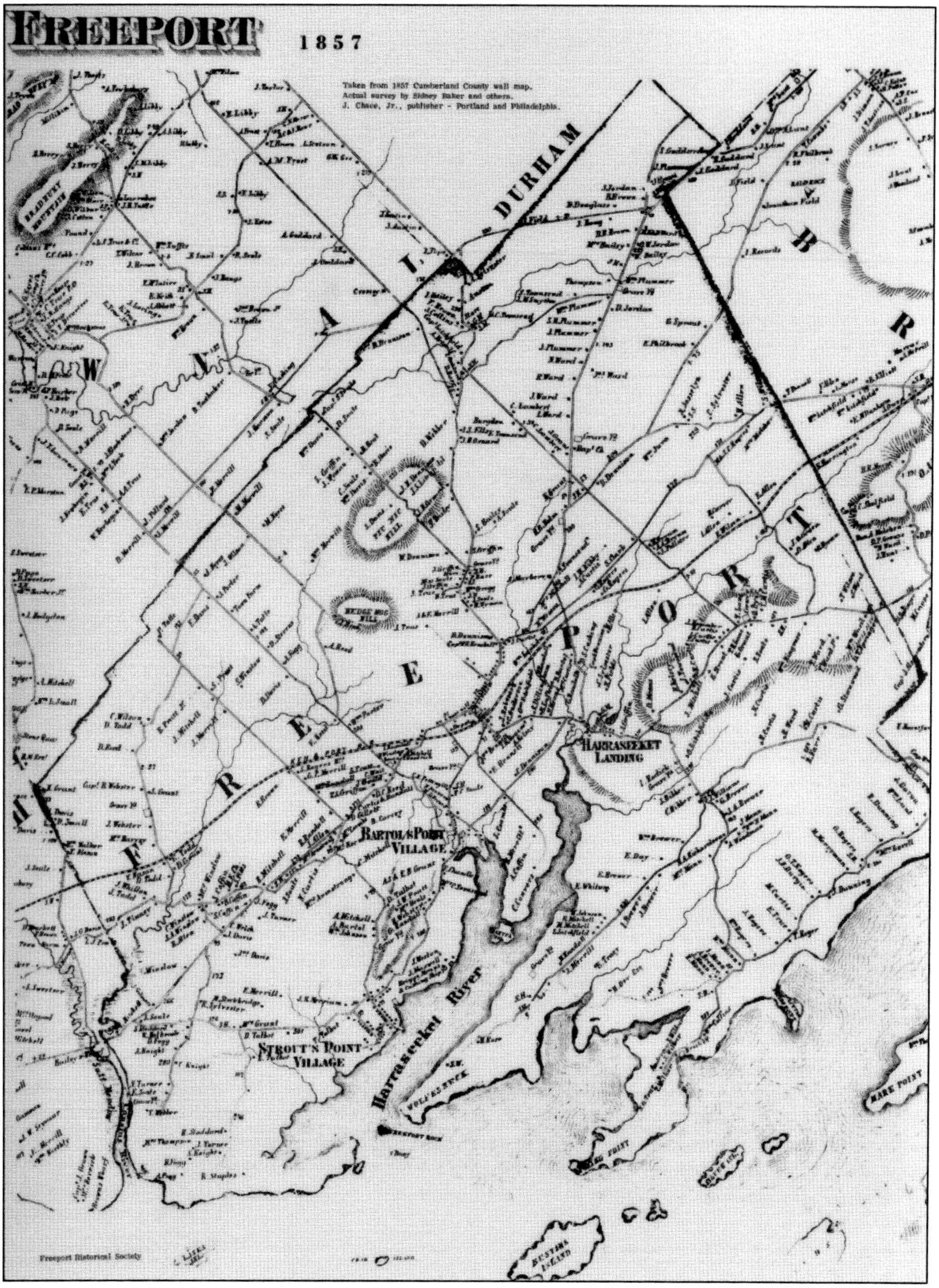

Freeport in 1857, from the *Cumberland County Atlas*.

IMAGES
of America

FREEPORT

The Freeport Historical Society
Freeport, Maine

ARCADIA
PUBLISHING

ISBN 978-0-7385-4507-3

Published by Arcadia Publishing
Charleston, South Carolina

Printed in the United States of America

Library of Congress Catalog Card Number: 2006920723

For all general information contact Arcadia Publishing at:
Telephone 843-853-2070
Fax 843-853-0044
E-mail sales@arcadiapublishing.com
For customer service and orders:
Toll-Free 1-888-313-2665

Visit us on the Internet at www.arcadiapublishing.com

Contents

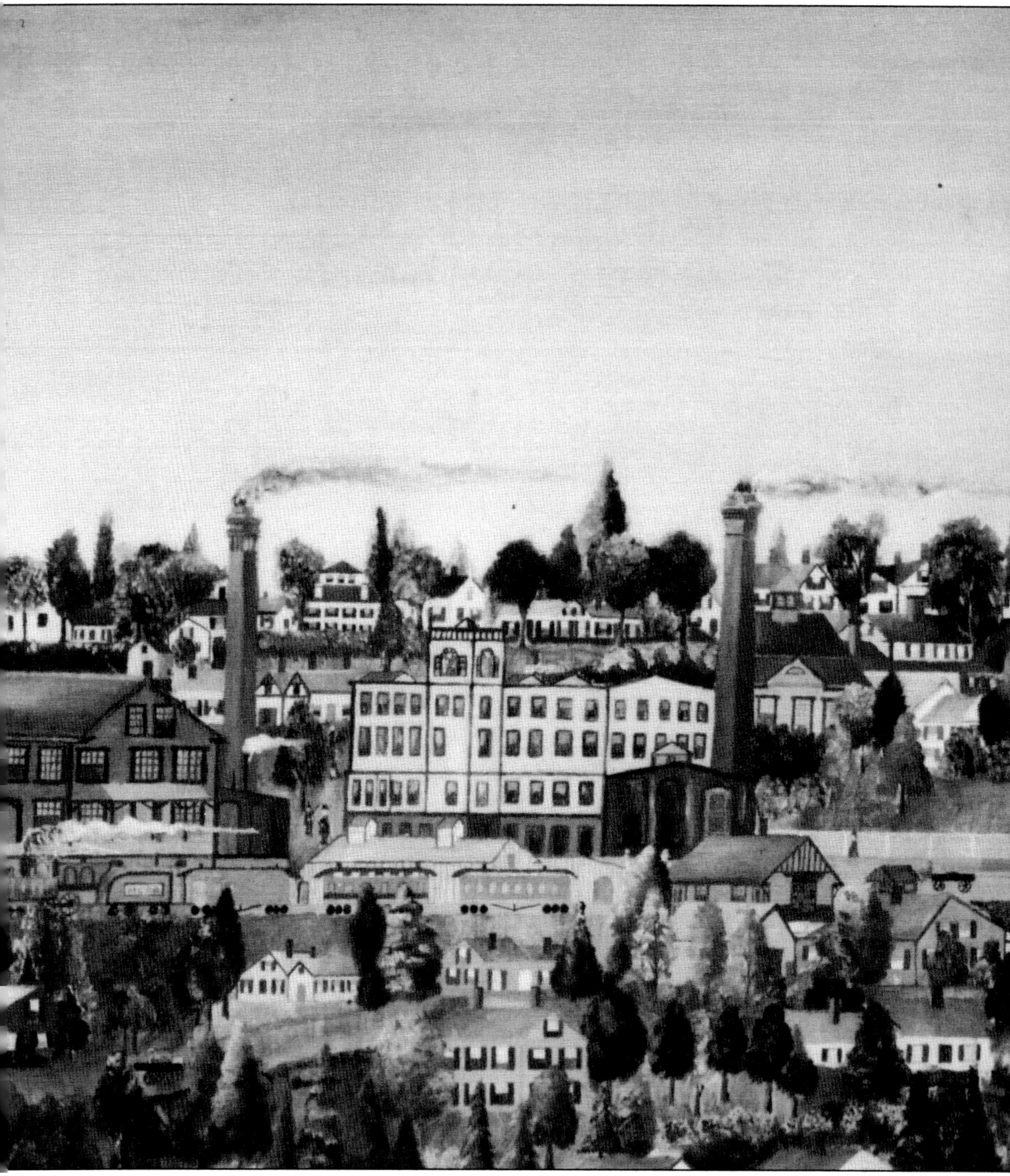

This panoramic oil painting of Freeport from Torrey Ridge Hill was painted by James L. Berkeley in 1946. It was a copy of a painting originally done by George T. Griffin in 1887, now owned

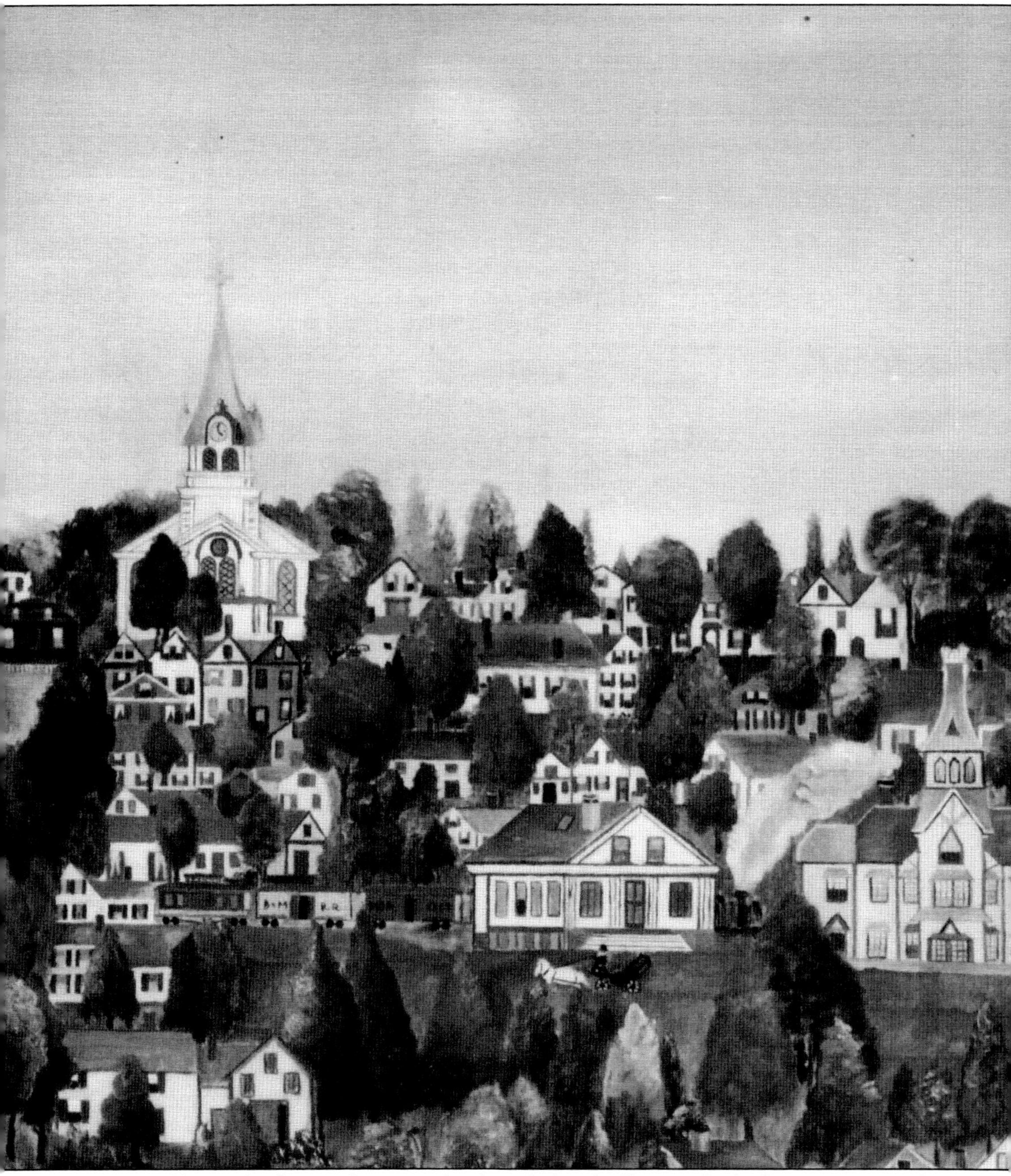

by Colby College. The factory, houses, school, and church illustrate both the economic and residential growth in Freeport Village at the turn of the century.

Introduction

The Fourth of July has always been well celebrated in Freeport by a parade and speeches, and in 1889 the holiday also marked the one-hundredth anniversary of Freeport's independence from North Yarmouth. For the occasion, Henry Koopman, native son, writer, and university librarian, read this poem:

Beloved town, with gladness we discern
How fortune smiles on thee at every turn.
And trust that all its present favor brings
Is but the promise of still goodlier things;
Yet on this day, the fullness of thy years
One word the poet brings not free from fears
Dear home town, let men ever call thee so;
Guard well the font from which thy virtues flow,
Only thy homes can rear thee manly sons
And daughters gentle, as thine earlier ones
Can bring thee love like ours from future men.
A land of Homes amid the storms to fall
No fear be thine if thou hast homes for all.

The poem is found in *Three Centuries of Freeport, Maine*, by Florence G. Thurston and Harmon S. Cross which was published in 1940 and which gracefully weaves history and reminiscences together and puts into print those things everyone is sure will never be forgotten. That 1889 Fourth of July celebration, like all similar celebrations in Freeport to this day, followed a Main Street route with its focus in Freeport Village where Bow Street enters. The street was widened here in the eighteenth century to allow tall mast timbers to make the corner as they were moved from the forest to the shore for shipment.

When the new town of Freeport was "set off" from North Yarmouth in 1789, it finally had enough families to support its own church. Although settlement had begun in the late seventeenth century, the pace accelerated in the eighteenth century. Access from the Corner to Porter's Landing was completed in 1770 when the County Road was built from the Landing to the Androscoggin River in Durham along today's Route 136. It was the sea and the character of this stretch of upper Casco Bay, with its deeply indented peninsulas that frame the Harraseeket River, that made continued settlement attractive. The sea was the highway until the coming of the railroad in 1849; today the sea is the playground as well as home to the local fishing industry. Where ships were once built at South Freeport there is today a flourishing marina; the 1830s fish packing plant has been replaced by the Harraseeket Yacht Club.

The three villages which today form the National Register Harraseeket Historic District, Mast Landing, Porter's Landing, and South Freeport, were for the first half of the nineteenth century self-contained. Mast timbers cut in the adjacent forests were shipped from Mast Landing at the head of tide of the Harraseeket River. Industries in this small village included a brickyard, a grist mill, a sawmill, and a fulling mill—all powered by the dammed-up stream which fed into the estuary. Salt hay was harvested from the marshes; there was modest shoe manufacturing and woodworking; and there were both a store and a school. Upper Mast Landing Road which connects to present-day Route 1 shows on the eighteenth-century DeBarres chart. Headstone carver Noah Pratt lived on nearby Pleasant Hill Road and made many of the early stones in several local cemeteries. The Pettengill saltbox house, on its remaining 140 acres near Mast Landing, is on a true salt water farm. It is owned and cared for by the Freeport Historical Society.

Porter's Landing was the port for Freeport before the arrival of the railroad and it served as a goods conduit as far inland as the Androscoggin River in Durham. Seward Porter's shipyard, established in 1782, was the site where the famous privateer *Dash* was launched during the War of 1812. She was built for speed on the coastal run to the Caribbean islands. After extraordinary fortune privateering, she set out early in 1815 with three Porter sons and a crew of sixty and was lost with all hands in a gale. In another twenty years, the shipyard was acquired by Rufus Soule, a prolific shipbuilder: his last, the *Daniel L. Choate*, was launched in 1859. Like Mast Landing, this village had its own industries; a saltworks, a brickyard, and a crab meat factory; and it is also similar in retaining a grouping of Federal and Greek Revival-style dwellings with a cemetery which records names of local families.

The four shipyards in South Freeport, the largest of the villages, capitalized on the deep water, and attracted the necessary artisans and labor force. Fishing, canning, and farming contributed to the economy. The concentration of early-to-mid-nineteenth-century houses attests to the prosperity of the village during this period. The last ship of this era was launched in 1880, with a brief revival of wooden boat building during World War I and World War II. The Casco Castle Hotel, built in 1903, was reached by a newly built trolley line and provided amusements and accommodations for day visitors and vacationers. The wooden hotel burned in 1914, but the stone tower remains a landmark.

Freeport Corner, at least until the coming of the railroad in 1849, was an inland village known as a farming and trading center. Its identity became fixed after the Civil War with the gradual introduction of manufacturing. However, as the architecture attests, there were stores and professional services, as well as many handsome dwellings from the early period. The Harrington House, owned by the Freeport Historical Society, was built on Main Street of brick c. 1830 by a trader, Enoch Harrington, who was in business with his father-in-law, Nathan Nye. Sea captain Josiah A. Mitchell acquired his father's house on upper Main Street, built c. 1804, nine years before his famous voyage on the *Hornet* in 1866. What began as a trip around the Horn to San Francisco became a tale of forty-three days survival in life boats which traveled 4,000 miles to land on Hawaii with all hands alive.

Freeport retained the size and feel of a small town while turning out a great deal of manufactured goods during the 1870s and 1880s because much of the work was done at home. Shipments of material for men's and boys' clothing came from New York and Boston to be made into garments by women and girls. In the old Oxnard Block there were only twelve employees in the shop; the other eighty worked at home. Life, in fact, was sustained then as now by piecing together several jobs. Perhaps the most colorful exemplar of this model—and an important developer of nineteenth century Freeport—was E.B. Mallet. Because of a large inheritance, he left Pownal for Freeport where he bought land, built buildings, and developed sources for building materials in granite quarries, a saw mill, and a brickyard, as well as food production in a grist mill, energy in a coal yard, and consumer goods in a general store. The large shoe factory he built launched Freeport into an industry which persists, although in diminished form. His factory buildings were, in turn, occupied by companies such as A.W. Shaw, where the first telephone was installed in 1904. Mallet, not surprisingly, was given the right to develop the water district in 1891 when he laid 14,400 feet of pipe and installed eighteen hydrants. Mallet was the chairman of Freeport's celebration of the centennial of Maine statehood in 1920 which included ball games, a free clambake, "pictures" and dancing at the Nordica Theater, and a lecture at the Baptist church by Captain (later Admiral) Donald B. MacMillan, renowned arctic explorer and graduate of Freeport High School.

The man in charge of publicity for the centennial was Guy Bean, brother of L.L. Bean, the outstanding entrepreneur of the generation after Mallet. L.L. and G.C. Bean ran the Walkover Shoe store in the Davis Block, across Main Street from the future L. L. Bean's. The design of the Maine Hunting Shoe by L. L. Bean set into motion his energetic and practical imagination. Bean was canny enough to understand the importance of the automobile and its effect on sportsmen and at the same time appreciate the possibilities of selling by catalogue. Bean first occupied the upper floors of the Warren Block, the site of the present retail store, before 1920. Many people still remember getting into Bean's by way of an exterior stairway, even at midnight when the twenty-four-hour-a-day policy began in 1951.

Freeport's awareness of its history crystallized with the founding of the Freeport Historical Society in 1969. The completion of an inventory of historic structures in 1977 led to the establishment of two National Register Historic Districts, one for part of Main Street and the other for the three historic villages. Many dwellings, churches, the B.H. Bartol Library, old schoolhouses, and the Soldiers and Sailors Monument visually memorialize the industrial era. The old railroad depot is gone, and the car barn and trolley tracks have disappeared as well as several historic houses. For these aspects of the past, the many local photographers and the "savers" who gave archival material to the Freeport Historical Society must be appreciated.

Patricia Anderson
July 1996

One

Early Freeport

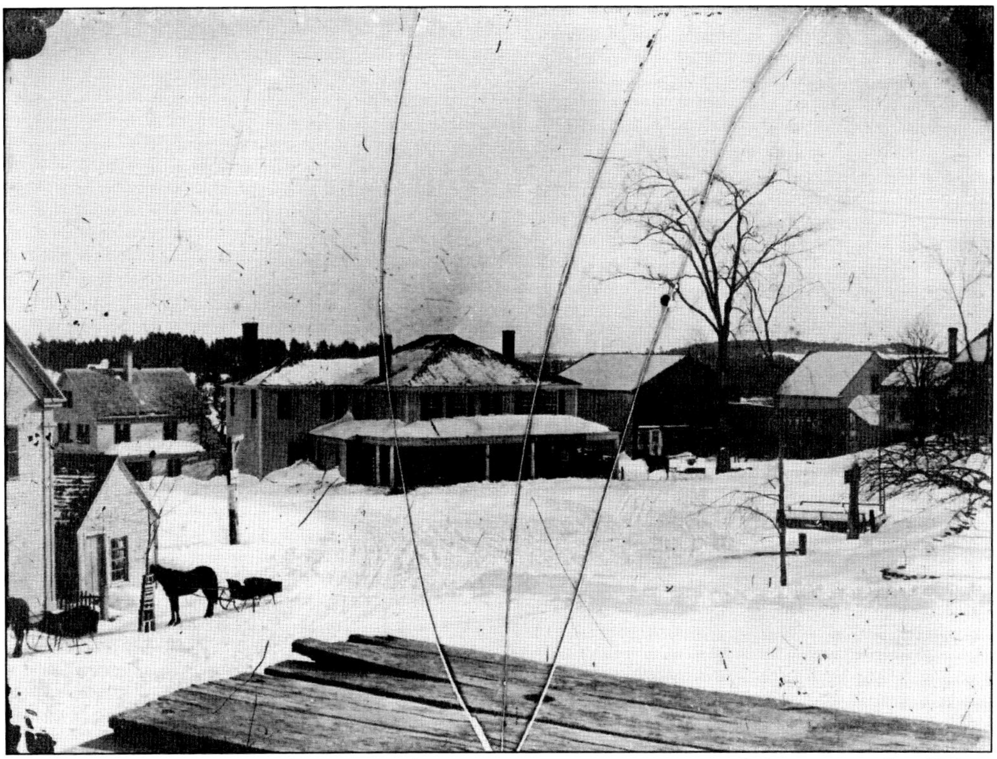

The village which is now the center of town activities grew up around the crossroads of Main and Bow Streets, pictured here between 1860 and 1871, then referred to as Freeport Square. One of the landmarks on the Square was Holbrook's Block, known successively as the Bliss Tavern and the Patterson Block. Built as his residence by Freeport's first minister, Reverend Alfred Johnson, it was later run as a tavern by Major Thomas Means and succeeding owners were Nathaniel Josselyn and Samuel Bliss. In this photograph the tavern had been replaced by Thing & Litchfield, one of three general stores in Freeport during that period.

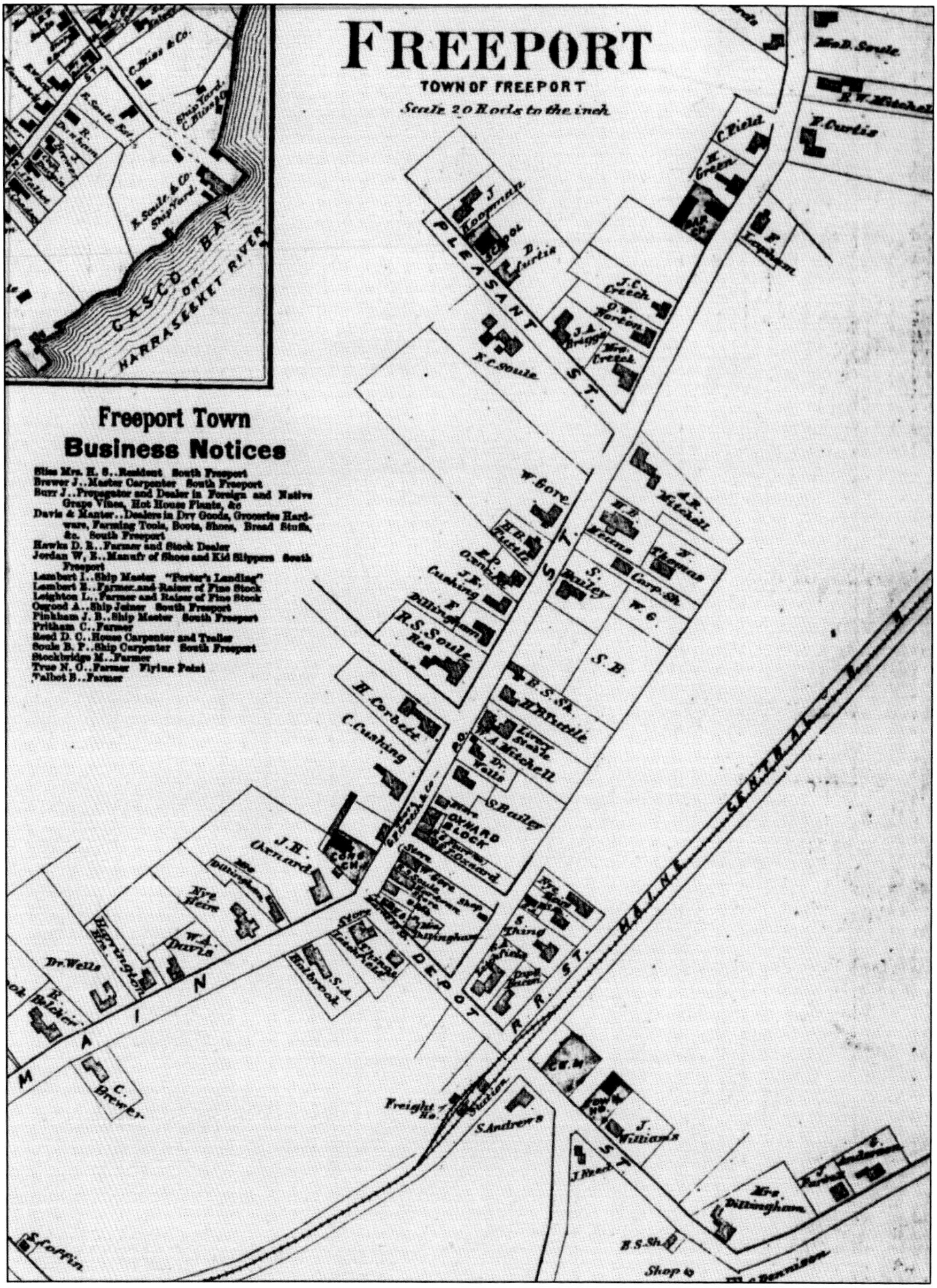

The 1871 map gives the names of the businesses and residences on Main Street. Bow Street, then called Depot Street, with Thing & Litchfield on one corner and a harness shop on the other, was considered to be the town square. It is said that the unusual shape of this intersection is directly related to the mast trading of the eighteenth century, when huge white pines were cut to be sent to England and the large area at the corner of Bow Street and Main Street was necessary to safely swing these logs as the turn was made on their way to Mast Landing.

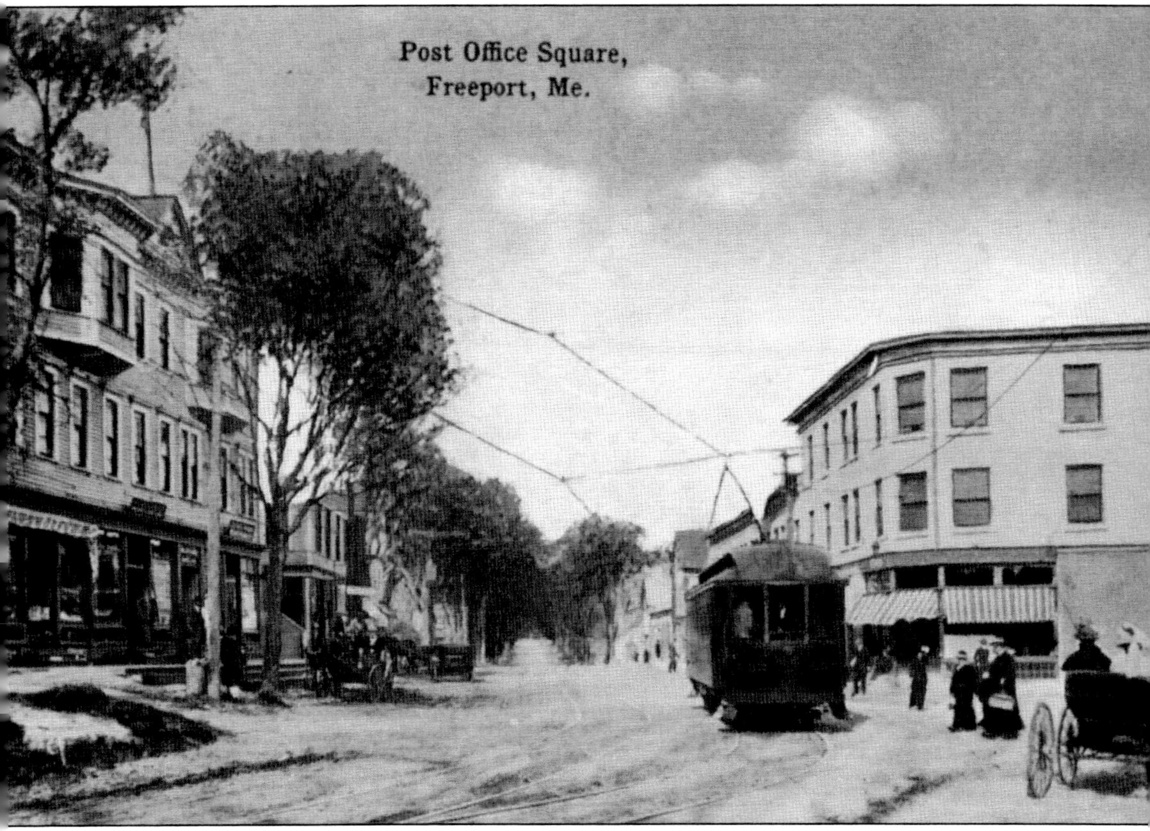

Freeport Square, also referred to as Post Office Square, is shown in this *c.* 1910 photograph featuring the trolley car, a popular mode of transport during the early part of the twentieth century.

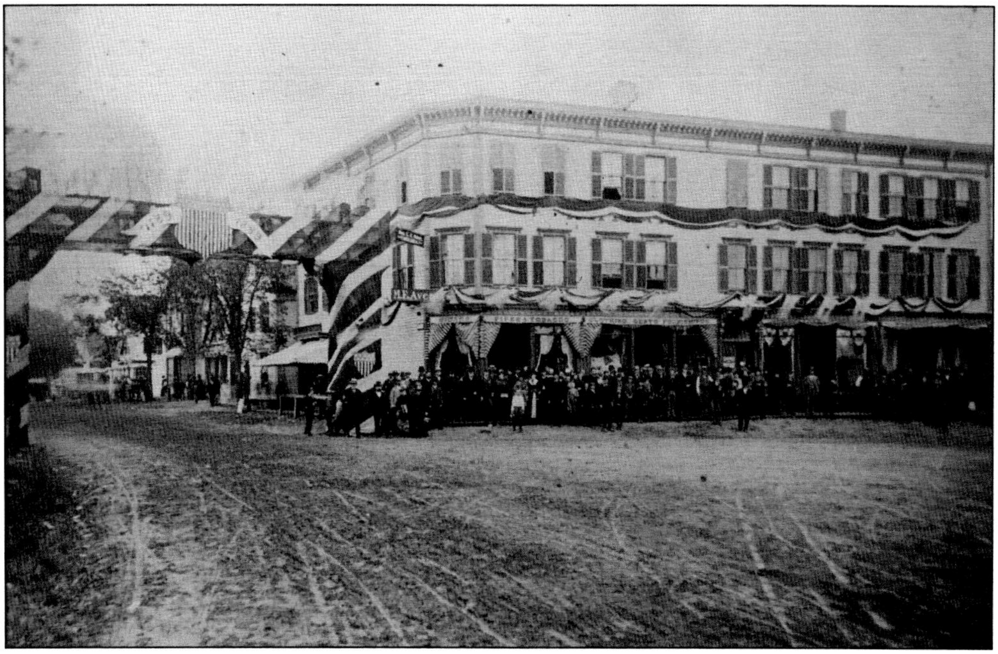

On the opposite corner of Bow Street, across from the Holbrook Block, was the group of buildings referred to as the Davis/Clark Block. Before 1909 the Harraseeket House provided lodging upstairs while different businesses occupied the ground floor. Clark's Hotel later replaced the Harraseeket House. Here, the decorations of the 1889 centennial celebrating the incorporation of Freeport festoon the building.

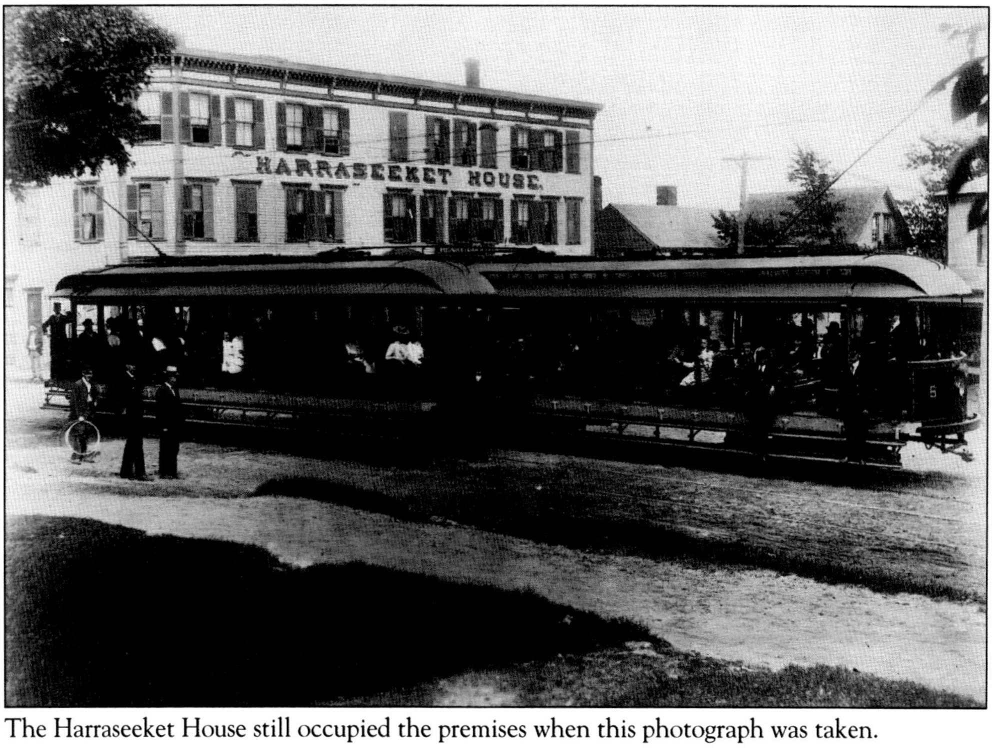

The Harraseeket House still occupied the premises when this photograph was taken.

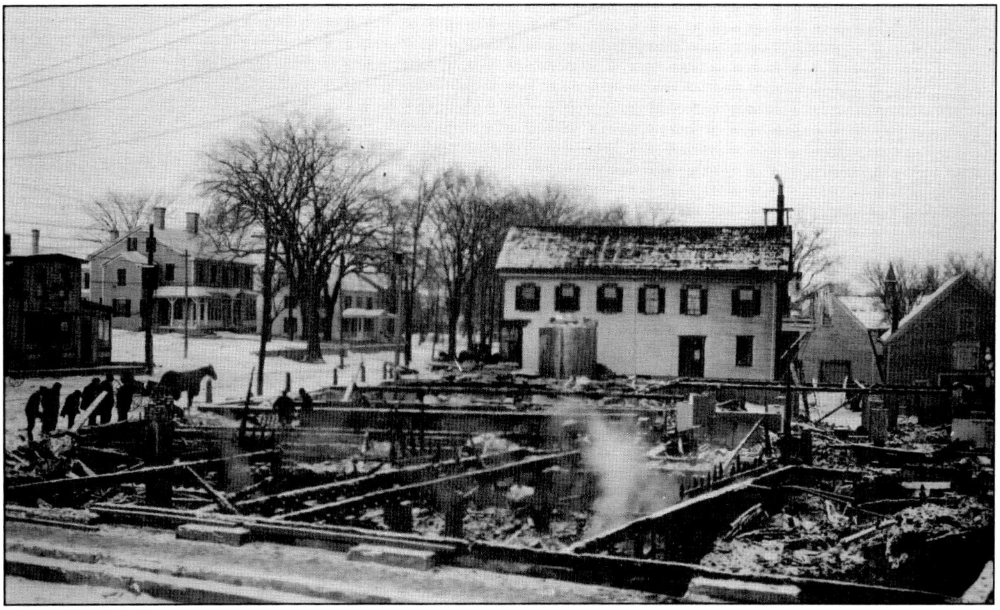

On the morning of December 28, 1909, a fire destroyed the Davis/Clark Block, which at that time housed Clark's Hotel, Curtis & Morton Grocery Store, and twelve other businesses.

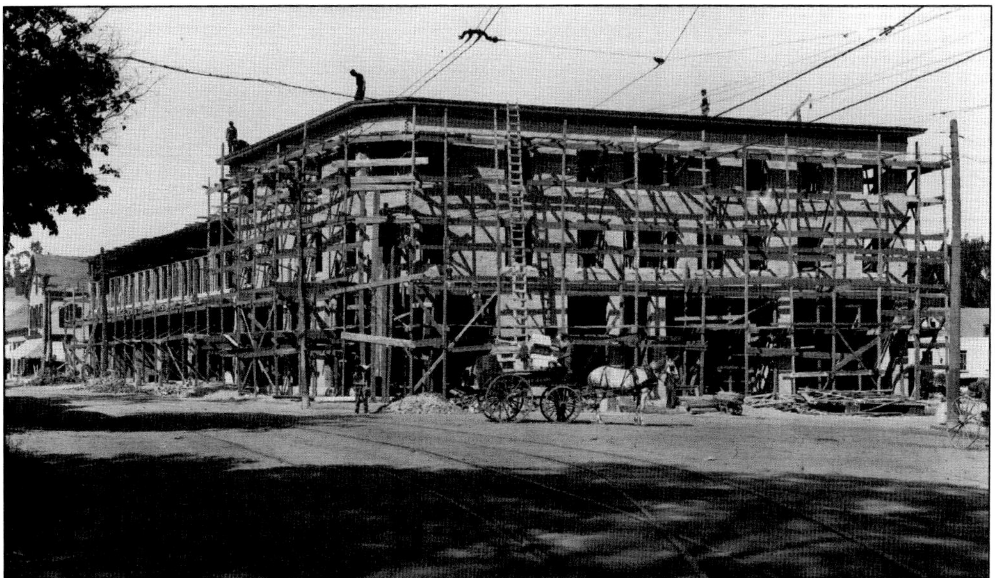

The businesses quickly re-established new quarters and in 1910, the date of this photograph, the block was rebuilt with "modern" brick. Other major fires destroyed the block in 1946 and 1980, and each time it was rebuilt.

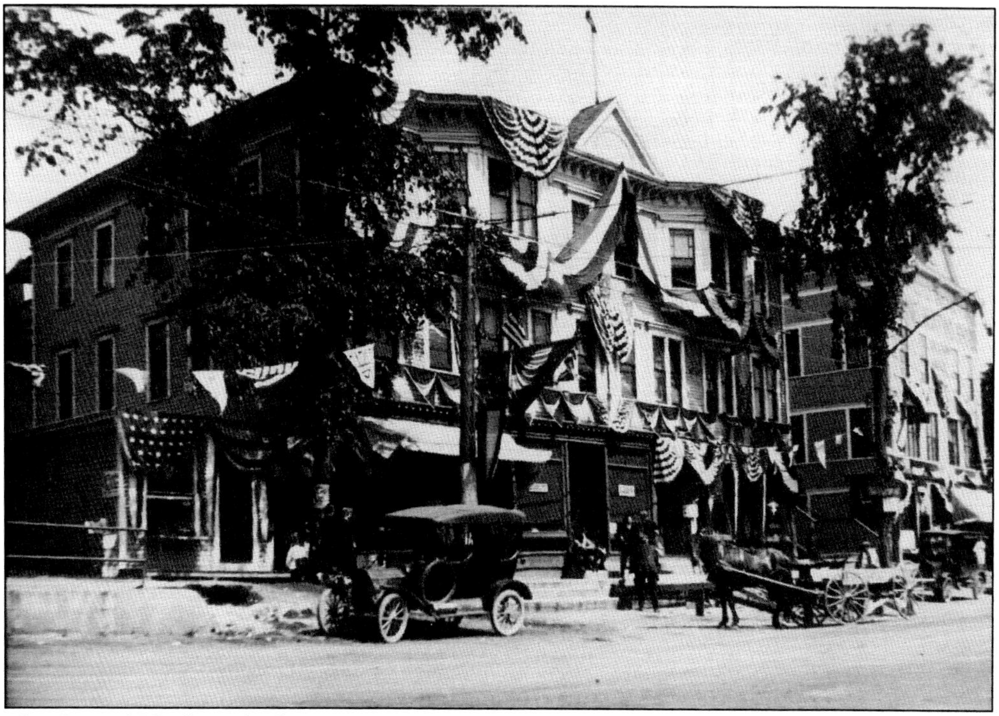

The Oxnard Block was built in 1893 on Main Street across from Bow Street. The Warren Block, on the extreme right in this photograph, was later home to the L.L. Bean Retail Store. In 1920, the centennial of Maine provided the opportunity for the community to gather and celebrate by covering the buildings with bunting and holding parades, picnics, sports events, and speeches.

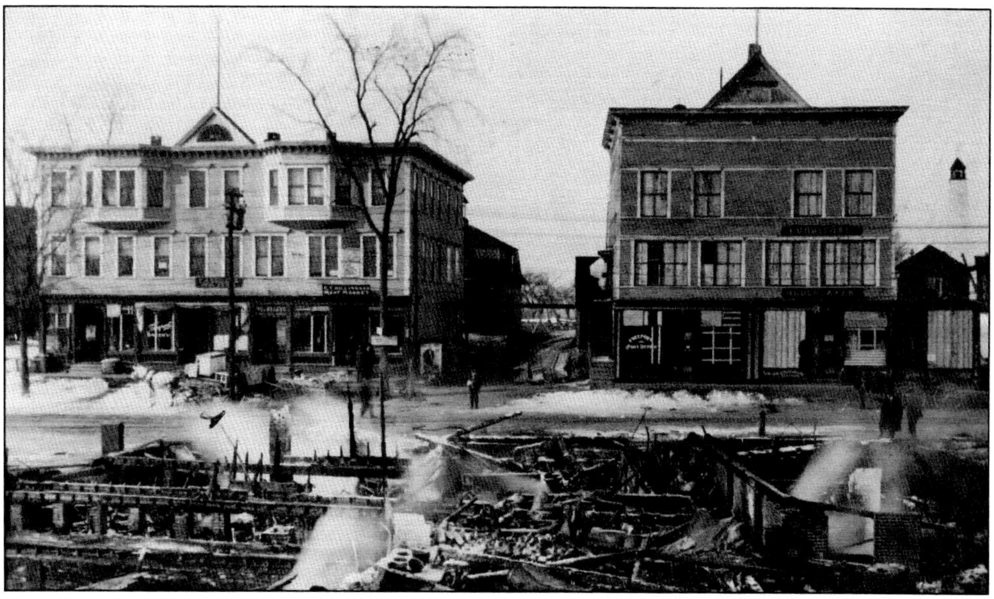

Another view of the Oxnard and Warren Blocks, taken in 1909, shows the burned-out structure of the Davis/Clark Block in the foreground.

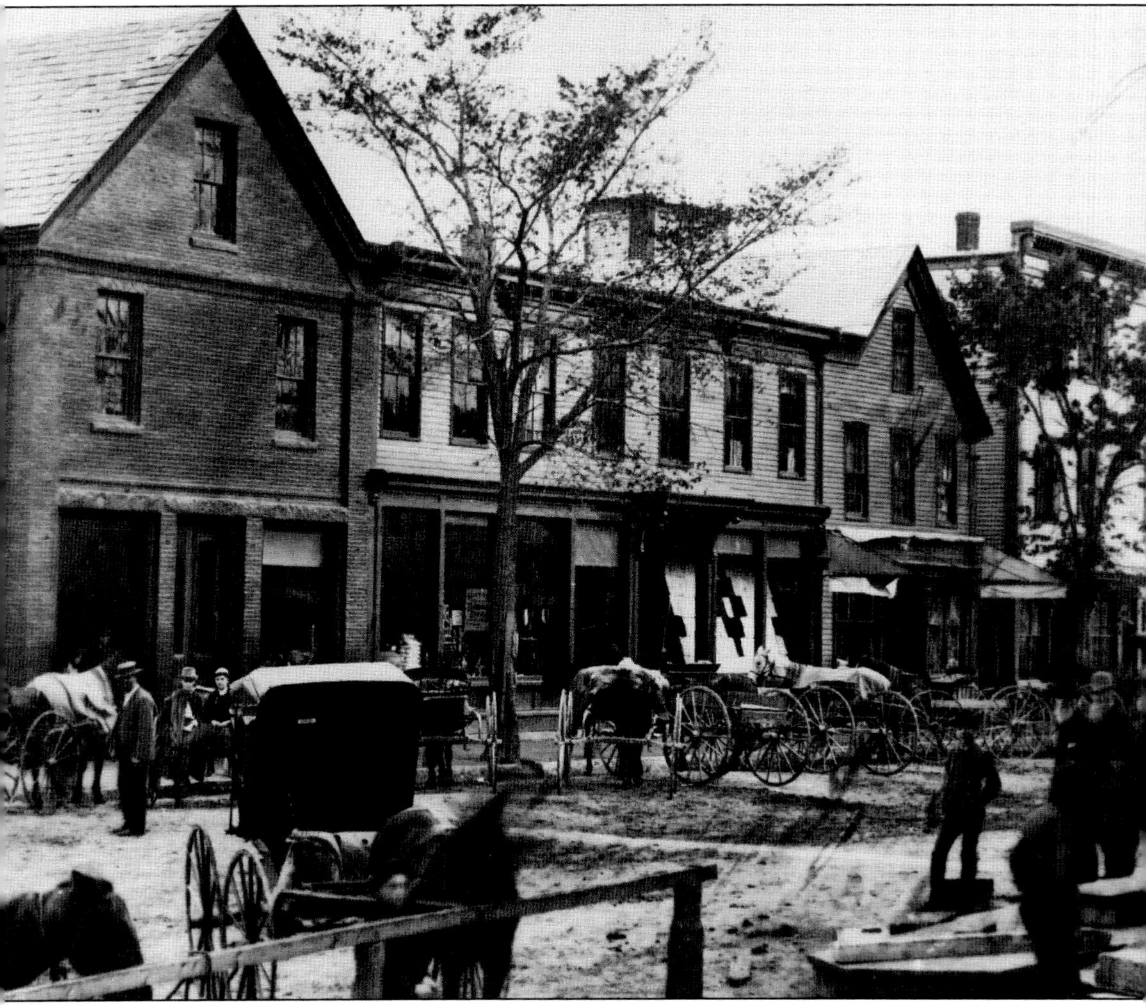

North on Main Street from Freeport Square stood a block of buildings which, during the 1830s, housed Captain Henry Green's harness shop, the office of E.C. Townsend, and a barbershop. This photograph, taken in 1890, shows the post office, a general store owned by E.B. Mallet, and a pharmacy occupying the block. The man in the foreground is identified as John Burr, founder of Burr Greenhouses.

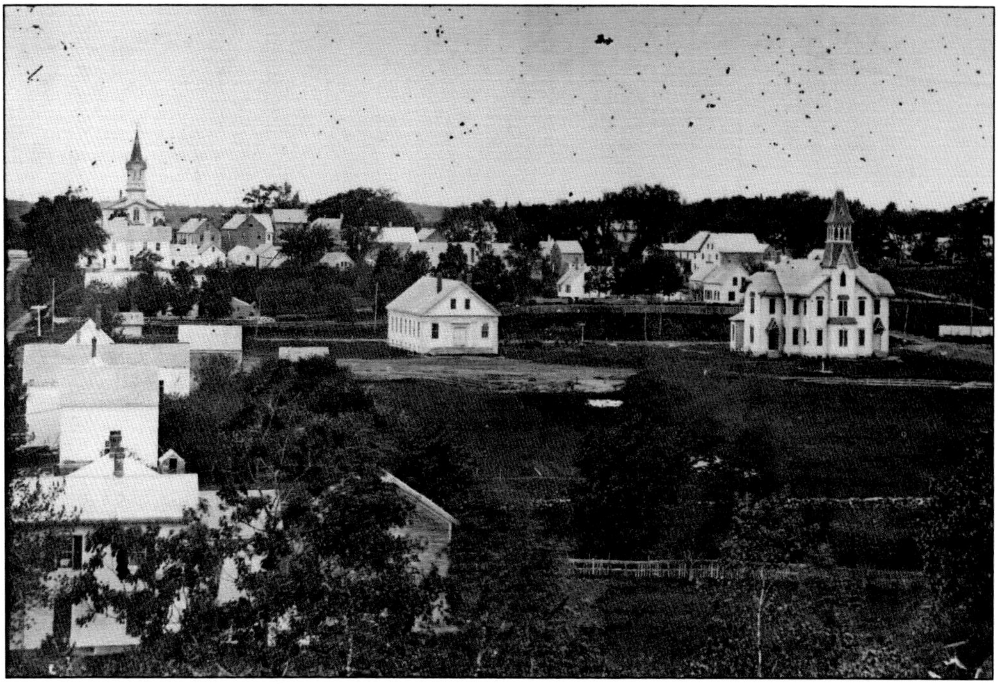

An 1890 view of Freeport from Torrey Hill Ridge shows Main Street and Park Street. Prominent buildings, from left to right, are: the Congregational church, the Freeport Town Hall, and Freeport High School.

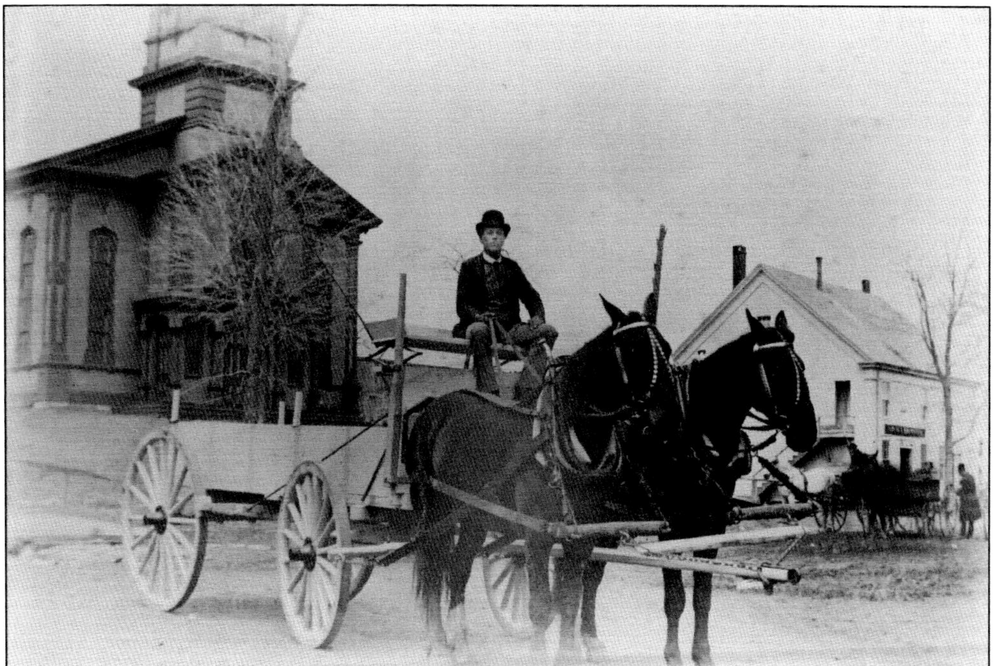

Elmer Welch is shown in front of the Freeport Congregational Church, which burned on April 13, 1894. The church, built in 1819 and remodeled in 1867, occupied the space where the L.L. Bean store now stands.

Freeport High School, designed by noted Portland architect Francis H. Fassett, was built in 1873 on Park Street for a total cost of $11,000. The school tower was a notable part of the streetscape before it burned in the 1930s.

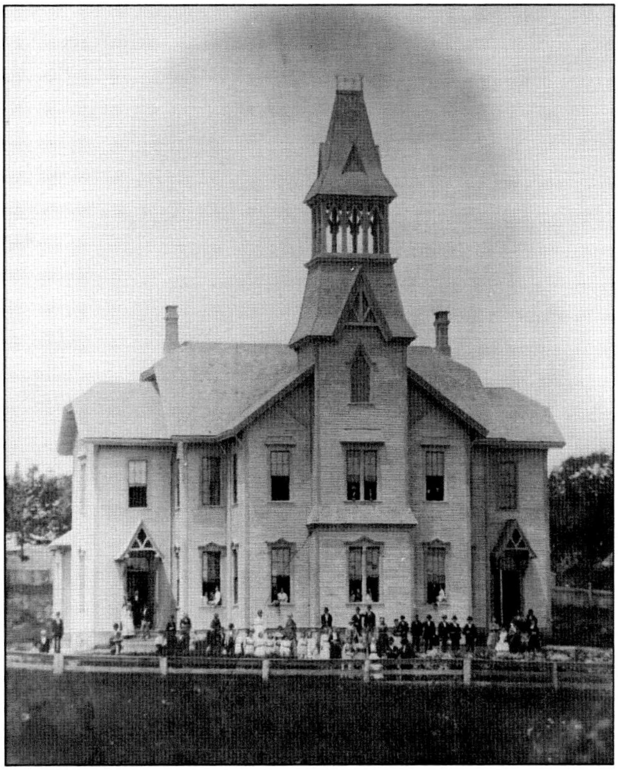

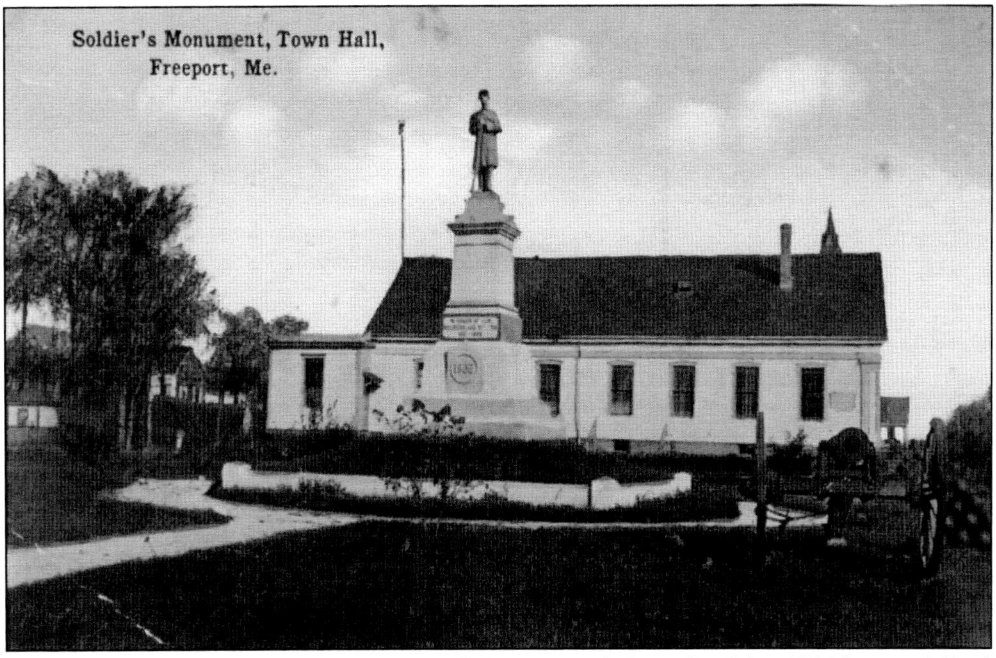

The Sailors and Soldiers Monument on Park Street was dedicated in May 1906 by noted Civil War General Joshua L. Chamberlain. The cannons are thought to have been used at the First Battle of Bull Run at Shiloh and on Sherman's March to the Sea; the town hall is in the background and the high school nearby.

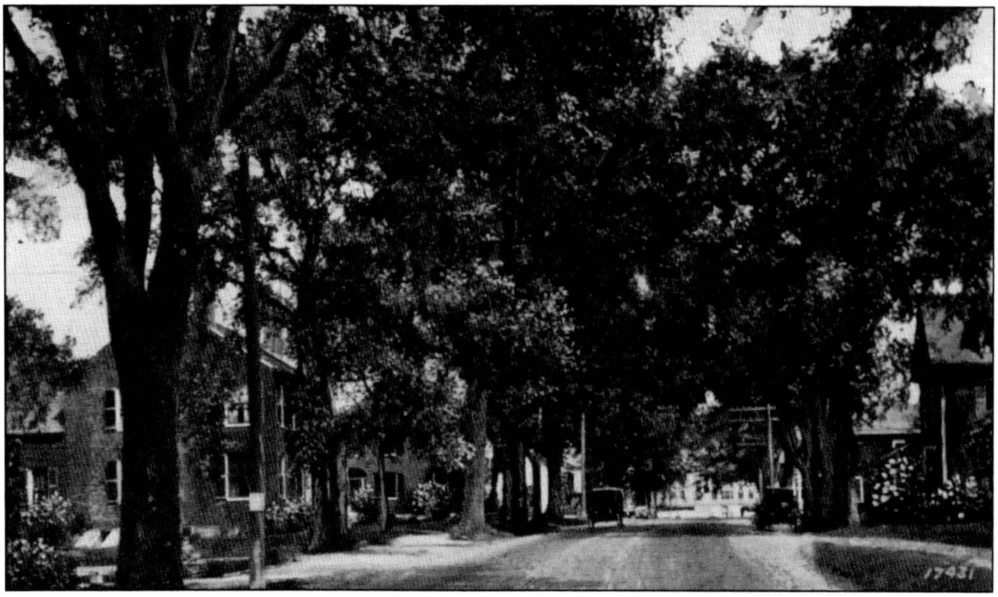

Main Street south of Freeport Square had numerous businesses as well as dwellings, all shaded by stately elm trees. This view, looking north, shows Main Street as it looked c. 1925. Harrington House, now home of the Freeport Historical Society, is the brick building on the left.

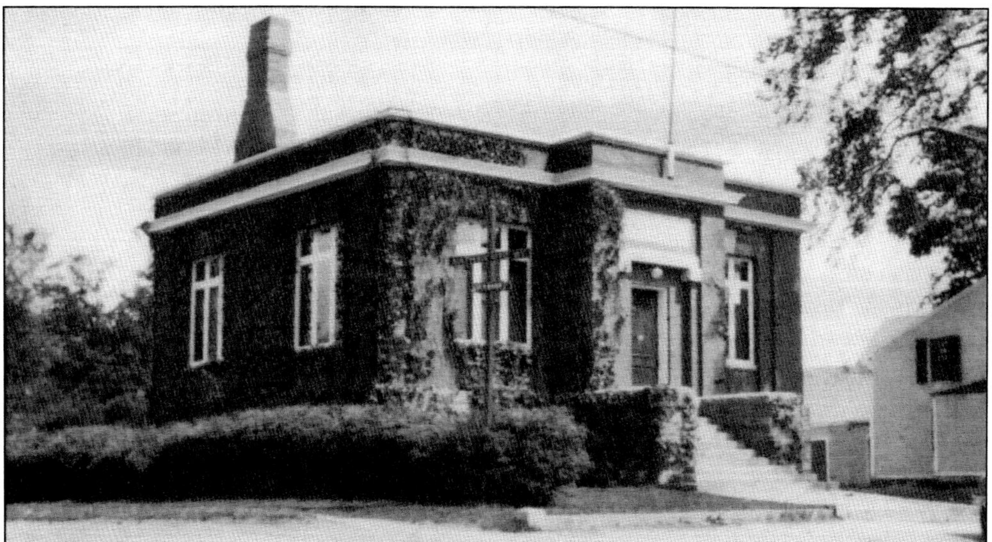

B.H. Bartol Library, designed by Portland architect George Burnham, was built in 1906 with funds from the Andrew Carnegie Foundation and books were purchased with money from the estate of Freeport-born Barnabas Henry Bartol. The granite used for the foundation was from a local quarry.

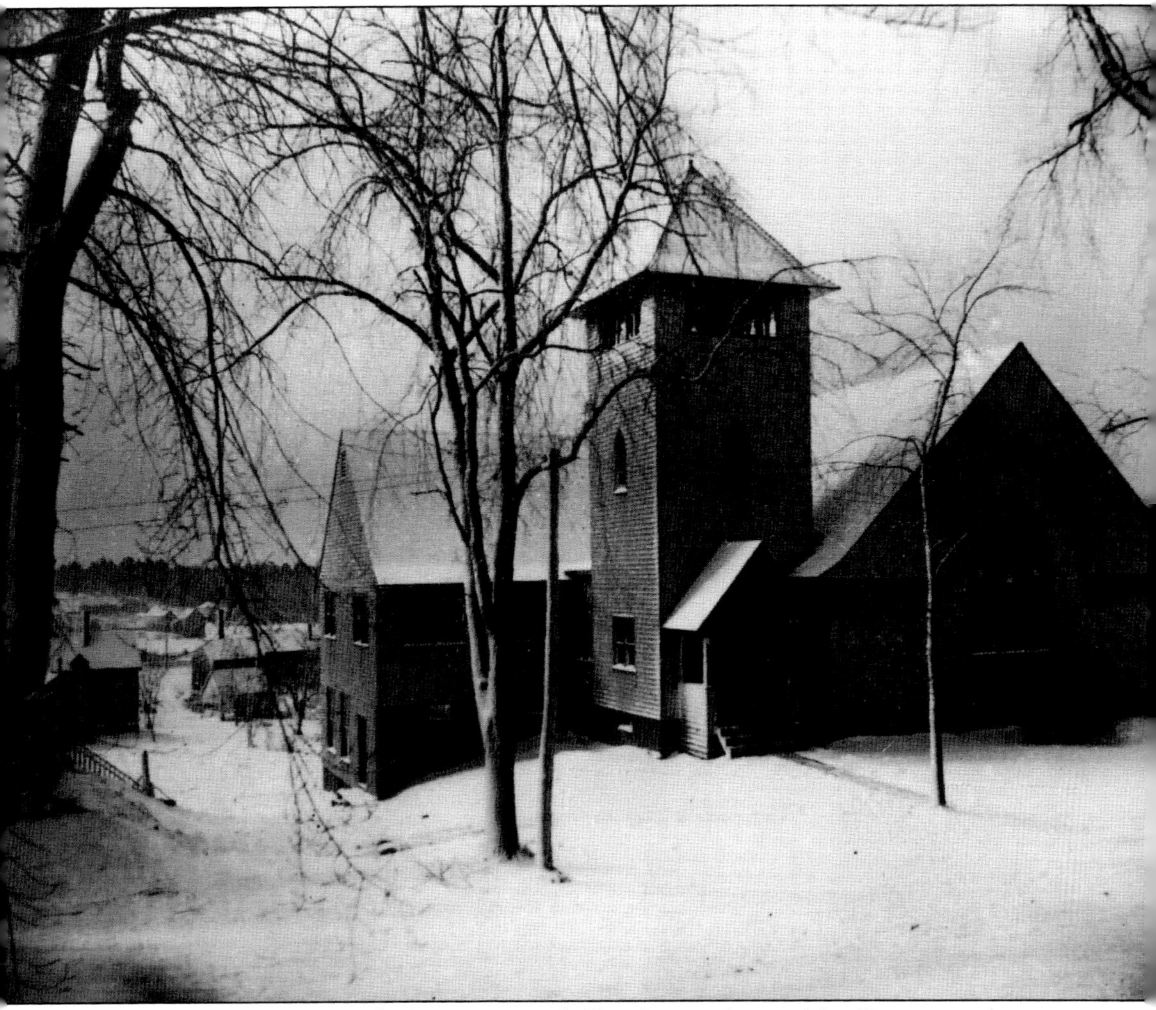

The new Freeport First Parish Congregational Church was designed by Freeport architect W.S. Aldrich in 1895 after the previous church on the present site of L.L. Bean had been destroyed by fire.

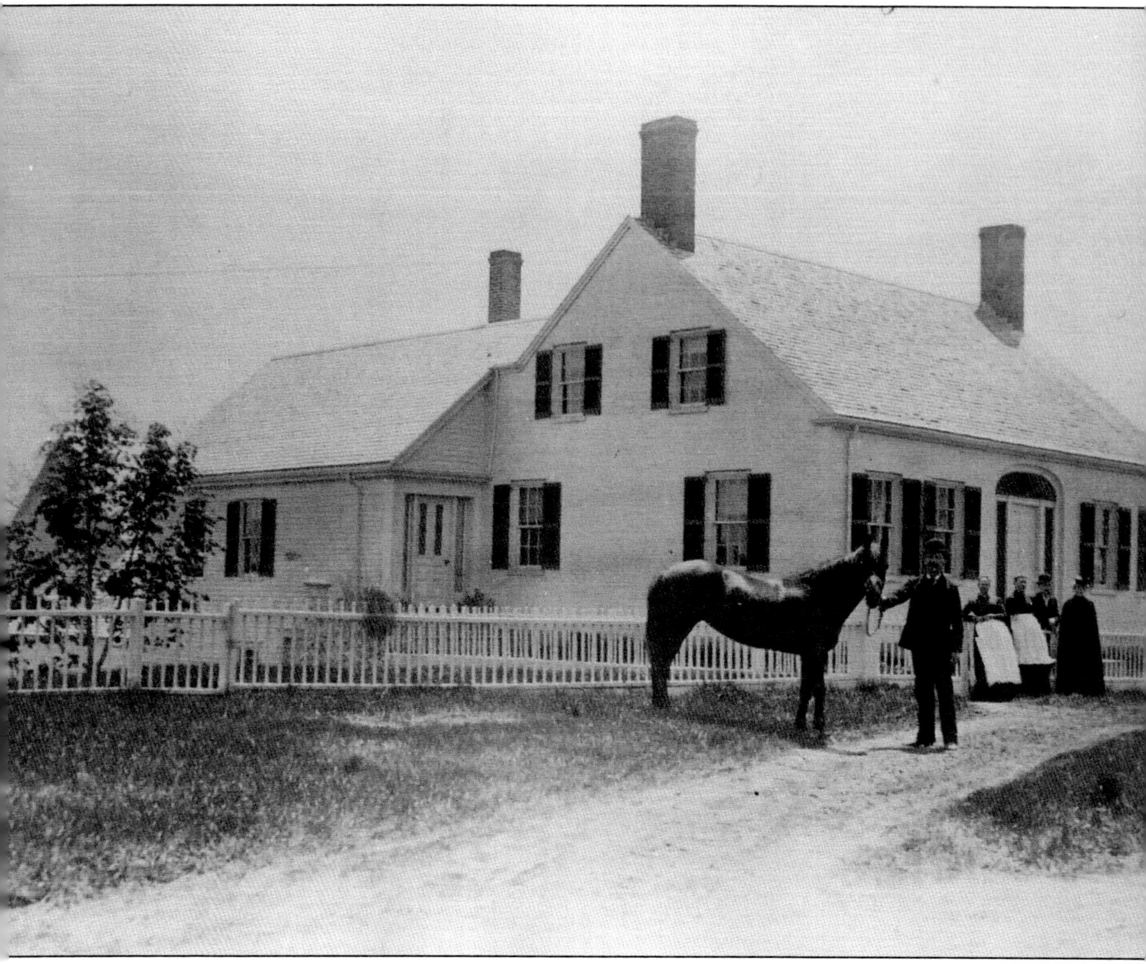

This small brick dwelling is known as the Andrew Brewer House, built in 1840 by the village blacksmith. It is one of the three original brick houses remaining on Main Street.

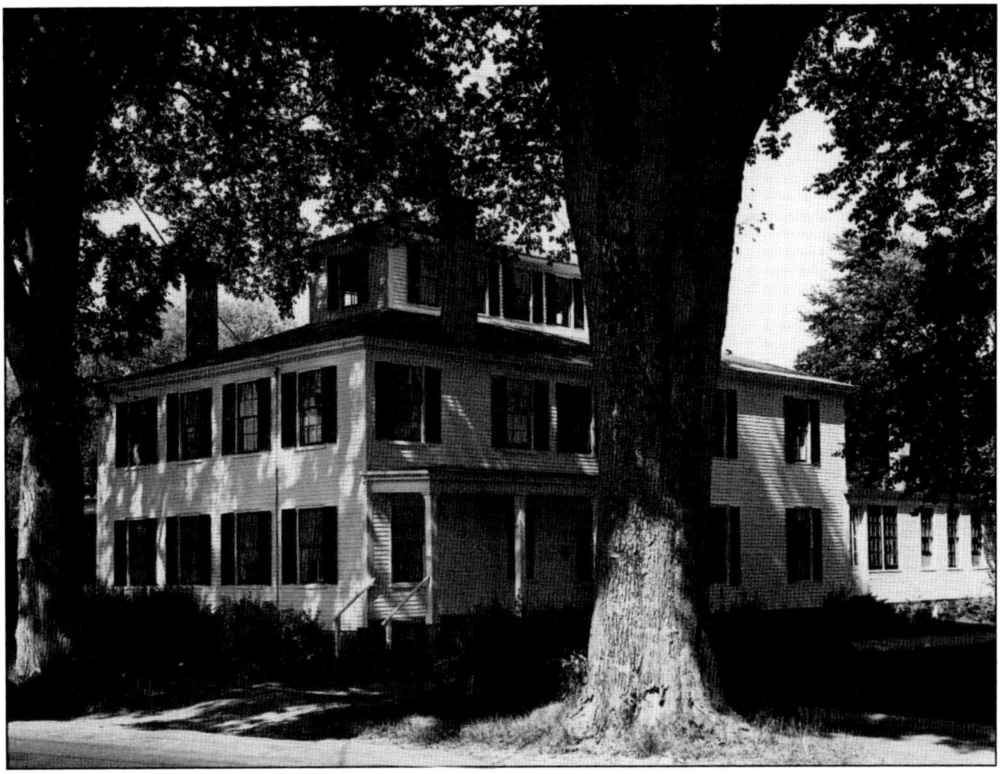

The Belcher House was built in 1828 by Richard Belcher, a Freeport lawyer. The monitor on the roof is original, although the spiral staircase in the front hall is gone.

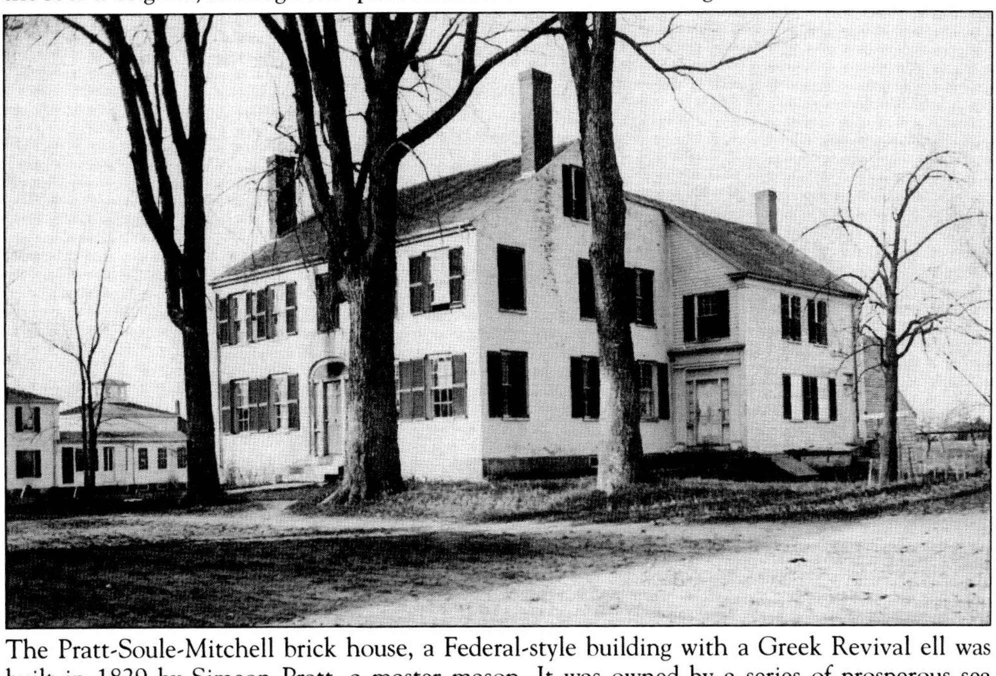

The Pratt-Soule-Mitchell brick house, a Federal-style building with a Greek Revival ell was built in 1829 by Simeon Pratt, a master mason. It was owned by a series of prosperous sea captains, ship owners, and shipbuilders.

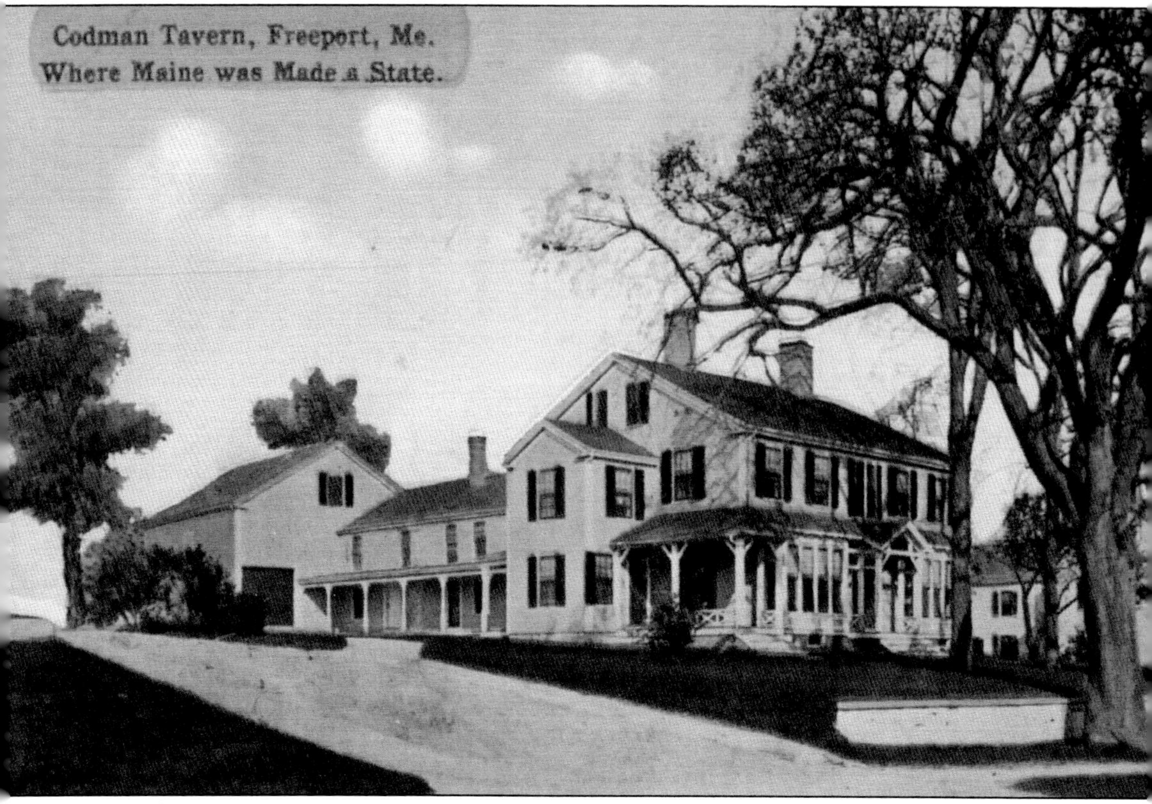

North of Freeport Square is the Jameson-Codman Tavern, built by John Angier Hyde in 1795. Purchased in 1801 by Samuel Jameson, it operated as a tavern and stagecoach stop until 1828 when it was sold to Captain Richard Codman. Codman continued to run it as a tavern until 1844 when the railroad diminished the stagecoach business and the tavern reverted to a private dwelling. The porch was added at some point late in the nineteenth century. Local legend has claimed that papers relative to Maine's statehood were signed here but there is no documentation to prove that this happened.

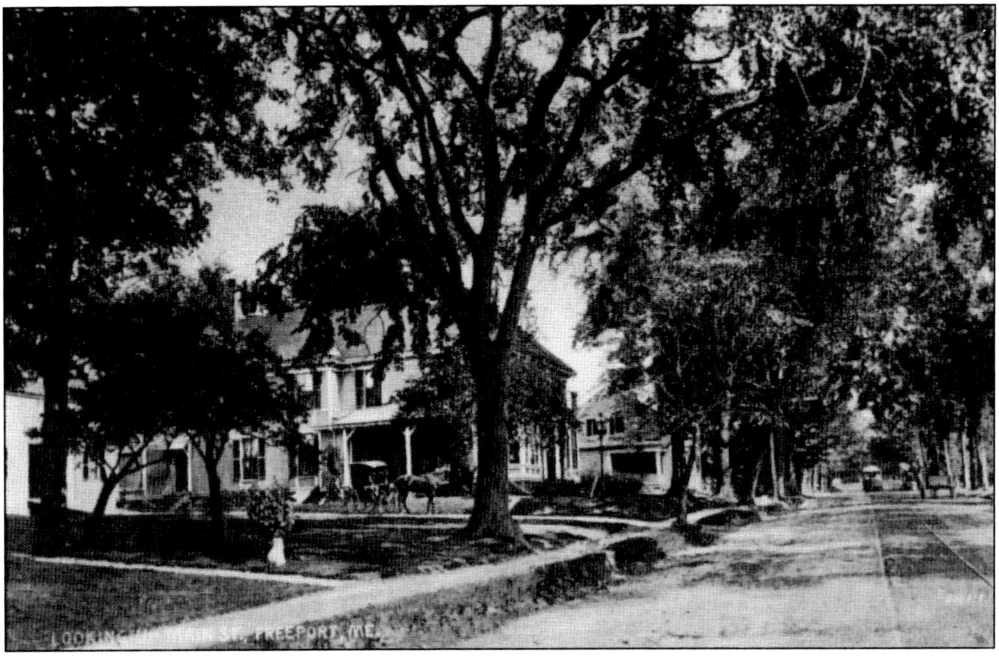

This is Main Street north of the square, as it appeared *c.* 1910.

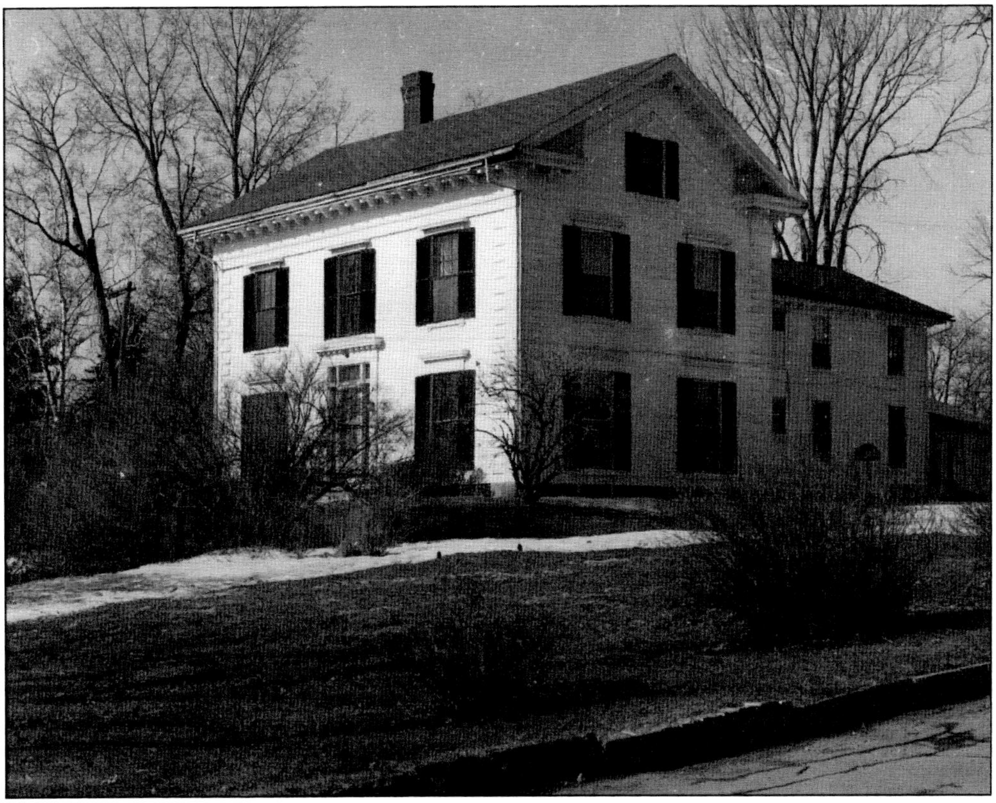

The Italianate dwelling known as the Soule-Sullivan House was torn down in 1973. It was designed *c.* 1858 by Freeport architect George W. Randall for Captain Robert S. Soule.

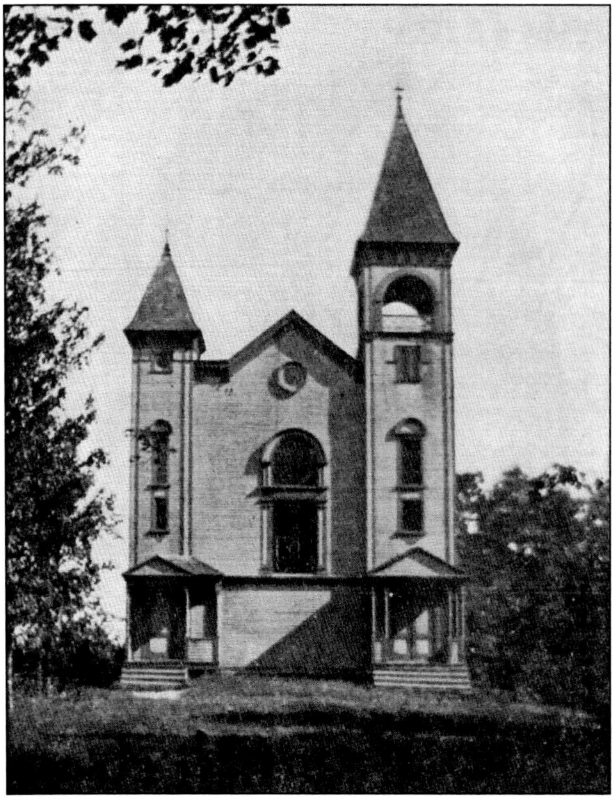

The Universalist church was moved to this site between 1874 and 1880. The original structure is said to have been built as an early North Yarmouth Academy building and moved several times, the last time being to this site. It was then purchased by the Second Universalist congregation in 1884 and the twin tower facade dates from 1890. In 1970 the church was dissolved and the structure later adapted as a residence and office.

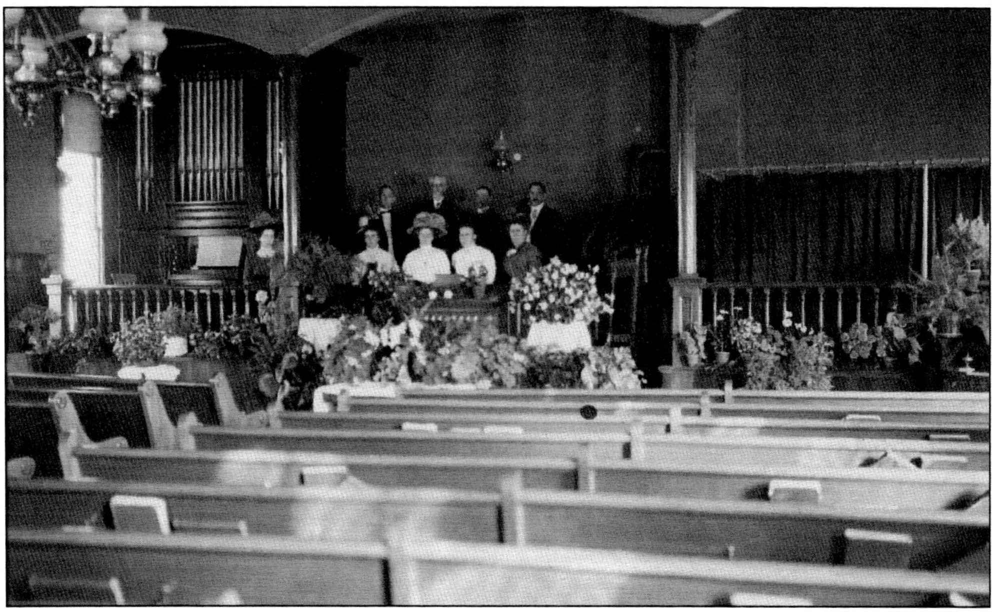

An interior photograph of the Universalist church on Easter Sunday shows the pews waiting to be filled.

Three successive Baptist church buildings have been constructed on the same site on upper Main Street. The earliest, shown on the right, is the first church building, built in 1808 and remodeled in 1861. This building was moved in 1896 to the old Freeport fairgrounds and converted into an exhibition hall. After the old church was moved, the shingle-style church pictured below, designed by Portland architect John Calvin Stevens, was erected and served the congregation until it burned in 1944.

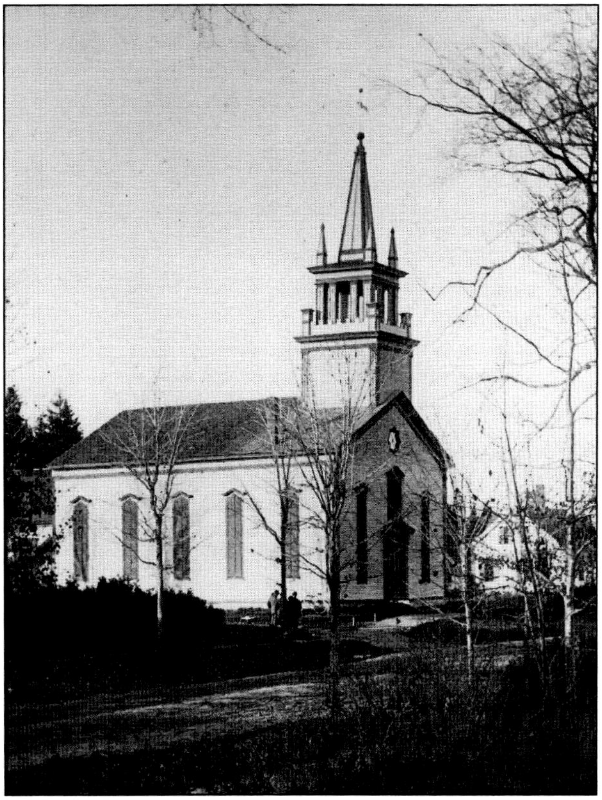

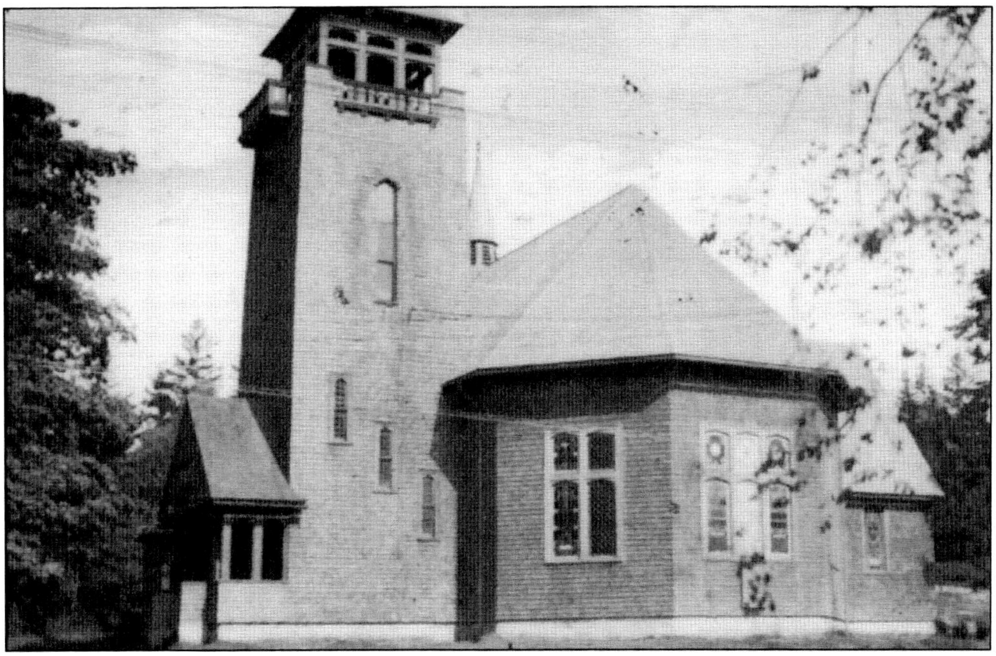

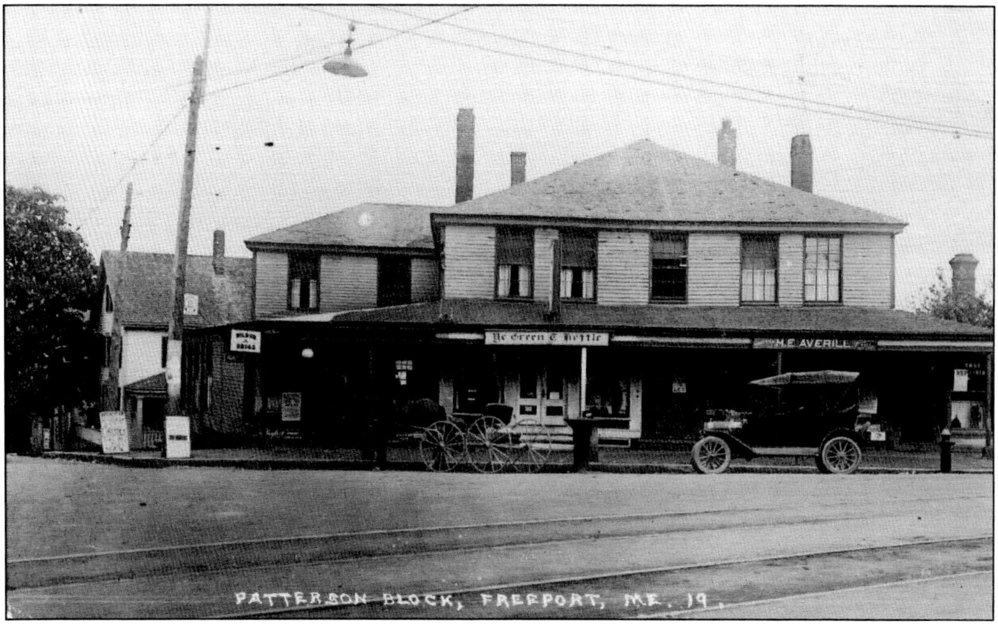

Over the years, Freeport Square prospered. A picture of the Patterson Block shows three modes of transportation—horse and buggy, automobile, and trolley.

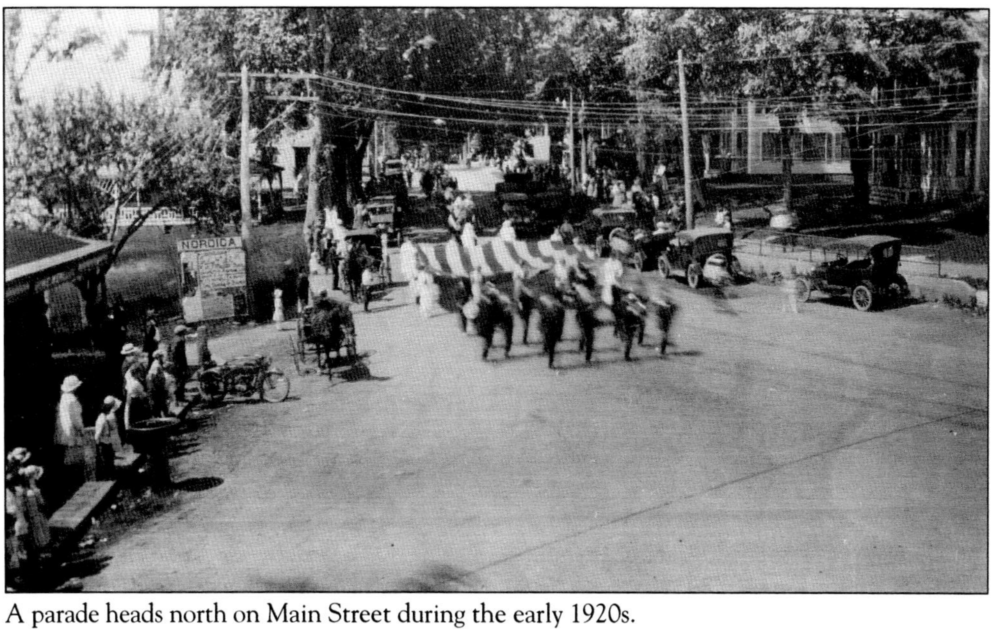

A parade heads north on Main Street during the early 1920s.

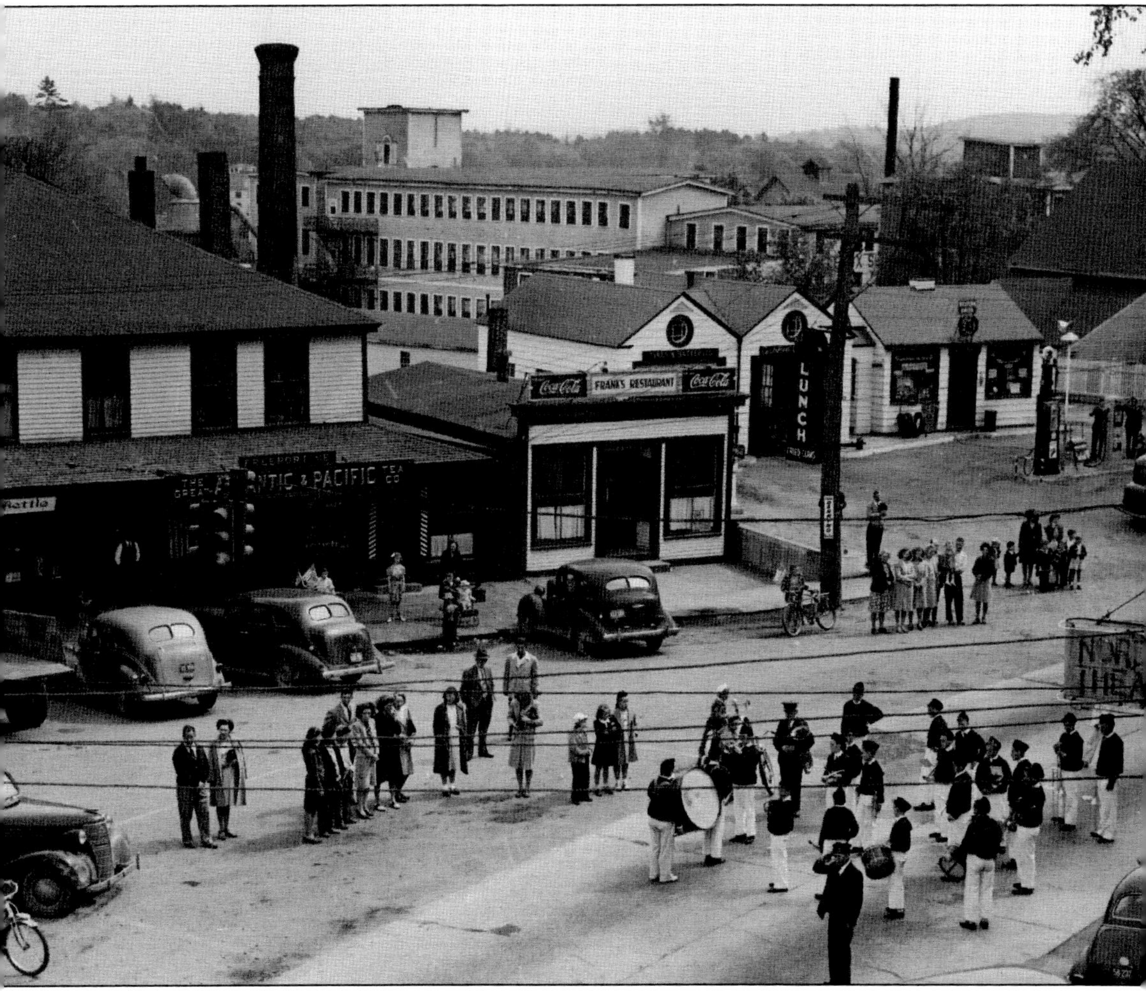

The Patterson Block, a Texaco gas station, and a shoe factory built by E.B. Mallet serve as the backdrop for a parade in 1944. This parade was poorly attended due to the many residents away at war.

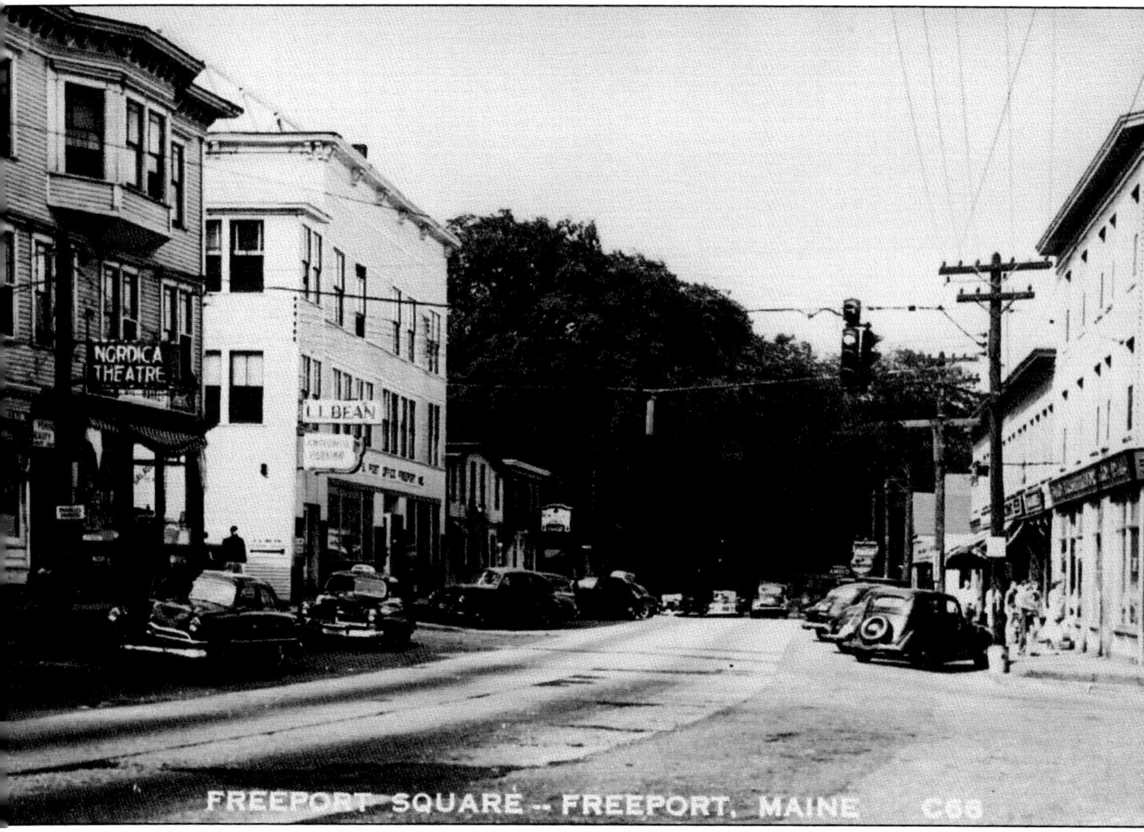

Freeport Square in the 1940s reveals automobiles, traffic lights, and the now-familiar L. L. Bean sign.

Two

E.B. Mallet

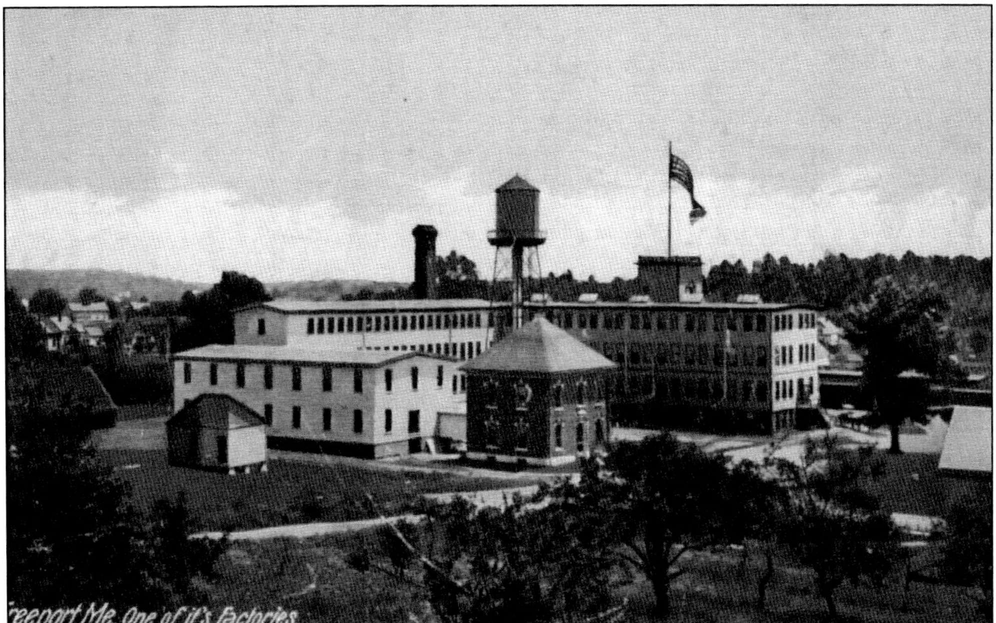

A shoe factory built by the entrepreneur E.B. Mallet in 1886, was his first venture. A three-story factory with an entrance tower was built near the railroad depot. This 1910 postcard reads, "Dear Mother, I didn't have time to come in and say good-bye this morning. I just barely caught my train. This is the shop where I work. —Lester."

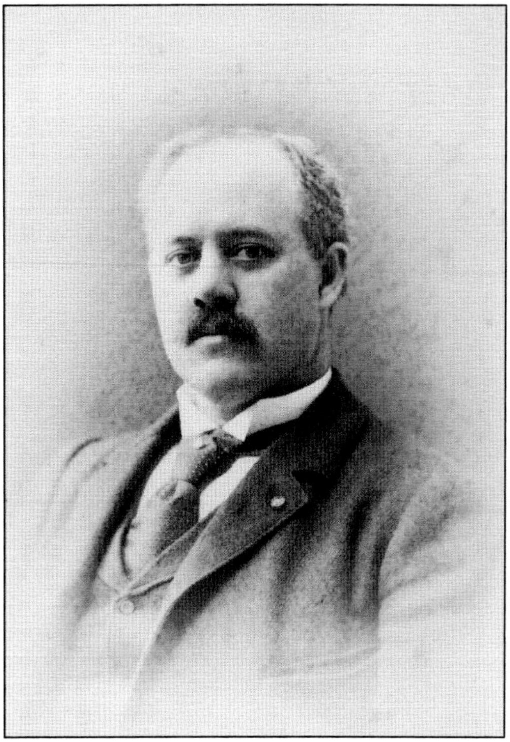

E.B. Mallet's photographic portrait was taken in 1893 while he was serving in the Maine senate. Mallet was born on September 3, 1853, on the ship *Devonshire* in the English Channel, and at thirty-one he inherited a great sum of money from his uncle, a retired sea captain. Mallet promptly moved from Pownal to Freeport and began an extraordinary course of industrial development including shoe factories, a quarry, and a sawmill. Eventually he lost his fortune due to bad investments, but his great works for the town of Freeport remained productive for many years and his impact on the town is still felt today.

Mallet leased his factory to A.W. Shaw & Co. of Portland, who put in the machinery and started manufacturing men's and boys' shoes on December 1, 1886. This group of workers is standing in front of Mallet's office.

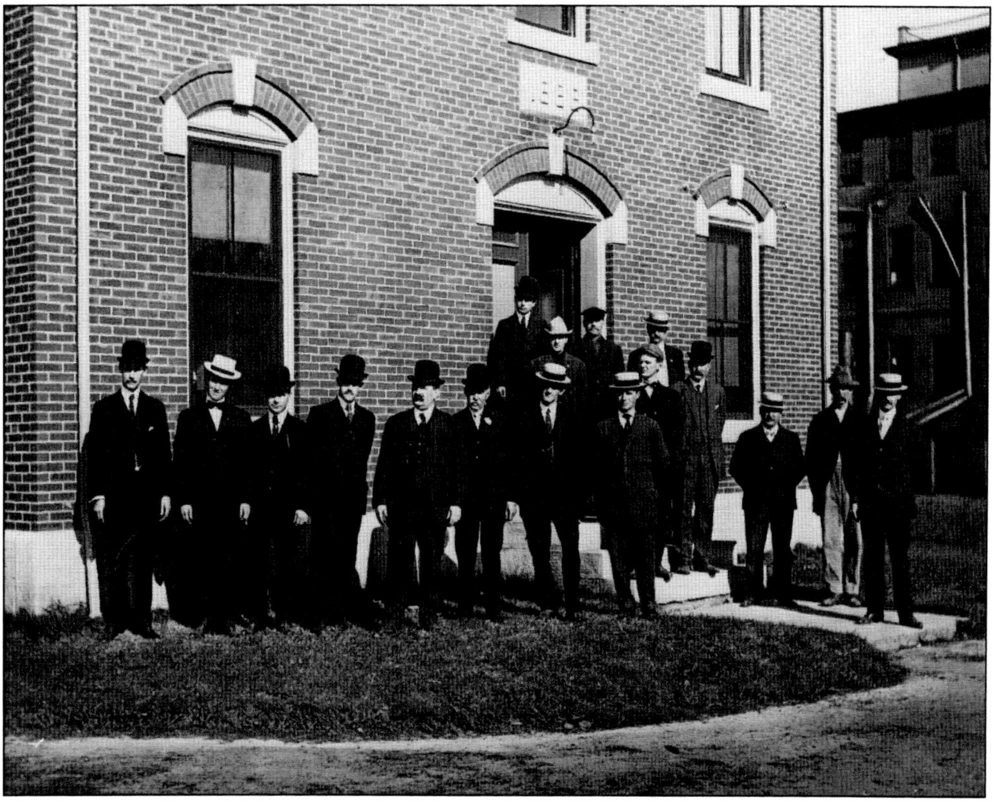

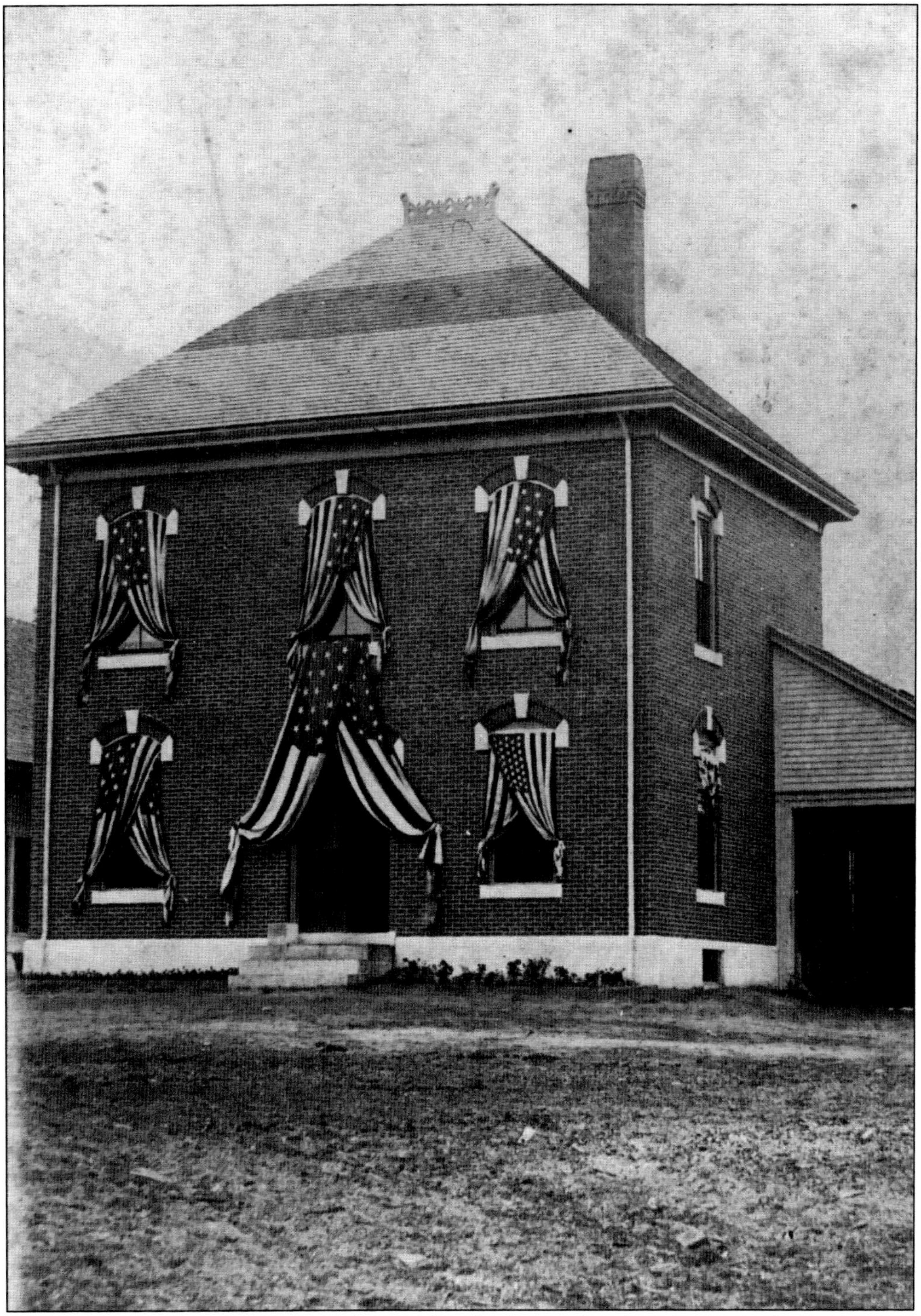

In 1888, E.B. Mallet had this handsome office built near his shoe factory with granite from his quarry, brick from his brickyard, and lumber from his sawmill. The building, designed by prominent Portland architect Francis H. Fassett, is shown here decorated for the Freeport centennial in 1889, of which Mr. Mallet was chairman.

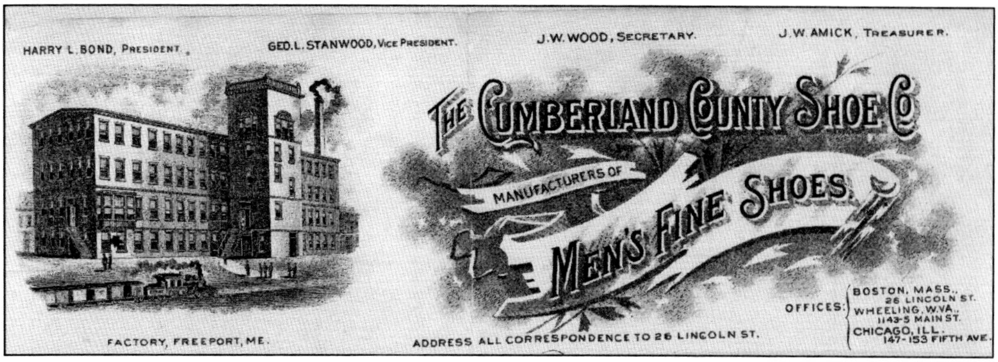

This letterhead is from the Cumberland County Shoe Co., one of the many shoe manufacturing companies that operated in Mallet's factory over the years. Some other manufacturers were Porter, E.E. Taylor, and Sears and Roebuck.

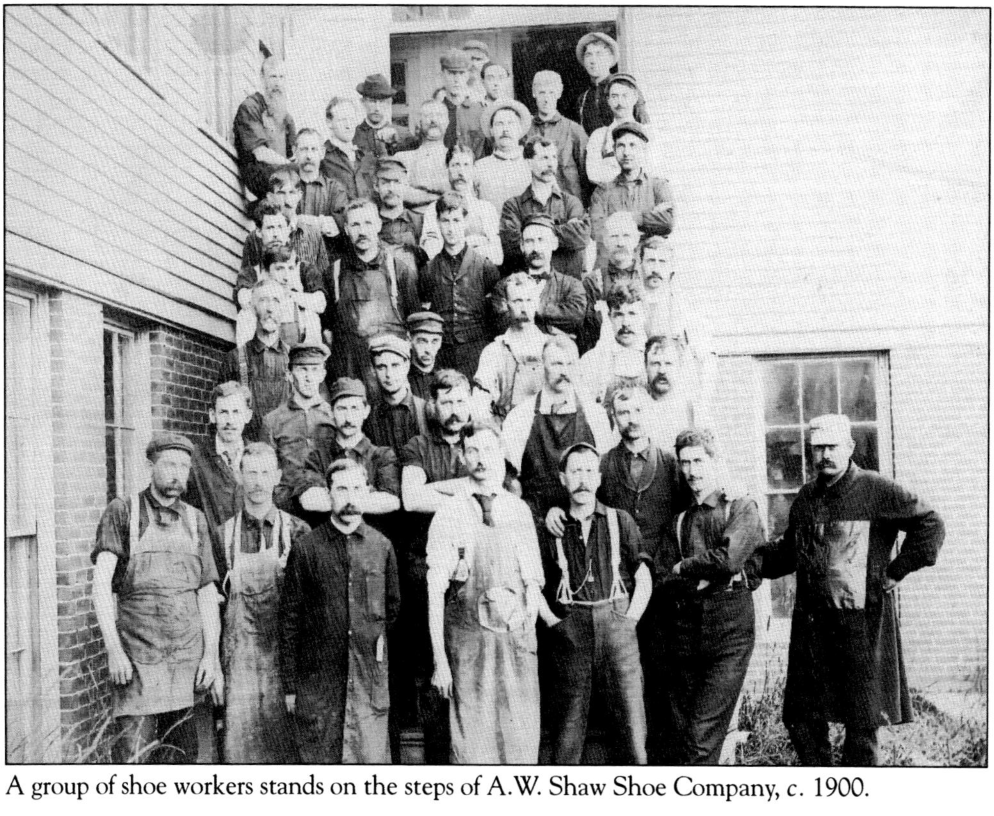

A group of shoe workers stands on the steps of A.W. Shaw Shoe Company, *c.* 1900.

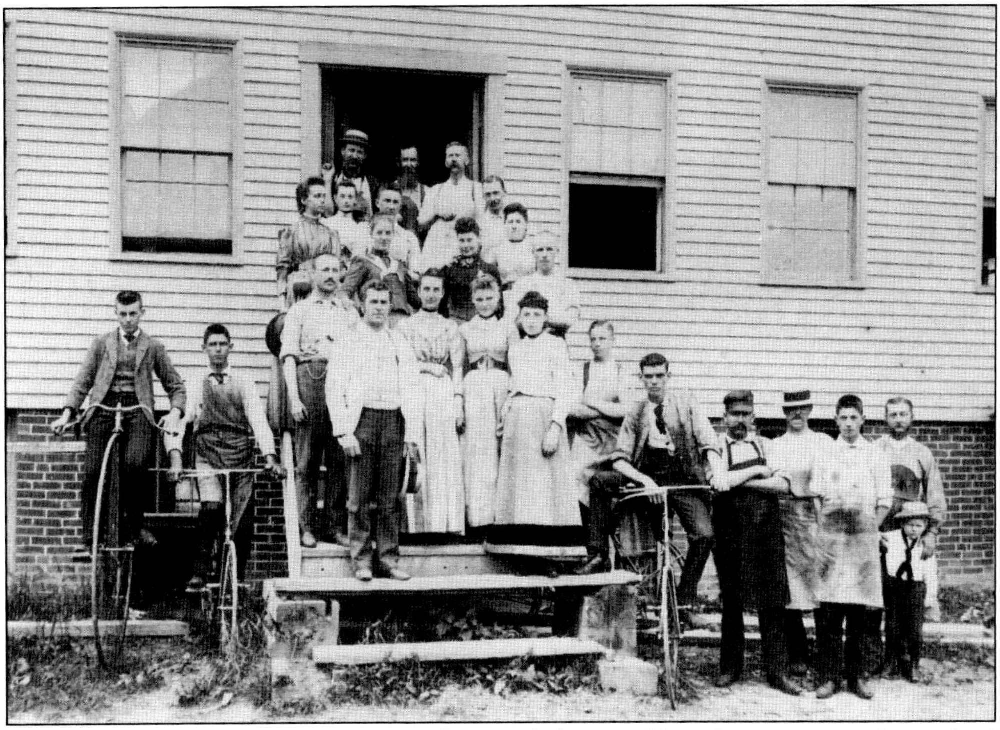

Women were always an important part of the work force and bicycles were a popular mode of transportation for many.

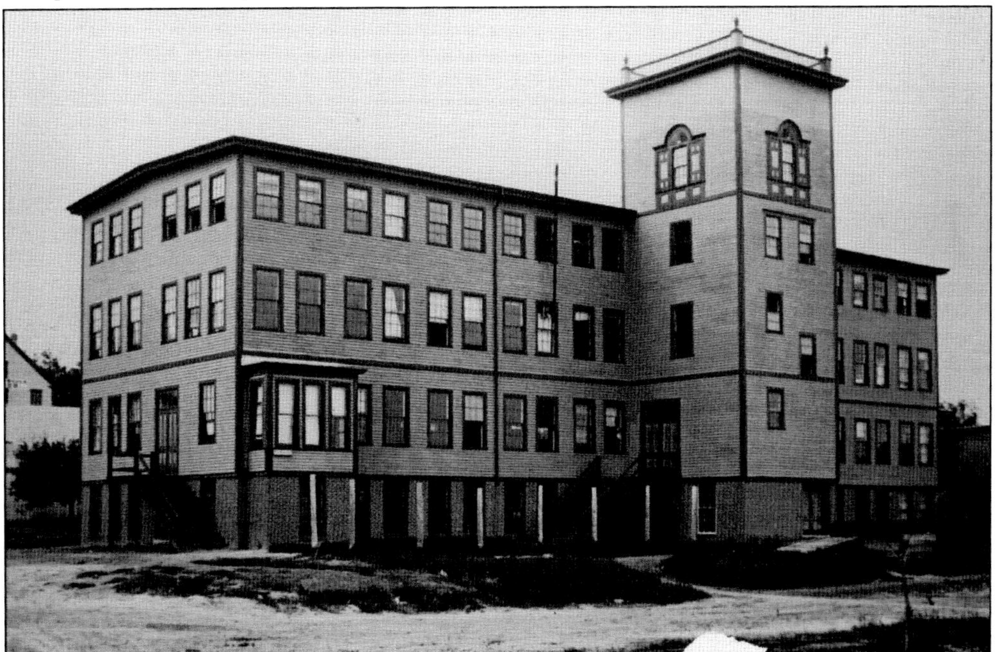

The Freeport Shoe Company operated here from 1962 to 1972. At its peak in the mid-1960s it employed over 500 people. The ninety-four-year-old building was eventually torn down in 1980.

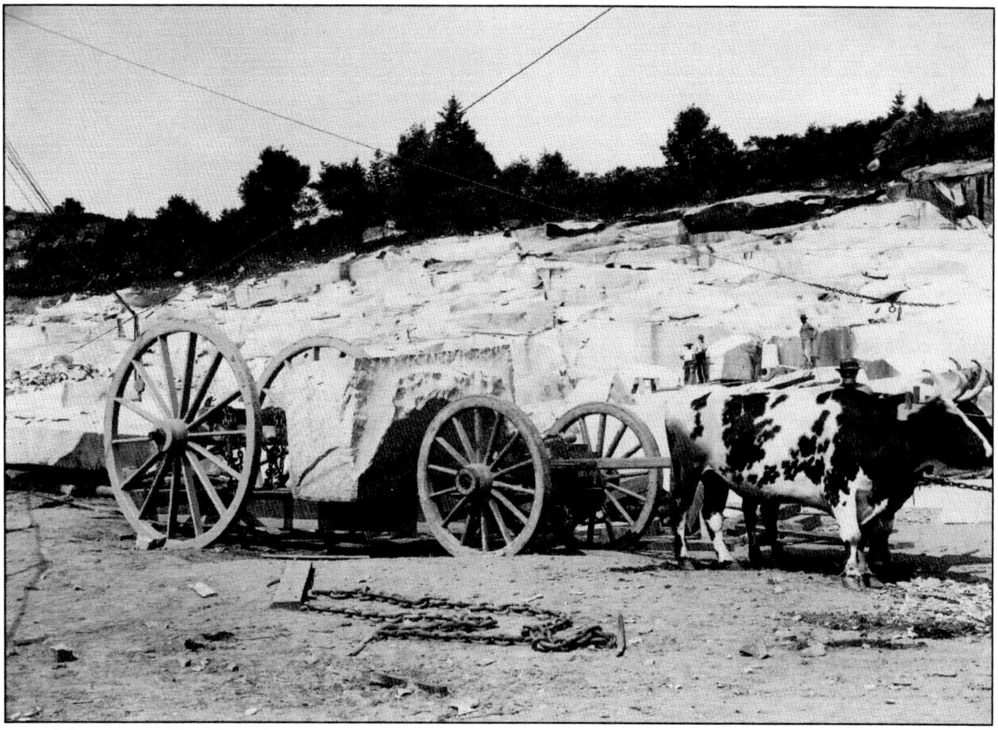

In addition to the shoe factory, Mallet owned an extensive granite quarry and marble works. He discovered the quarry in 1886 while looking for stone for the foundation of his shoe factory. Eventually quarrying thirty-five acres at Torrey's Hill behind Bow and South Streets, he provided granite for buildings in Freeport and the Portland area, as well as Boston, New York, and Philadelphia. Here, the oxen pull a galamander loaded with granite blocks.

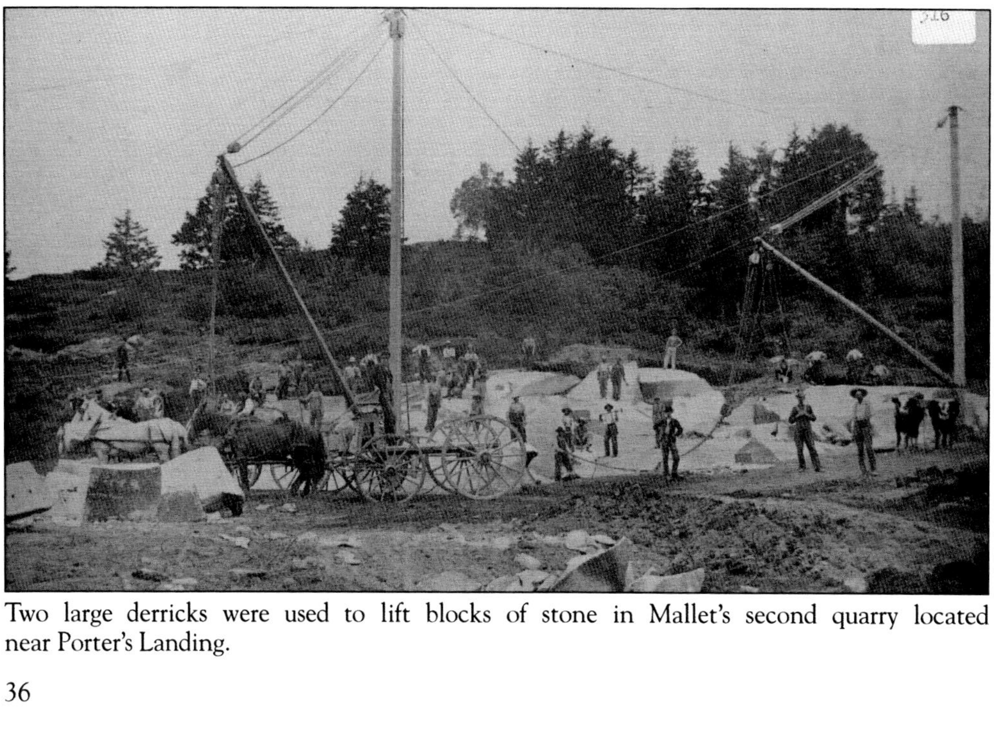

Two large derricks were used to lift blocks of stone in Mallet's second quarry located near Porter's Landing.

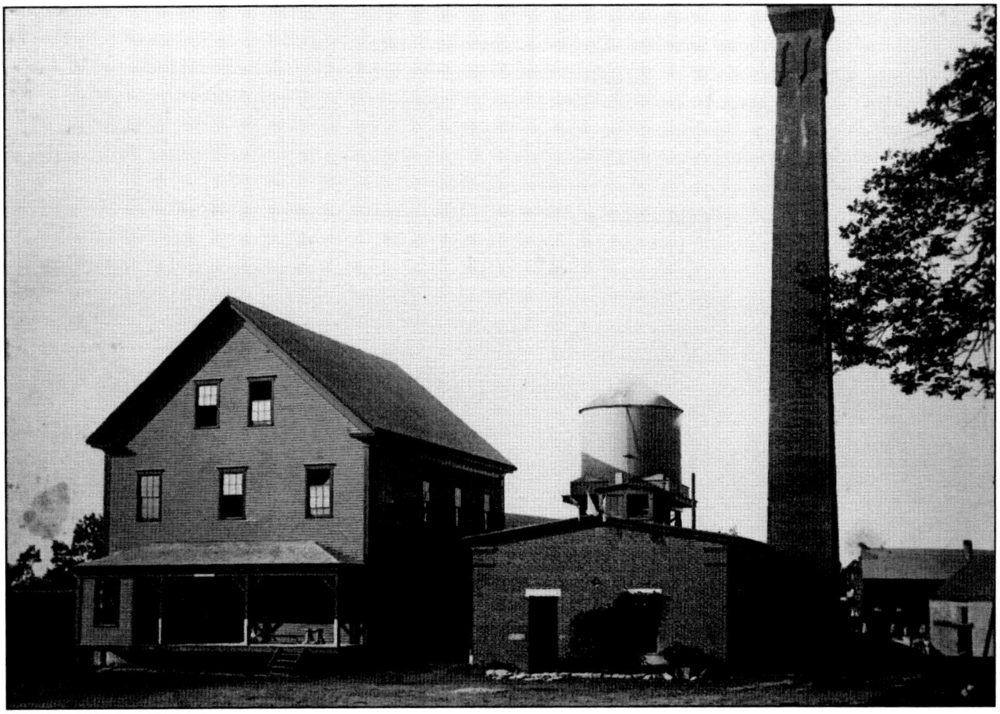

In 1886, across from the shoe factory, Mallet built a grist mill and steam engine house which also supplied power to the shoe factory. The grist mill ground corn, graham flour, and rye meal at the rate of 800 to 1,000 bushels of grain and feed weekly.

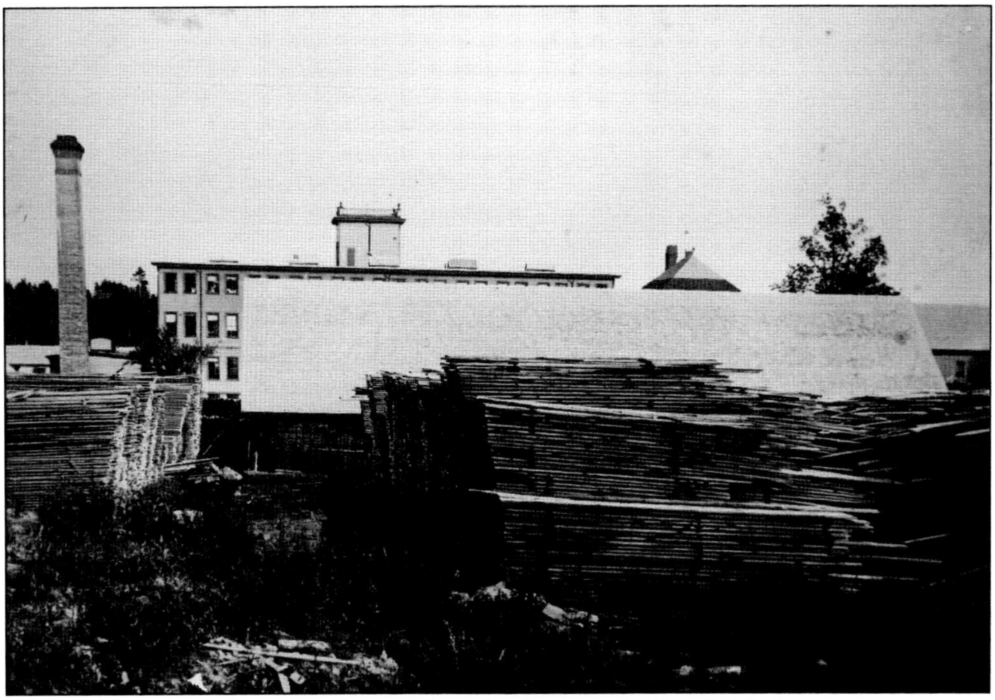

In 1887 Mallet built this sawmill across from the factory at Mill and Oak Streets.

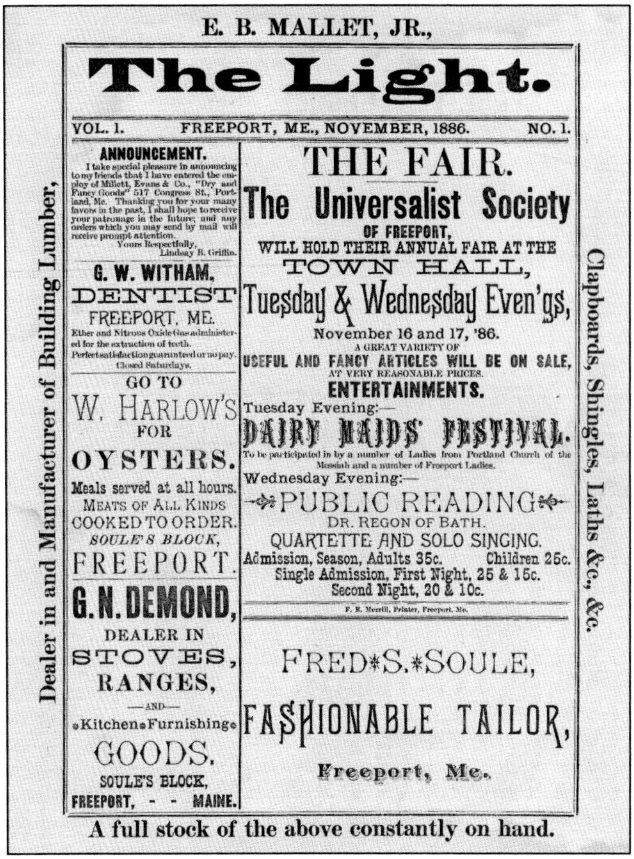

E. B. MALLET, JR.,

Dealer in and Manufacturer of Building Lumber,

The Light.

VOL. 1. FREEPORT, ME., NOVEMBER, 1886. NO. 1.

ANNOUNCEMENT.

I take special pleasure in announcing to my friends that I have entered the employ of Millett, Evans & Co., "Dry and Fancy Goods" 517 Congress St., Portland, Me. Thanking you for your many favors in the past, I shall hope to receive your patronage in the future; and any orders which you may send by mail will receive prompt attention.

Yours Respectfully,
Lindsay B. Griffin.

G. W. WITHAM,
DENTIST
FREEPORT, ME.
Ether and Nitrous Oxide Gas administered for the extraction of teeth.
Perfect satisfaction guaranteed or no pay.
Closed Saturdays.

GO TO
W. HARLOW'S
FOR
OYSTERS.
Meals served at all hours.
MEATS OF ALL KINDS
COOKED TO ORDER.
SOULE'S BLOCK,
FREEPORT.

G. N. DEMOND,
DEALER IN
STOVES,
RANGES,
—AND—
Kitchen Furnishing
GOODS.
SOULE'S BLOCK,
FREEPORT, - - MAINE.

THE FAIR.
The Universalist Society
OF FREEPORT,
WILL HOLD THEIR ANNUAL FAIR AT THE
TOWN HALL,
Tuesday & Wednesday Even'gs,
November 16 and 17, '86.
A GREAT VARIETY OF
USEFUL AND FANCY ARTICLES WILL BE ON SALE,
AT VERY REASONABLE PRICES.
ENTERTAINMENTS.
Tuesday Evening:—
DAIRY MAIDS' FESTIVAL.
To be participated in by a number of Ladies from Portland Church of the Messiah and a number of Freeport Ladies.
Wednesday Evening:—
PUBLIC READING
DR. REGON OF BATH.
QUARTETTE AND SOLO SINGING.
Admission, Season, Adults 35c. Children 25c.
Single Admission, First Night, 25 & 15c.
Second Night, 20 & 10c.

F. E. Merrill, Printer, Freeport, Me.

FRED S. SOULE,
FASHIONABLE TAILOR,
Freeport, Me.

Clapboards, Shingles, Laths &c., &c.

A full stock of the above constantly on hand.

The Light was an advertising flyer full of Freeport attractions published by E.B. Mallet. Around the border are advertisements for lumber from his sawmill.

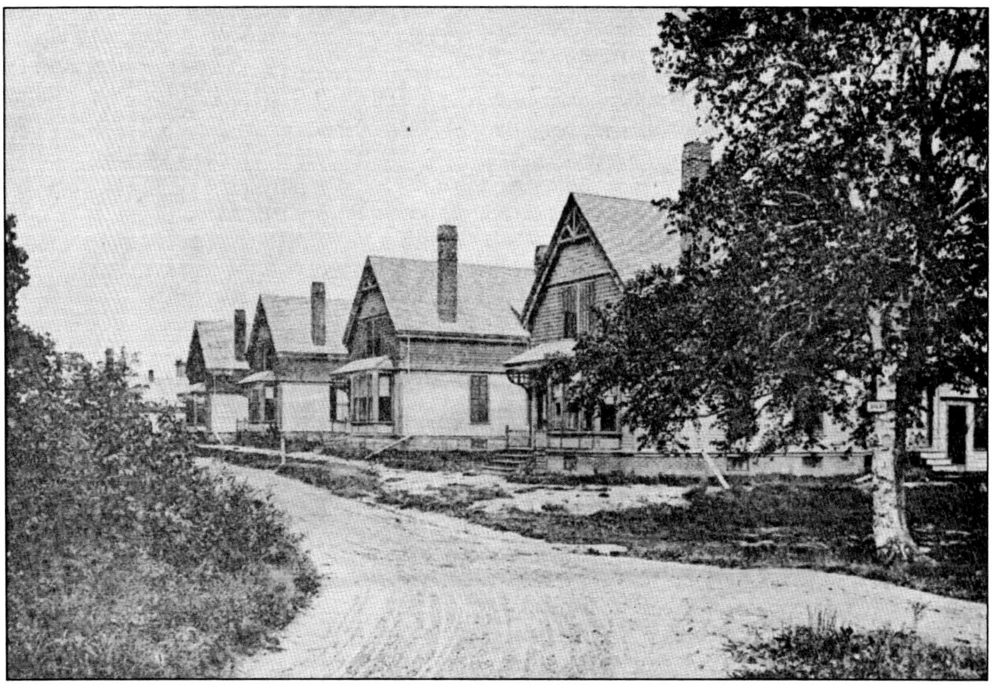

During late 1886 and early 1887 Mallet built "six pretty cottages and three double tenement houses, which are rented to men to whom his works give employment." Over the years he put up a dozen or so more houses. These houses on Oak Street are some of the cottages Mallet built.

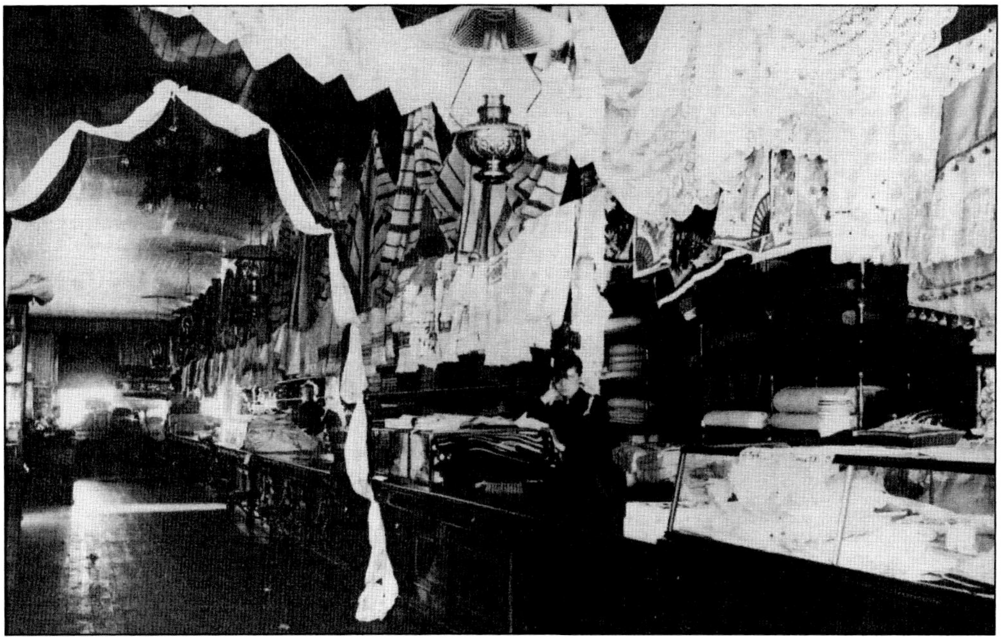

Another of Mallet's enterprises was a wholesale and retail general store mainly to furnish the food and clothing requirements of his more than 250 employees. It was then the largest retail store in Maine and was divided into departments. This display of dry and fancy goods was next to the grocery and provision department.

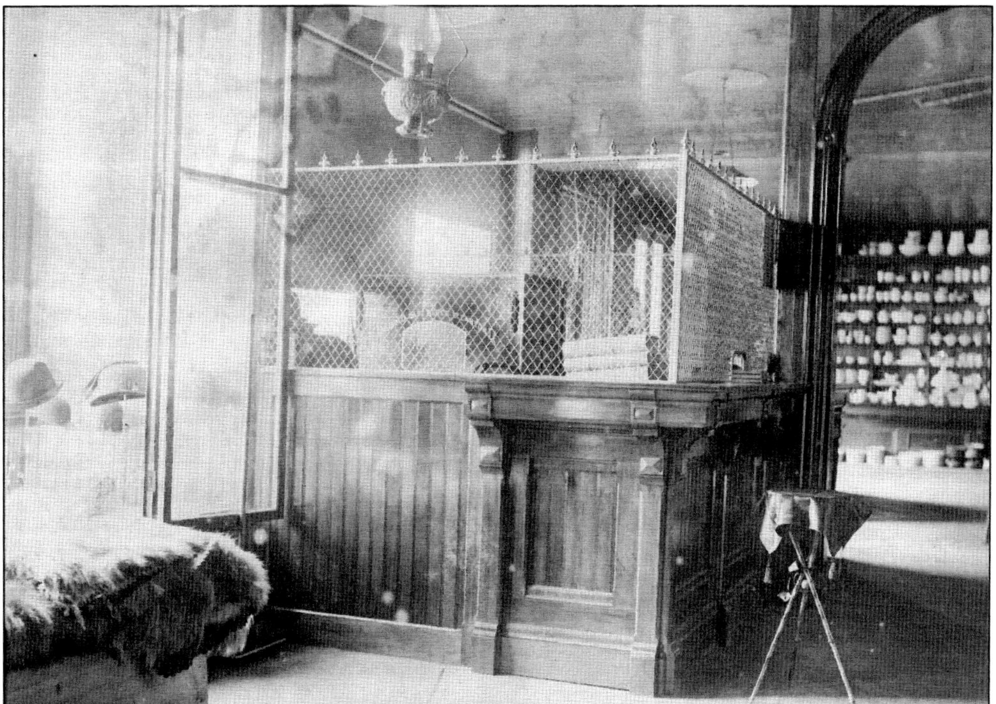

An interior view of Mallet's store with hats in the window and crockery displayed beyond a small office cage.

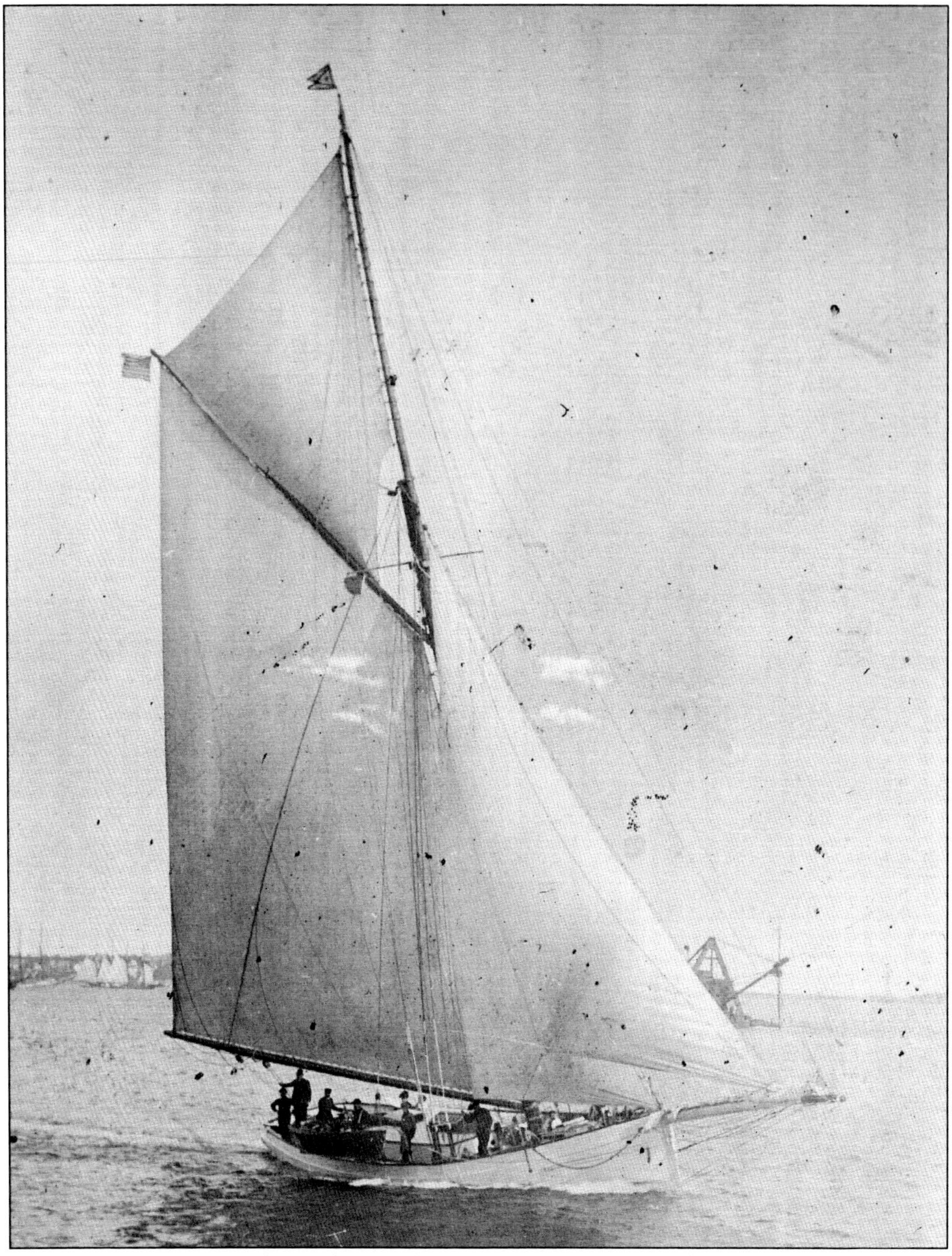

Mr. Mallet's sixty-foot yacht *Restless* was launched on July 9, 1887. This yacht, built in Bath by C.B. Harrington, was considered to be one of the fastest in the water at that time. Representing the Portland Yacht Club, Mallet won several races, but primarily used the yacht for cruising.

Three

Downtown Businesses

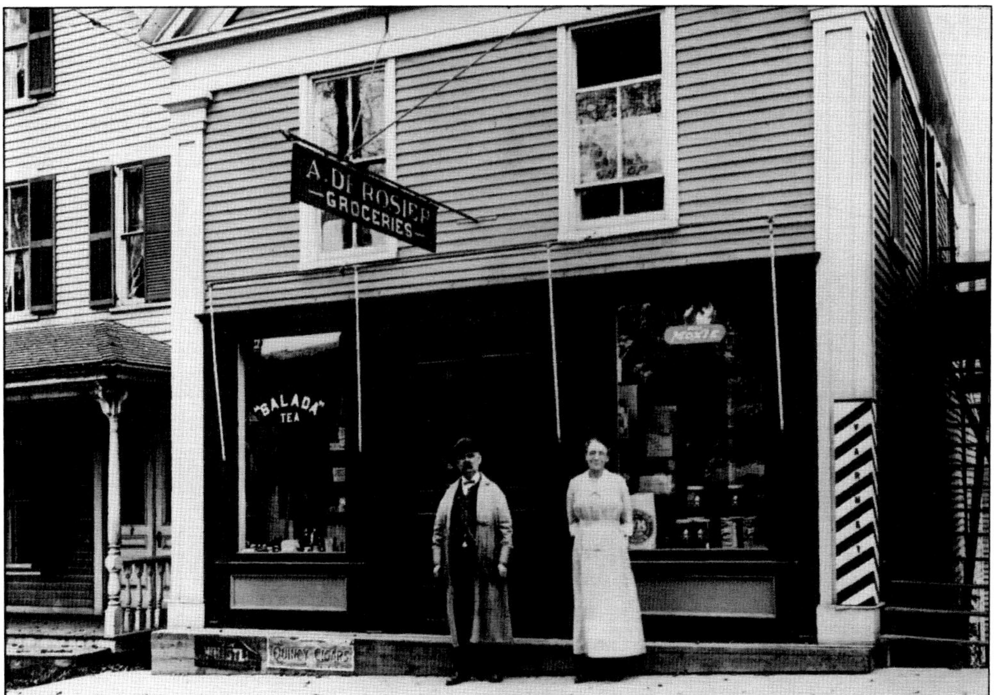

DeRosier's Grocery Store was photographed with the proud owners, Mr. and Mrs. Augustus DeRosier, c. 1920. The business, still located in the same building on Main Street, is the oldest family owned store in Freeport and is now run by the couple's great-grandson, Richard Wagner.

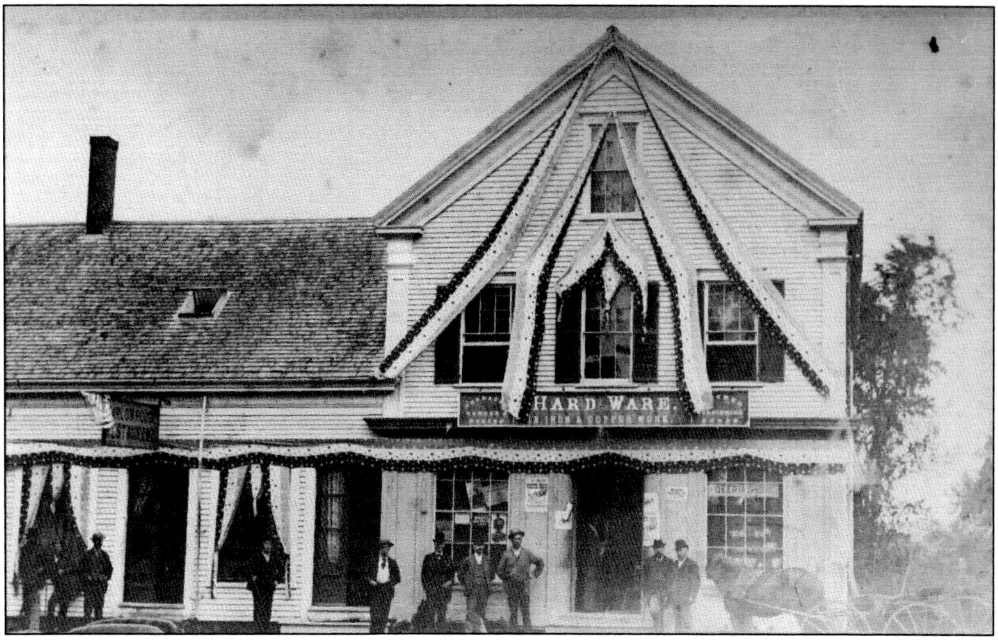

The Harlow House Restaurant and a hardware store were located on Main Street between Mechanic and School Streets around 1889.

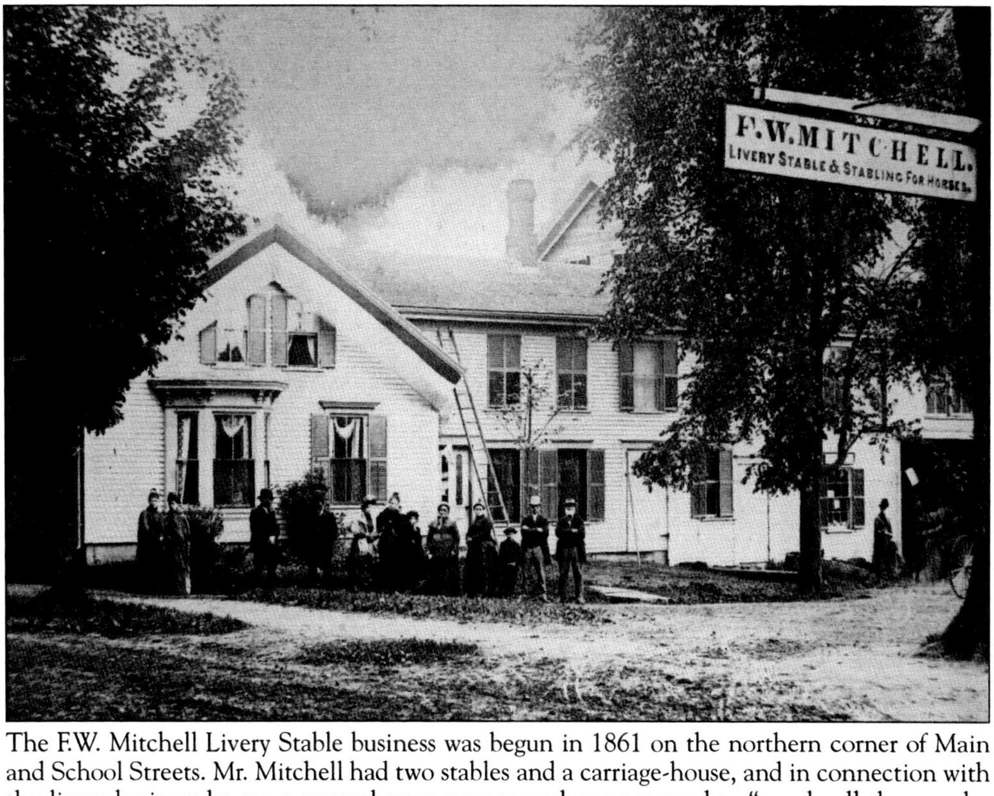

The F.W. Mitchell Livery Stable business was begun in 1861 on the northern corner of Main and School Streets. Mr. Mitchell had two stables and a carriage-house, and in connection with the livery business he ran a general news agency and was prepared to "supply all the popular publications of the day." The house was moved to Elm Street where it stands today.

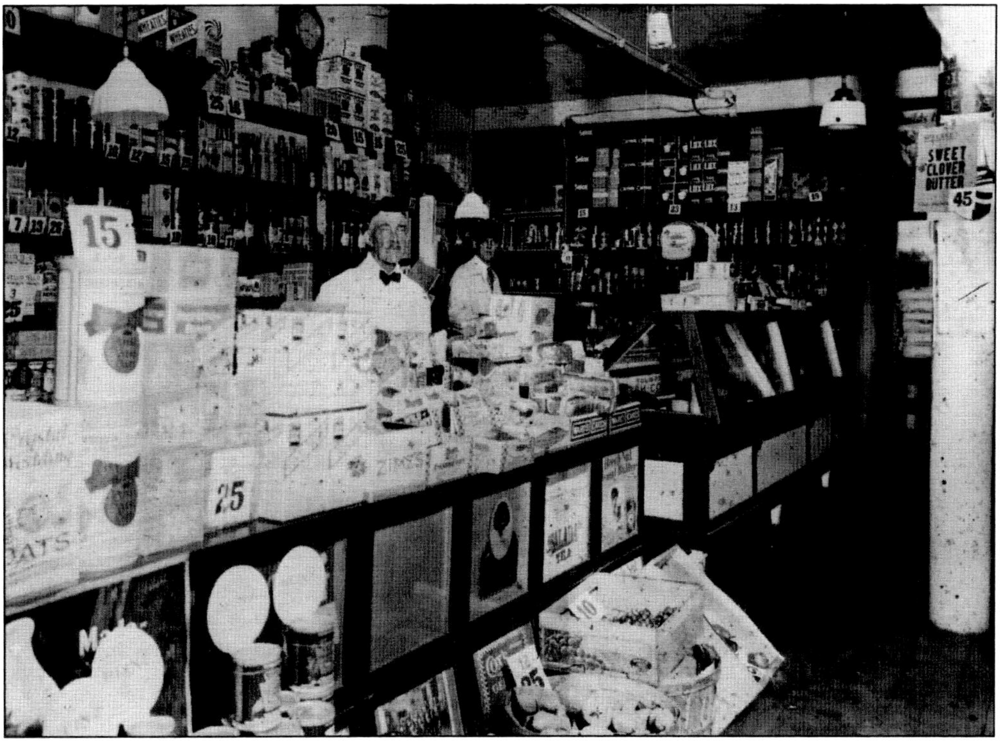

Mr. Charles T. Dillingham ran this neat and attractive grocery store in the Oxnard Block from 1902 to 1938. The store specialized in native products from surrounding farms and featured free delivery. Mr. Dillingham was famous in the community for his oyster stew.

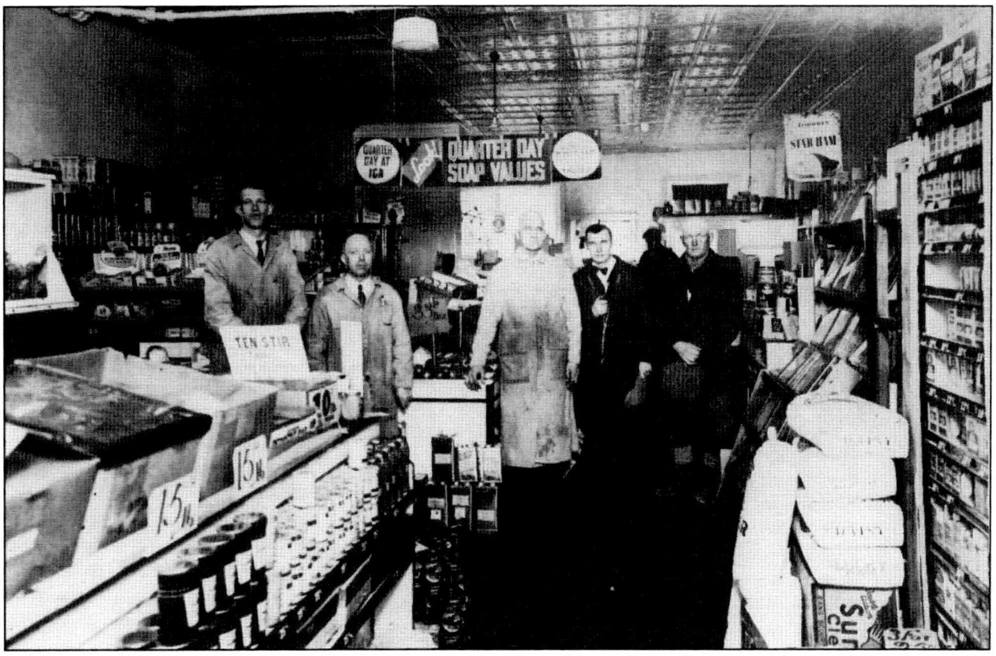

Raymond Thomas, Andy Coffin, L.E. Curtis, Jack Collins, and John Varney posed for this early 1920s picture in the IGA Grocery Store on Main Street between Bow and Mechanic Street.

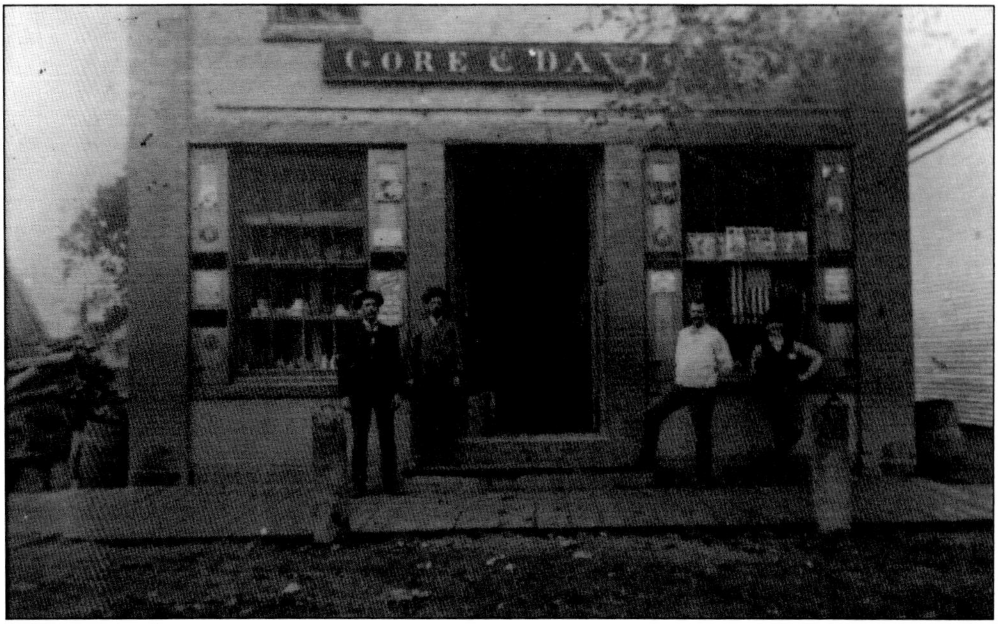

The Gore & Davis general store operated on the south corner of Main and Mechanic Streets from 1875 to 1890. William Gore began his partnership with Samuel Holbrook in 1831 and they ran the store together for nearly forty years. When Samuel Holbrook left the business in 1875, Mr. Gore formed a partnership with one of his clerks, William Davis. The store sold dry and fancy goods, groceries, boots and shoes, paints, and oils. At some point Mr. Gore added stock-raising to his mercantile business and sold cows in nearly all the New England states and New Jersey. The man in the white shirt was Presbury Dennison.

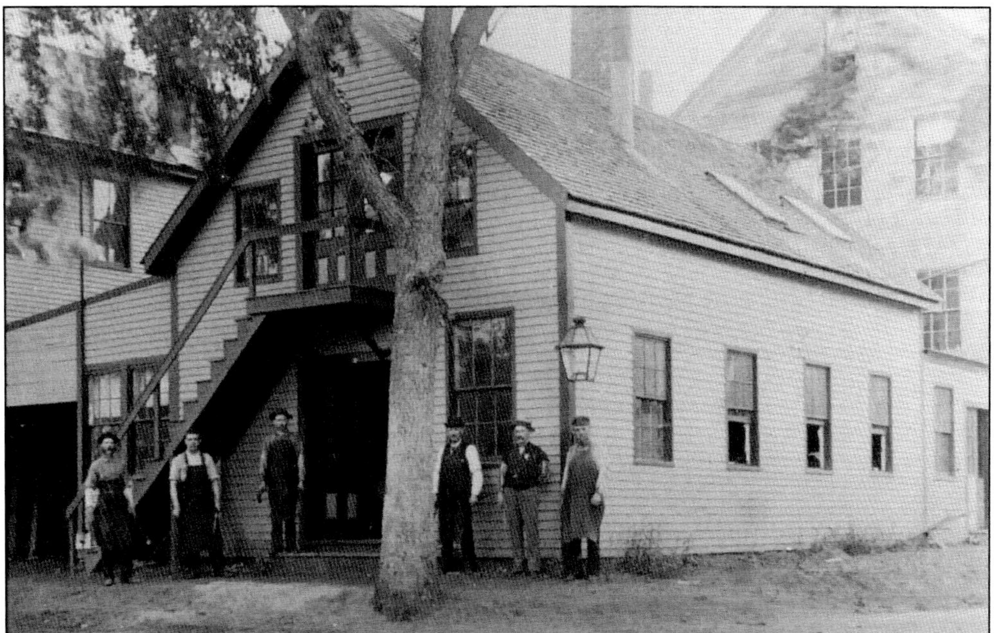

A machine shop stood on the corner of Mechanic and Middle Streets *c.* 1900. The building was at one time the home of Small Abbott Company, moccasin manufacturers.

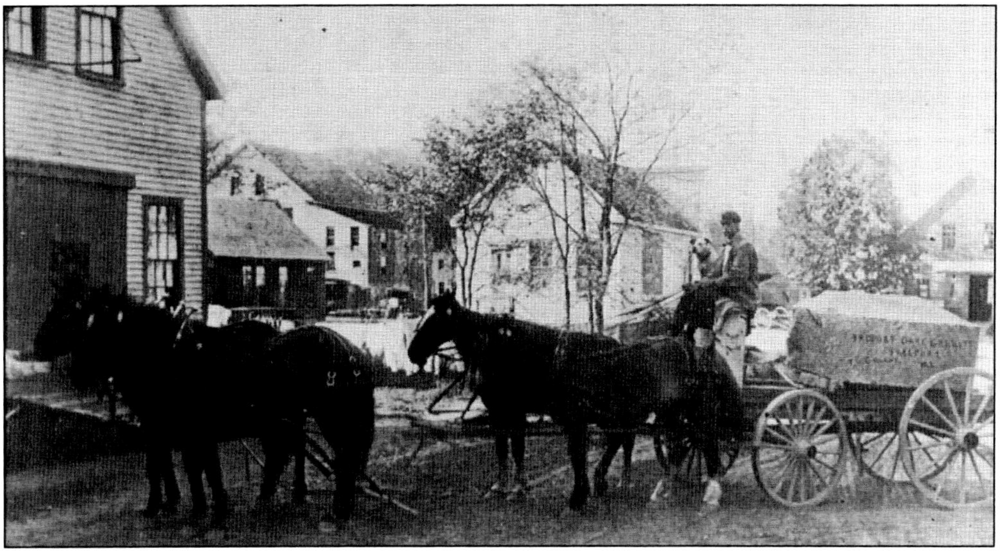

Fred C. Green is shown here making a delivery of a large piece of Freeport granite somewhere on Middle Street looking towards School Street.

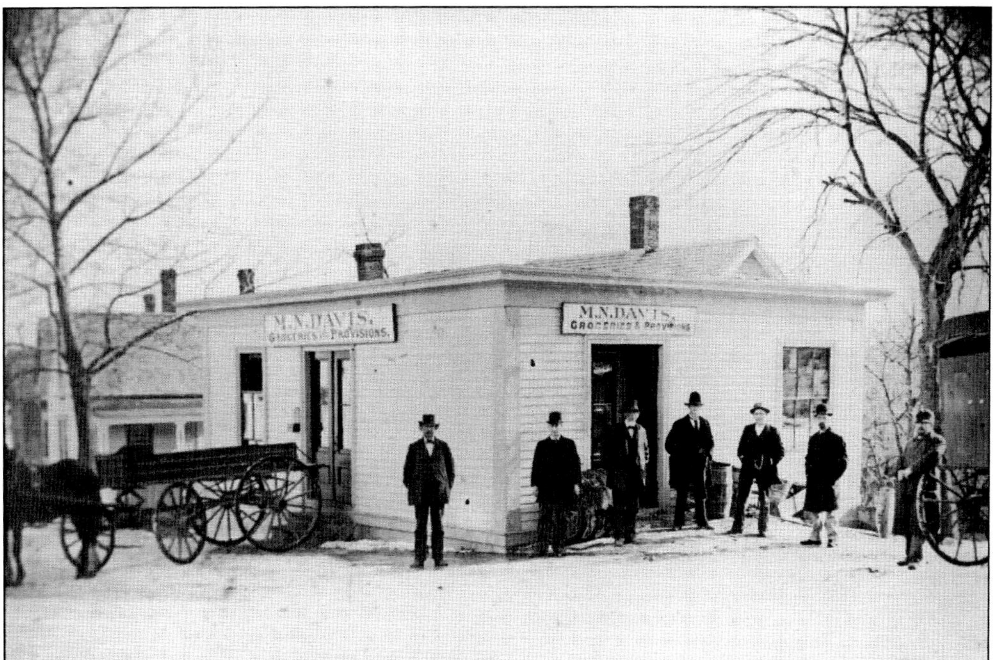

Another one of Freeport's grocery stores around the turn of the century was run by M.N. Davis. This store was located on Mechanic Street.

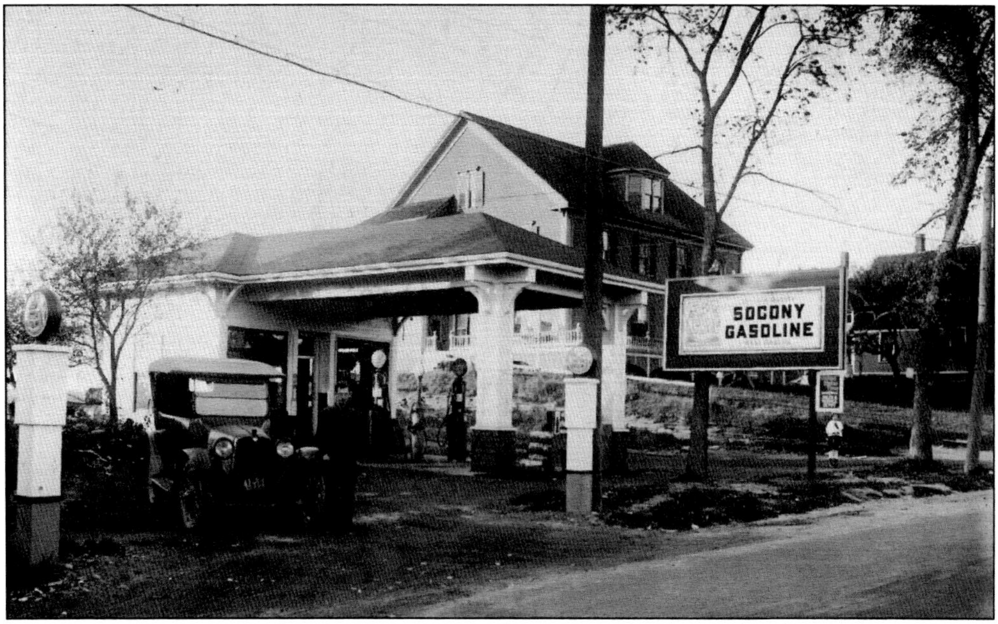

By the 1920s, gas stations had become a part of Freeport's downtown landscape. In fact, there were so many that the town passed an ordinance in the late 1930s preventing new stations from being built. This is Bob Hunter's Arcade Filling Station which was on Lower Main Street. The man standing beside the car is Linwood "Bun" Varney.

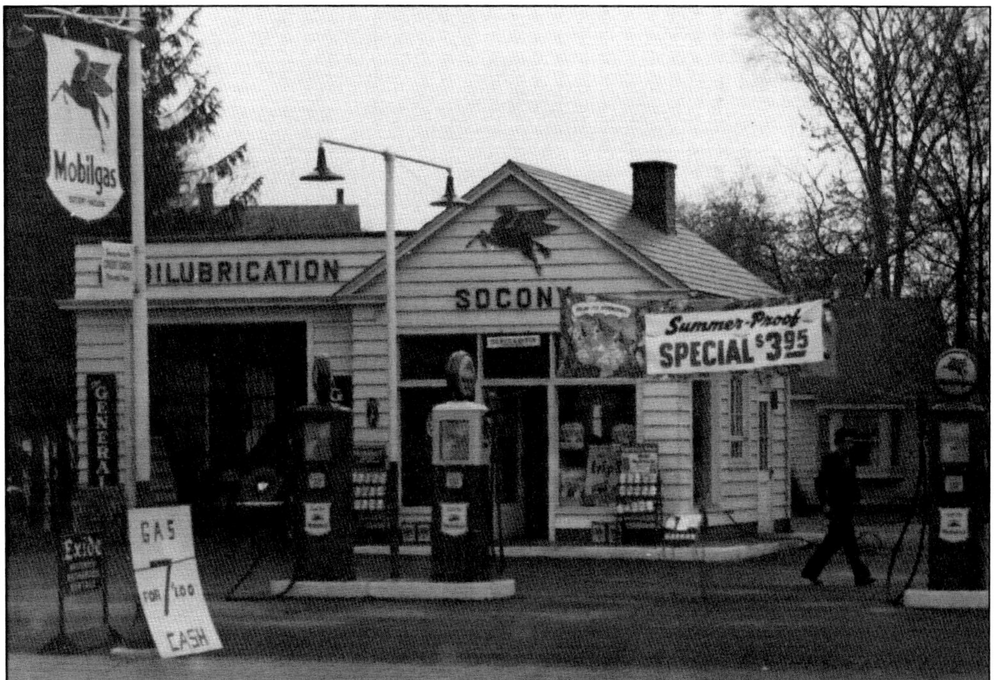

This SOCONY Filling Station was located next to the B.H. Bartol Library. It later became a Mobil Station and was torn down in 1972 to make room for a larger and more modern facility which, in turn, was torn down in the mid-1990s to make room for a larger commercial structure.

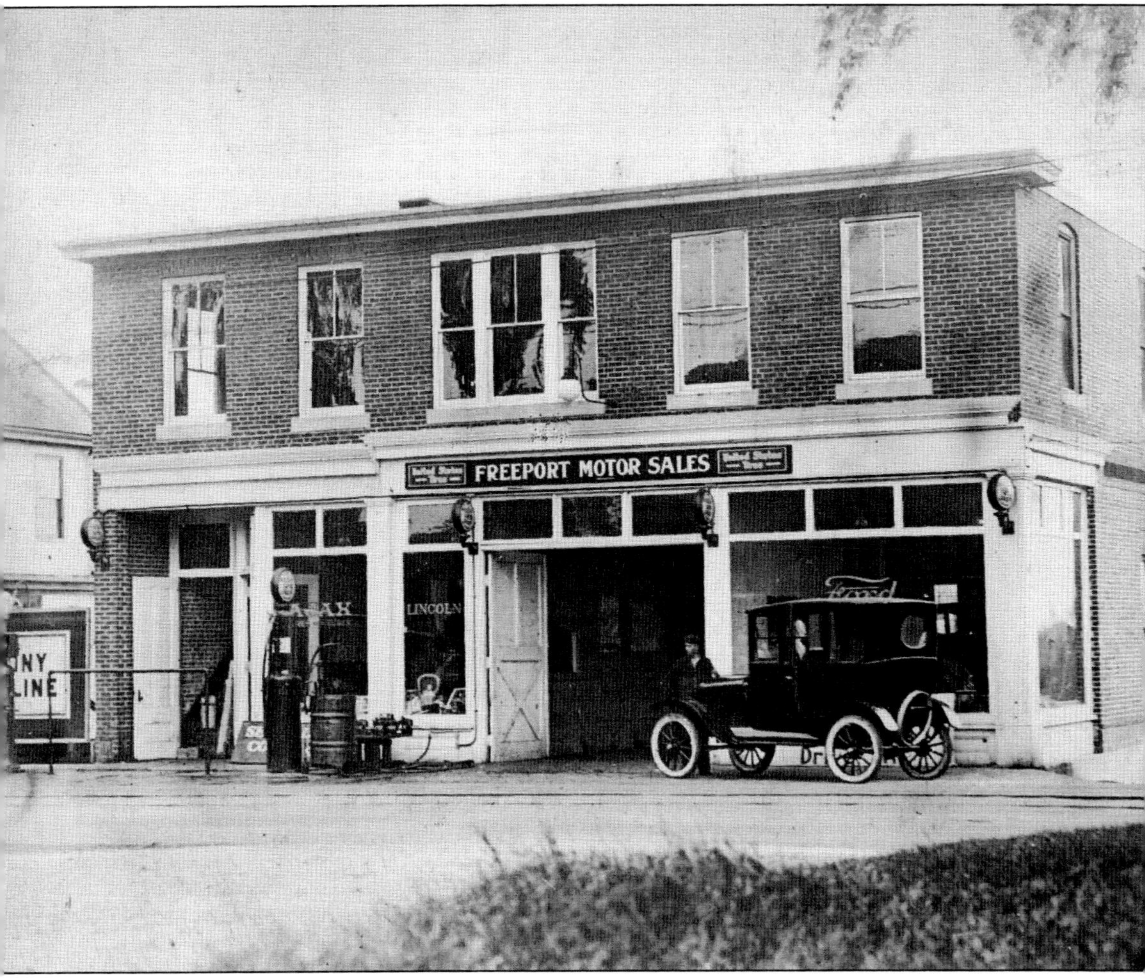

A third station on Main Street still stands today. Freeport Motor Sales was built in the 1920s by Luther Kennedy who sold Fords and later Chevrolets and gas. In 1982, the brick exterior was given a facelift by its owner and today the building is leased by a retail business. The demise of Main Street gas stations was the result of appreciated land values in downtown Freeport.

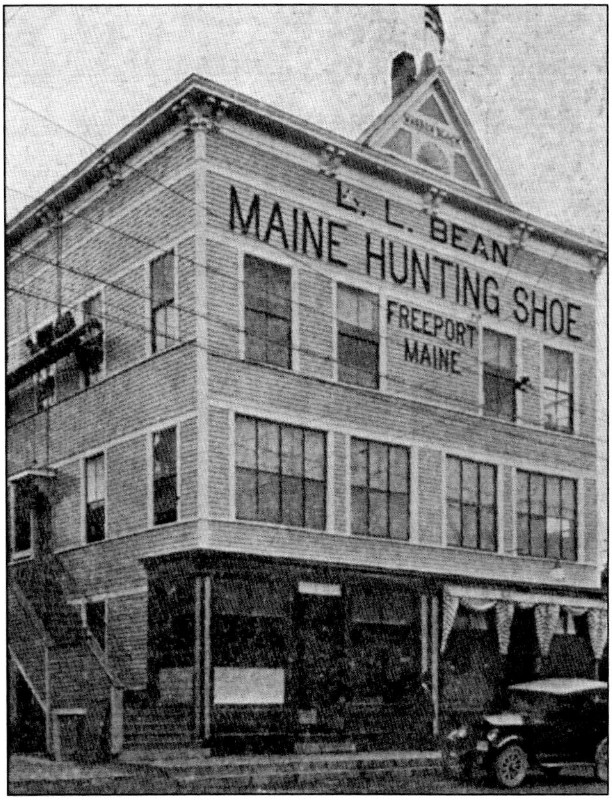

L. L. Bean was home of the Maine Hunting Shoe. In 1911 Leon Leonwood Bean began making his famous rubber and leather boots which he sold in his brother's Freeport store for $3.50 per pair. They were extremely popular and he was able to expand his business and move into this building known as the Warren Block in the 1920s. This was the beginning of the now-famous L.L. Bean mail order business, which has expanded over the years and now attracts over four million visitors each year to its retail store. Many people still remember climbing the exterior stairs to the second floor. The post office occupied the ground floor.

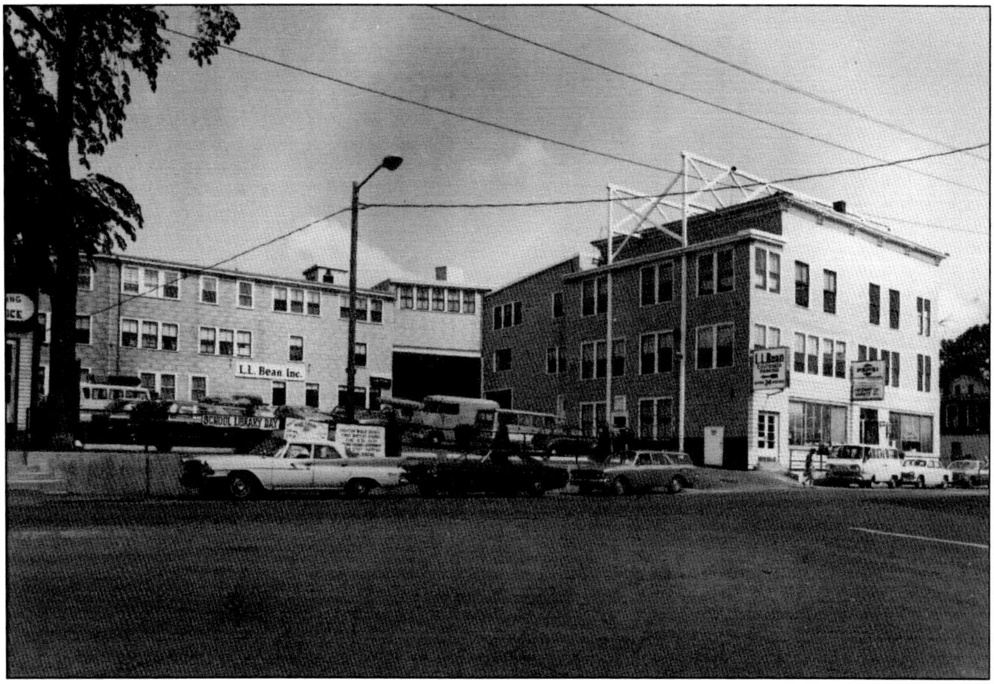

By the 1960s, L. L. Bean had enlarged its space and had done major renovations on the Warren Block.

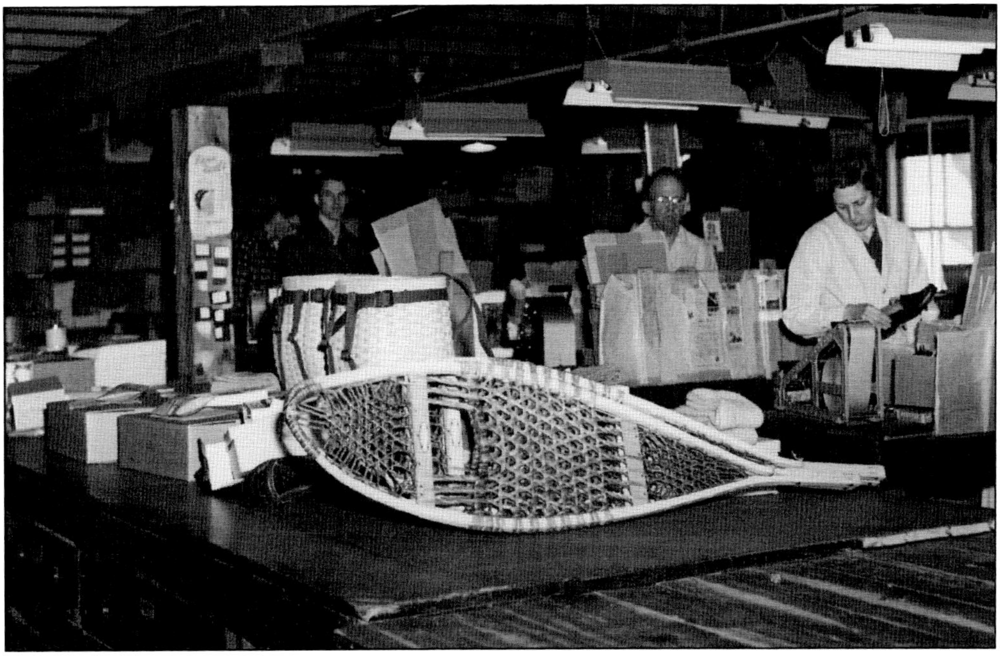

In this interior photograph of the shipping room at L. L. Bean, Don Finney, Jim Dorington, Ed Skillin, and Edna Hawes are shown packing items for mail order.

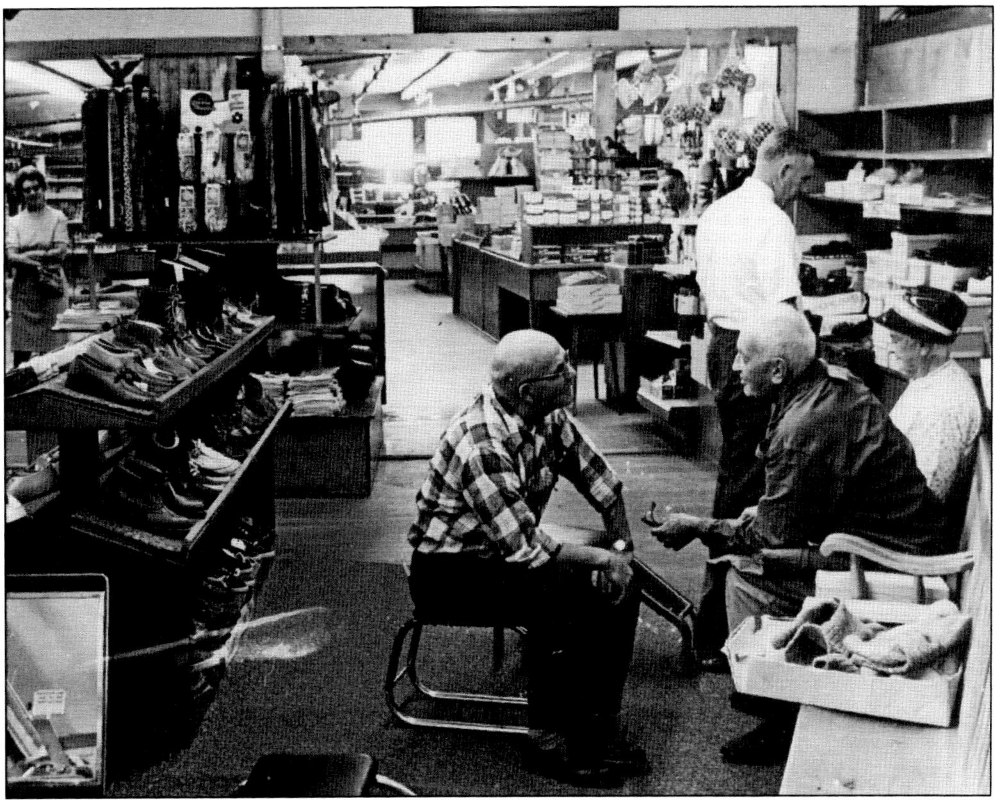

Another picture of the interior of L.L. Bean's retail store in 1968 shows the shoe department.

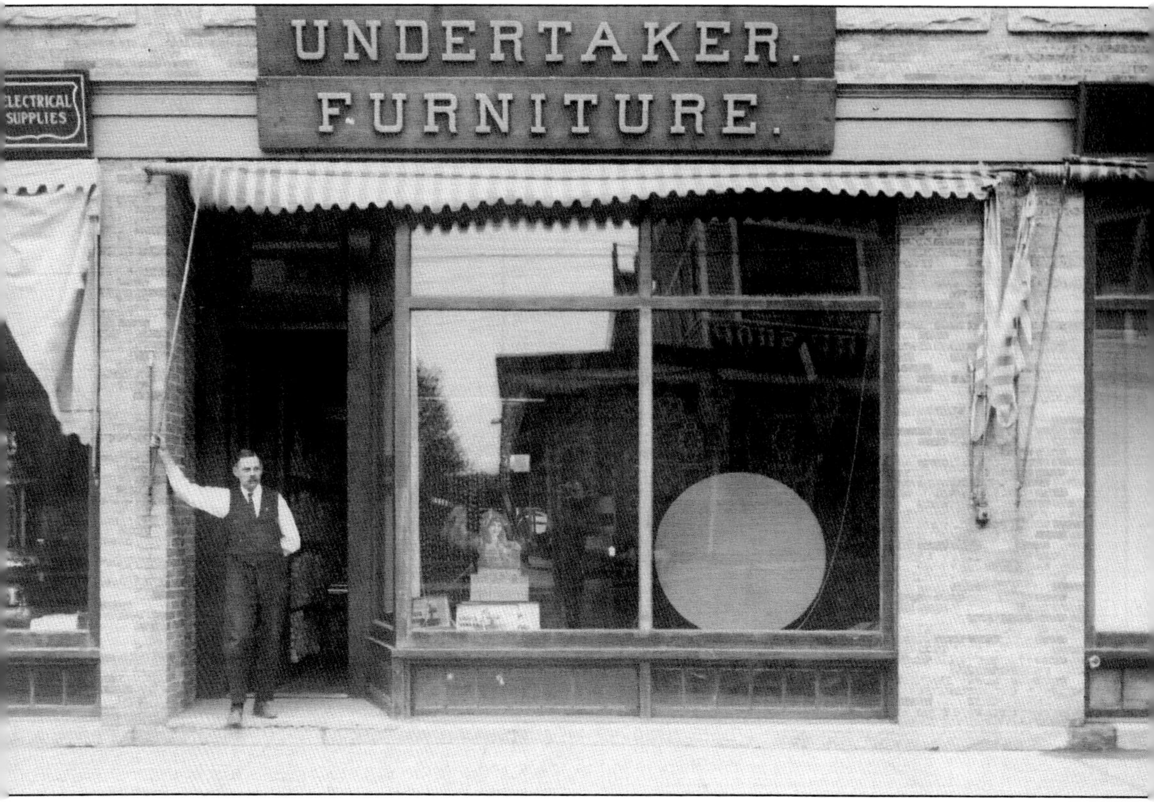

William W. Fish is shown standing in front of his undertaking and furniture business in the Davis Block around the turn of the century.

Four

Neighborhoods

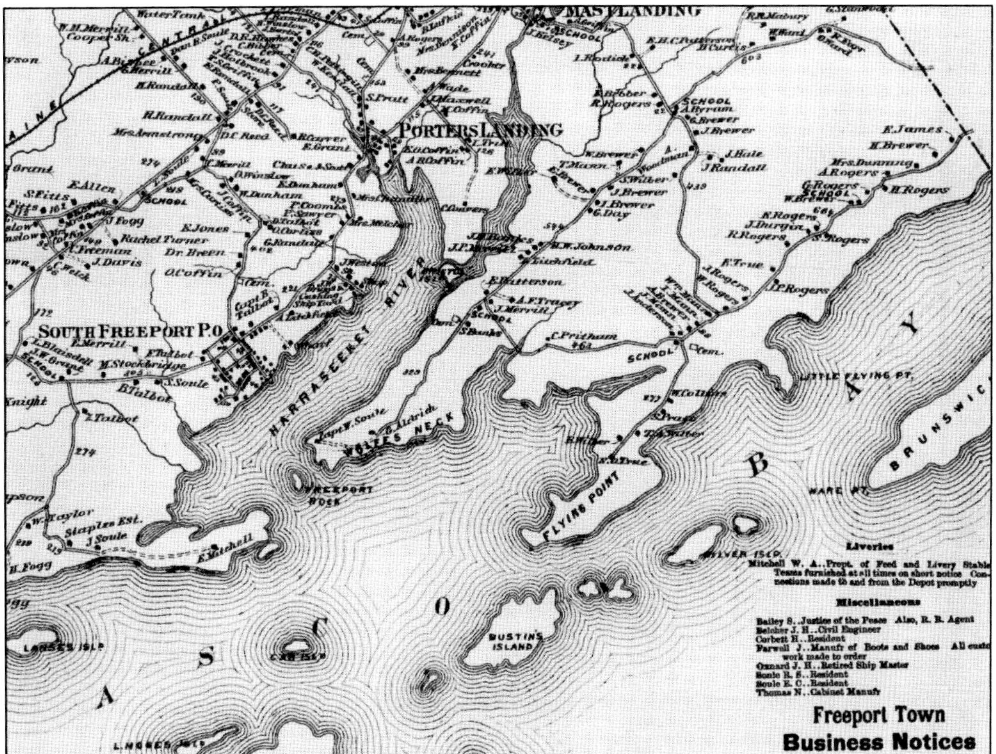

The peninsulas of Wolfe's Neck and Flying Point and the area around the Harraseeket River are shown on this detail of an 1871 map of Freeport. The little-changed historic landscape, early saltwater farms, and coastal villages of this section of town led to the establishment of the Harraseeket Historic District, listed in the National Register of Historic Places in 1974. Since the eighteenth century, self-sufficient landowners in this area of Freeport have relied on products of land and sea—hay from salt marshes and fields, farm produce from gardens and pastures, timber from their wood lots, and fish and shellfish from the bay and mud flats surrounding these points. Some of the men were mariners, leaving their wives to run the farms when they were away at sea.

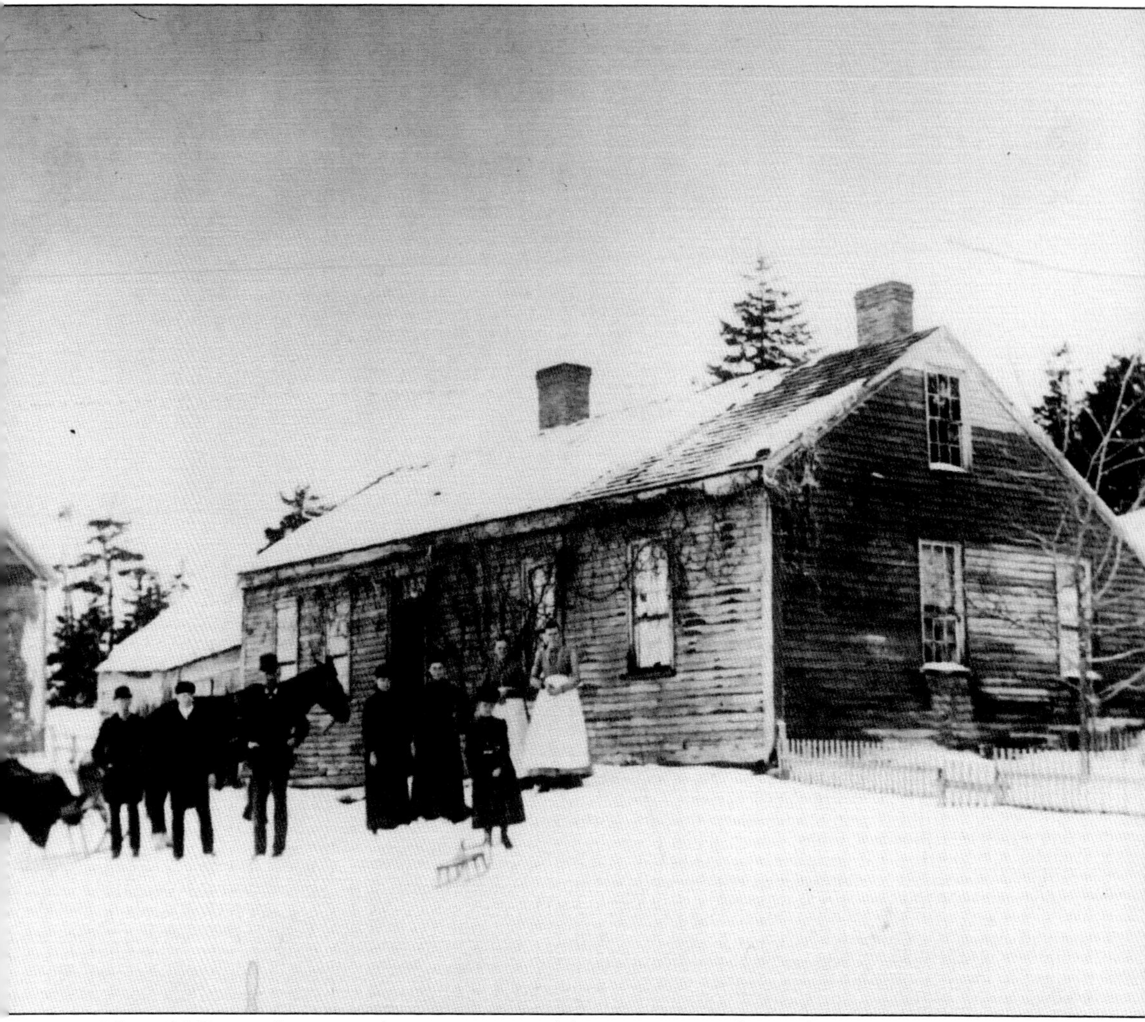

The old Rogers homestead, a one-story saltbox, once stood on Flying Point Road near the Brunswick line. This picture shows the family gathered outside with a sleigh. The little girl with the sled has been identified as Helen Farr.

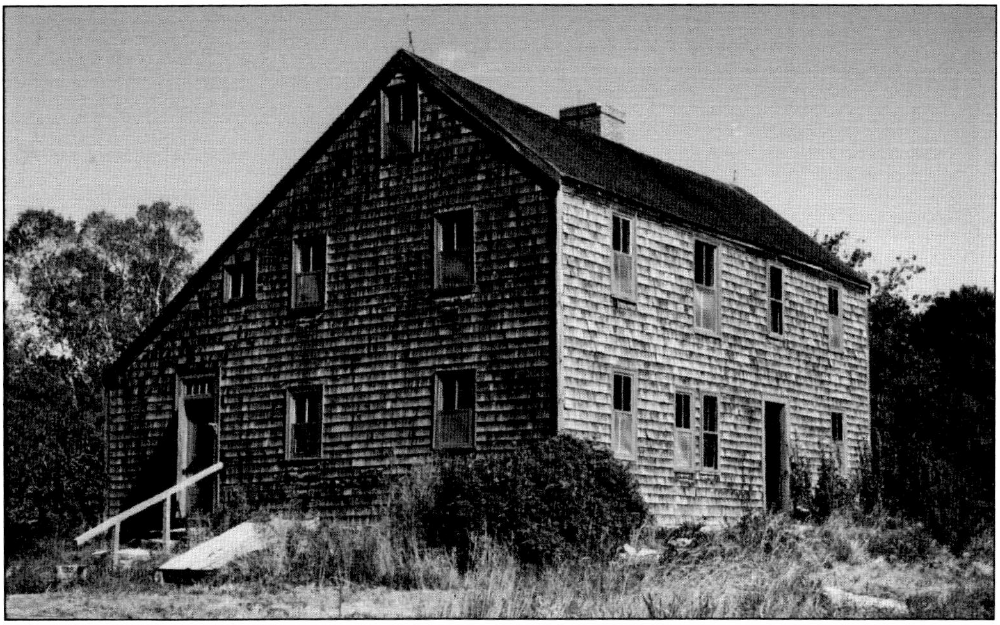

The Captain Greenfield Pote House was built c.1760 in Falmouth and moved by water to Wolfe's Neck around 1787 following a disagreement with the Town of Falmouth. The saltbox design was once common in Freeport and few, such as the Pote House, remain standing today. The house now belongs to the University of Southern Maine.

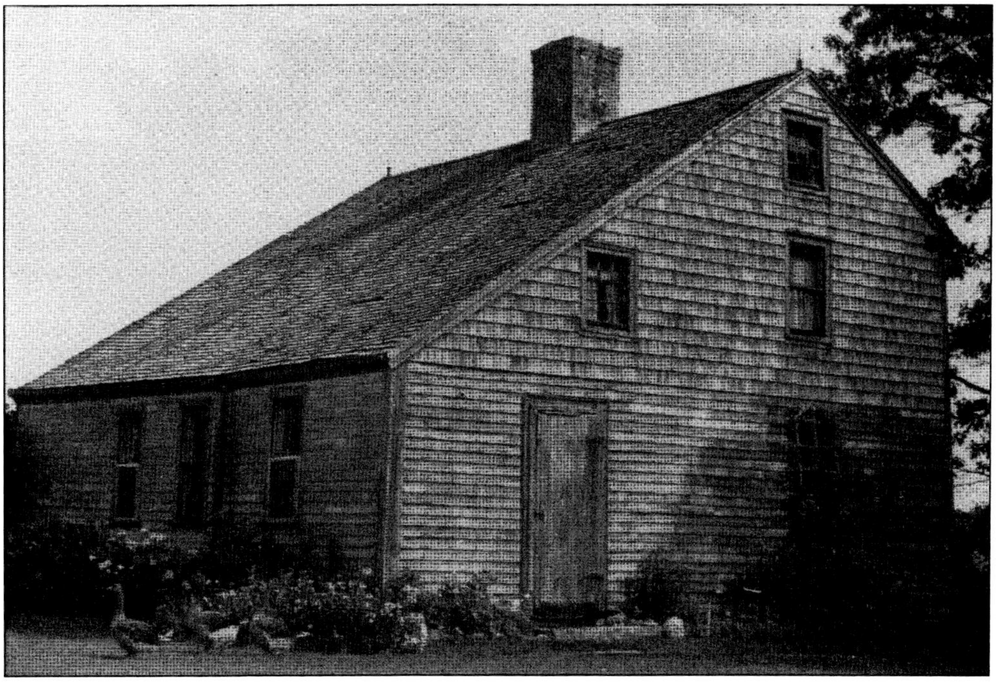

Near the village of Mast Landing, not far from the head of the Harraseeket River, lies the 140-acre Pettengill Farm, owned by the Freeport Historical Society. The farmhouse is a small Federal-period saltbox built c.1810 by former mariner Aaron Lufkin and later owned by the Rodick and Pettengill families. It remains in its original state with no electricity or plumbing.

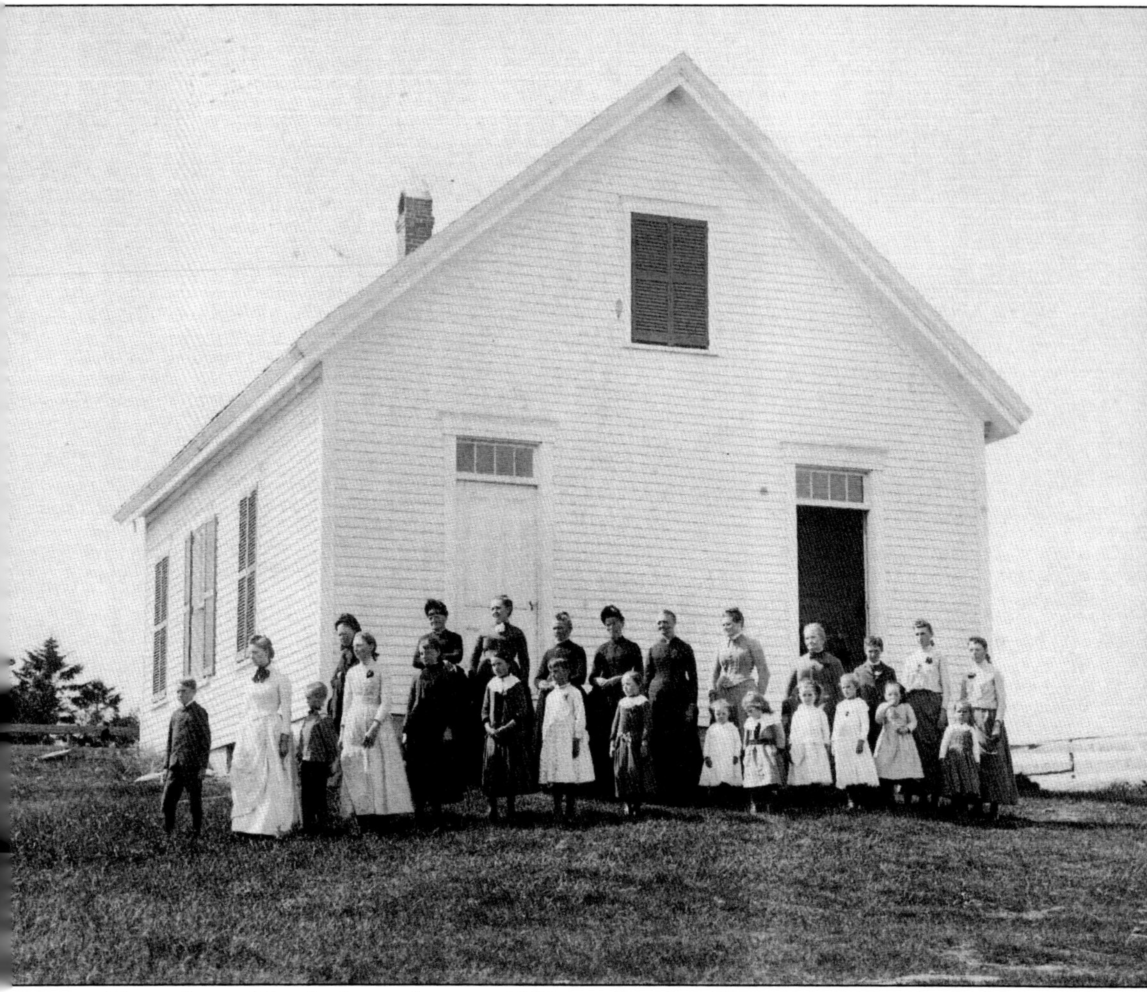

Flying Point School, shown here in 1887, was listed as "District # 13" and stands on land purchased for a schoolhouse by neighborhood families early in the 1800s. The families, including the Andersons, Manns, Brewers, Dunnings, Rogers, and Means, were early settlers of the Flying Point area and some of their descendants live there today. Closed as a school in 1924, the building has been owned and used for many years as a neighborhood center called the "Thomas Means Club," named after one of the victims of a 1756 Indian attack on his house nearby.

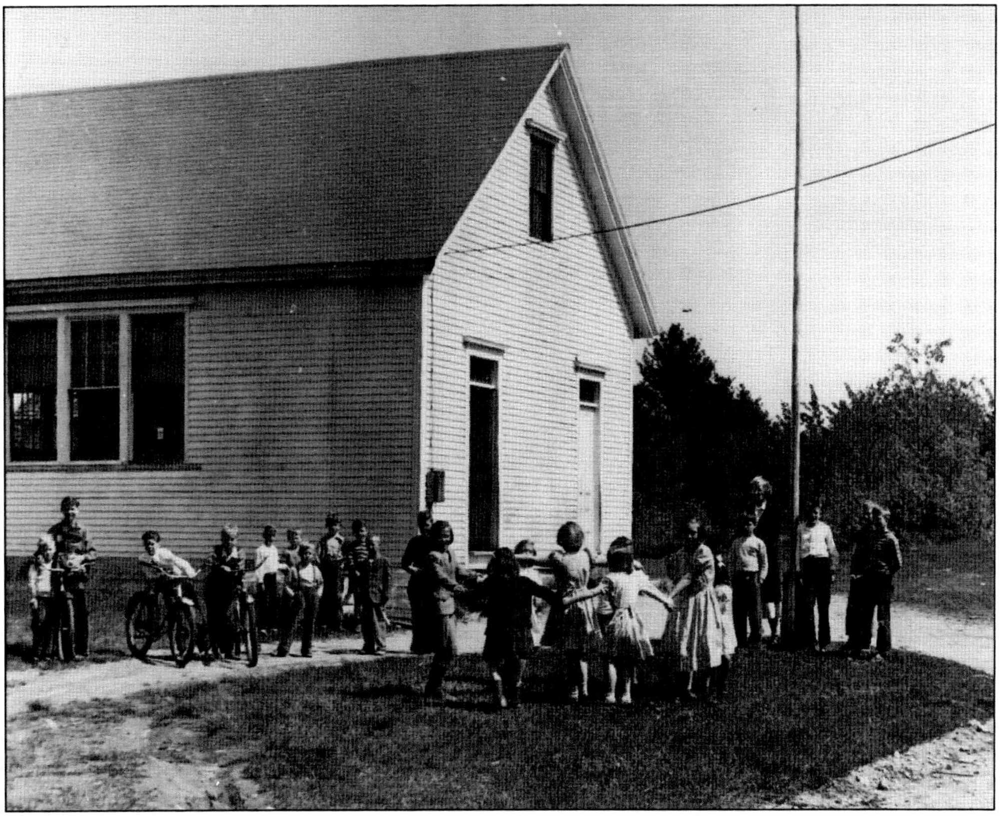

The Litchfield School, built in 1854 on a nearby site, was another one of Freeport's fifteen neighborhood schools, and was listed as "District # 16." It was moved a few hundred yards west away from Flying Point Road in the nineteenth century and closed in 1959 shortly after this photograph was taken. It is no longer standing today.

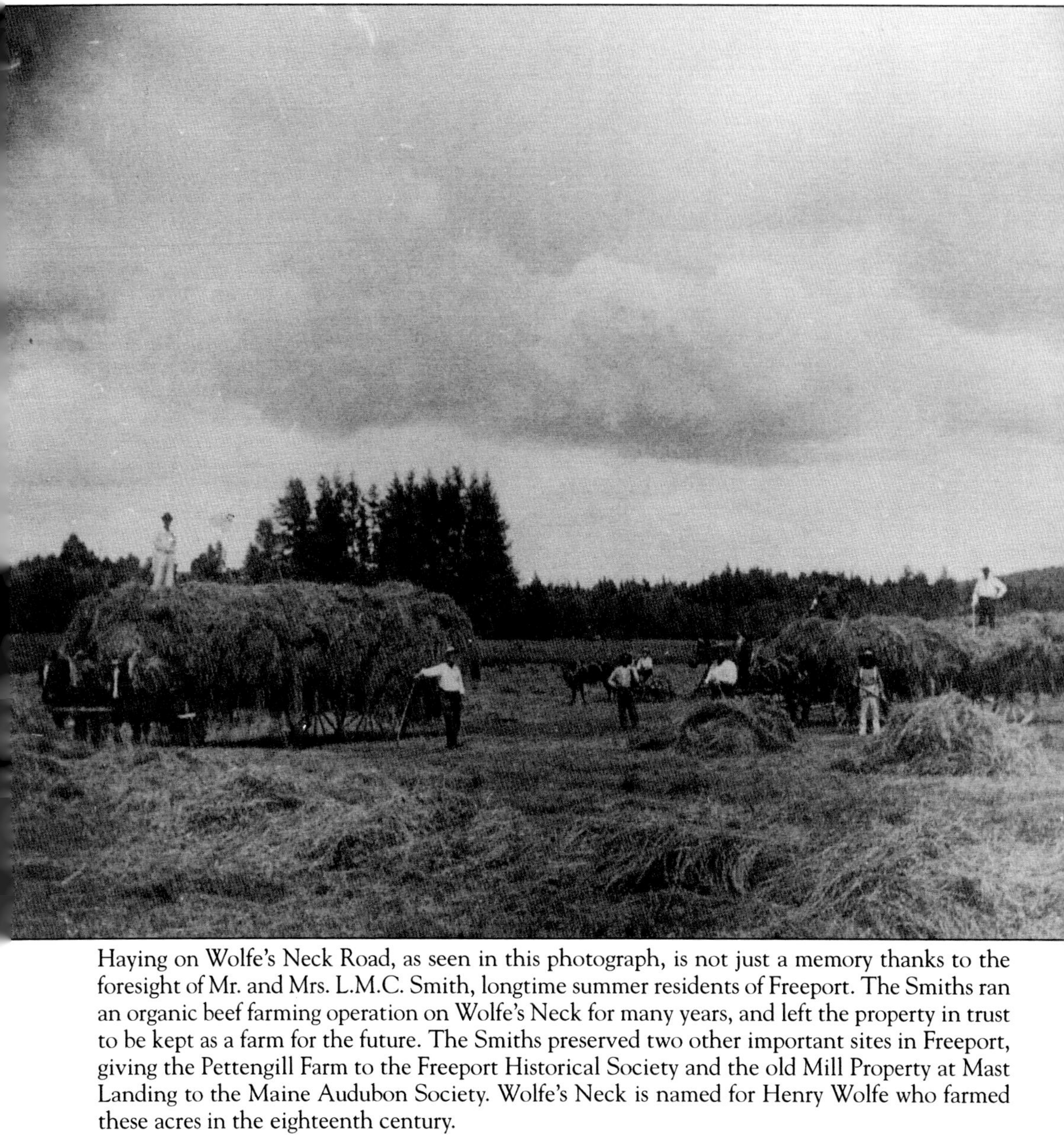

Haying on Wolfe's Neck Road, as seen in this photograph, is not just a memory thanks to the foresight of Mr. and Mrs. L.M.C. Smith, longtime summer residents of Freeport. The Smiths ran an organic beef farming operation on Wolfe's Neck for many years, and left the property in trust to be kept as a farm for the future. The Smiths preserved two other important sites in Freeport, giving the Pettengill Farm to the Freeport Historical Society and the old Mill Property at Mast Landing to the Maine Audubon Society. Wolfe's Neck is named for Henry Wolfe who farmed these acres in the eighteenth century.

A photograph of the Smith family enjoying a summer afternoon at the Wood-Smith House, now known as "The Stone House," their summer home on Wolfe's Neck Road.

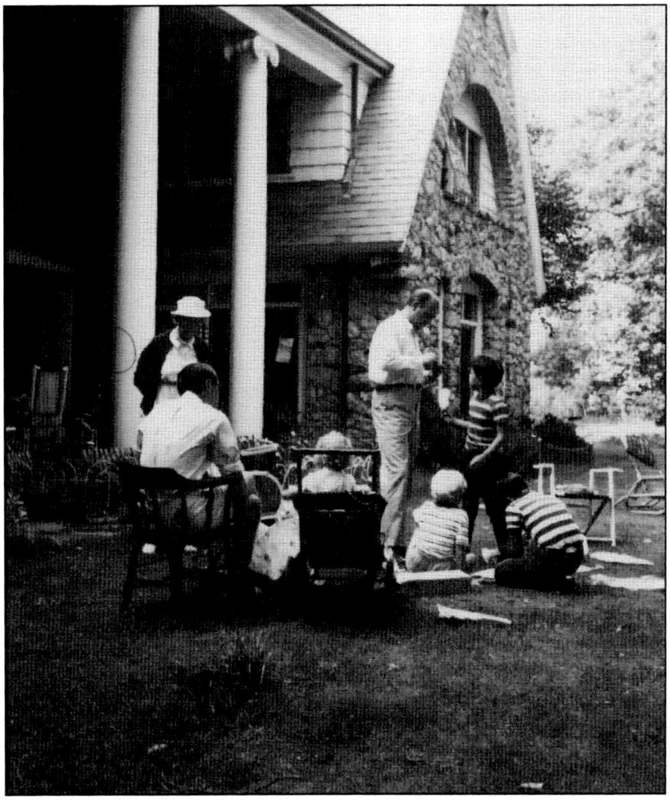

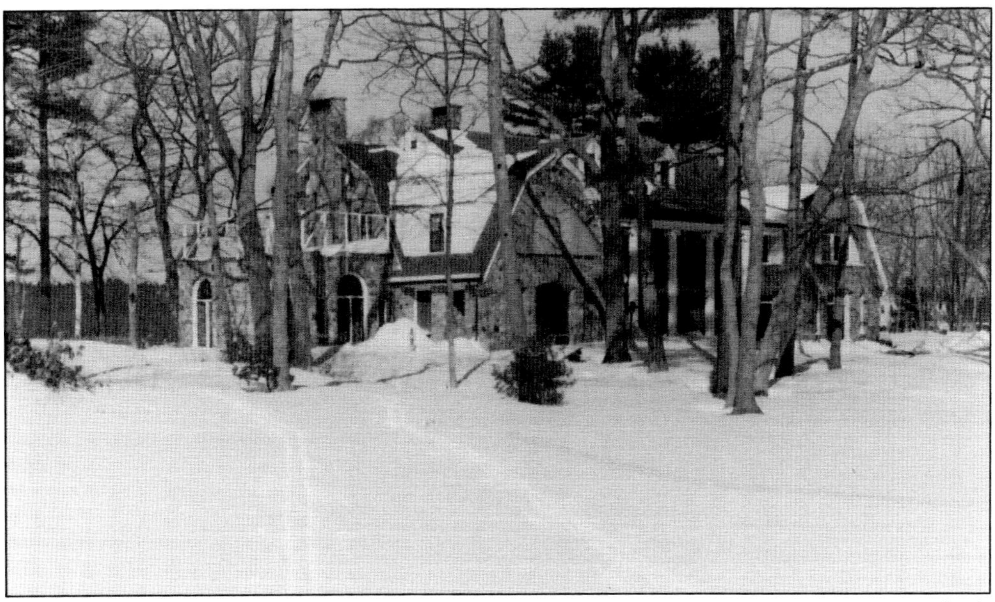

The Wood-Smith House, designed by Portland architect John Calvin Stevens, was built between 1918 and 1922 as the summer residence of Stanley Wood of the American Hoist and Derrick Co. The house was purchased in 1946 by Lawrence M.C. and Eleanor H. Smith who spent many summers there with their family. In the mid-1980s Mrs. Smith gave the house to the University of Southern Maine, and today it is used as a conference center.

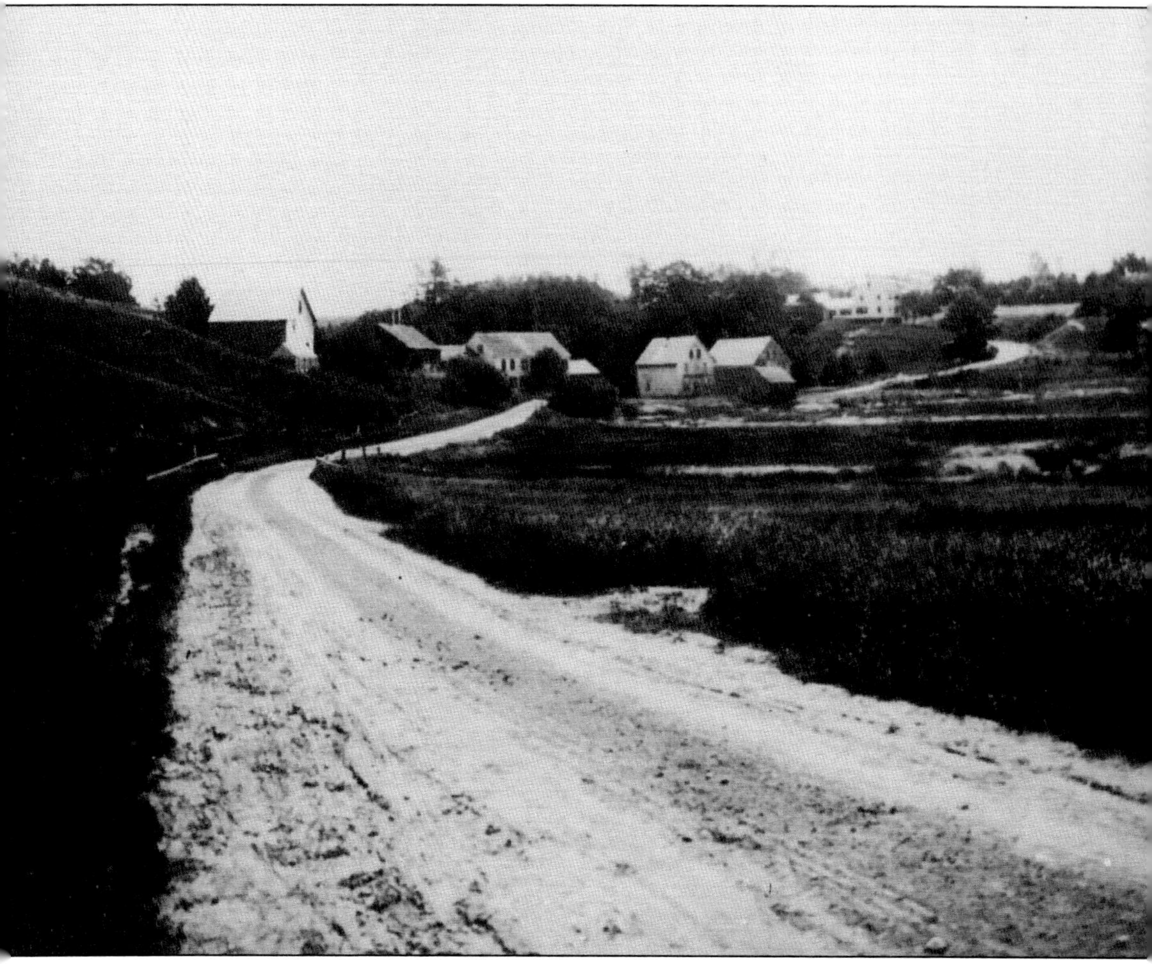

Mast Landing is located inland of the head tide of the Harraseeket River. In the eighteenth century, masts and spars from surrounding and inland forests were brought here to be floated out for shipment from Portland. This 1902 view of the village shows the old road winding by the salt marshes towards the small village above the river. On the top of the far hill the village consists primarily of small, center-chimney capes built between 1800 and 1850. Dennison's mill and dam (1804) operated in this area first as a grist mill and later as a saw, shingle, and woodworking mill.

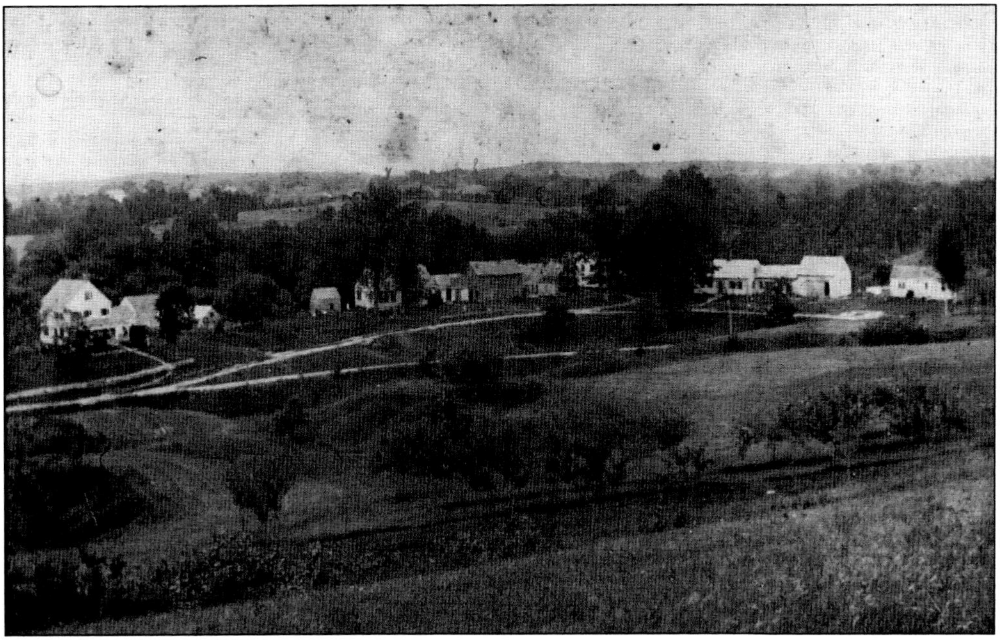

This view offers another perspective of the Mast Landing Village.

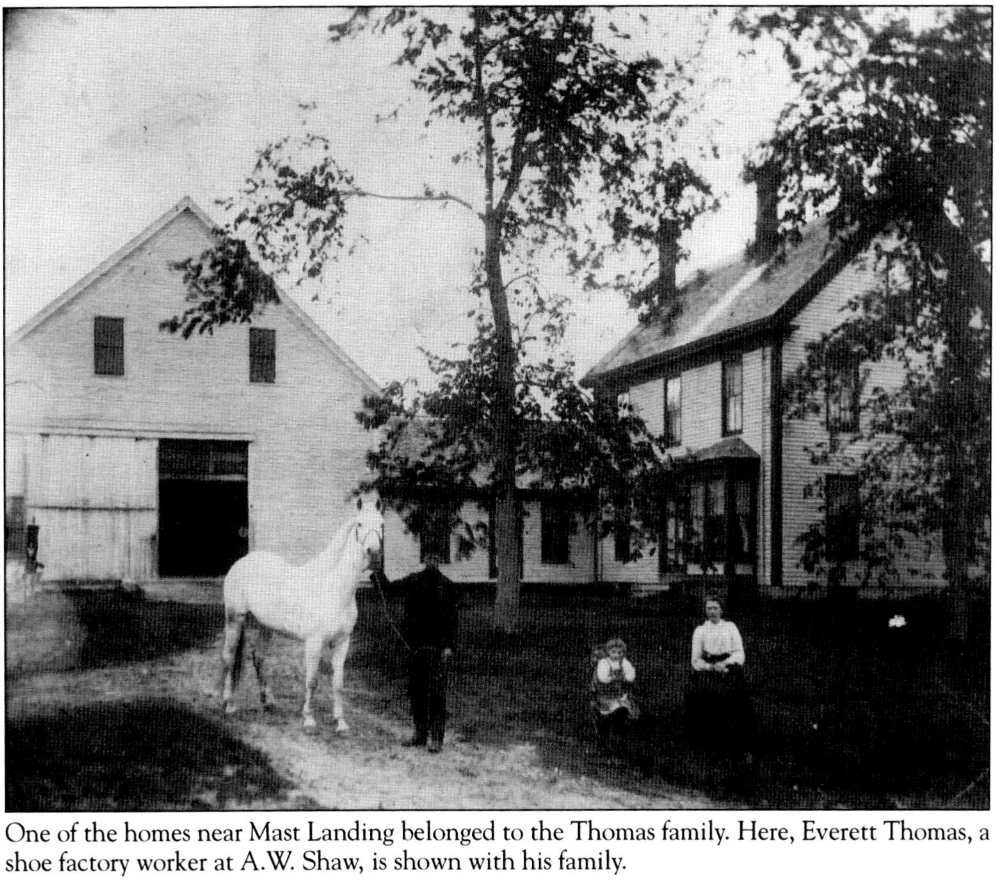

One of the homes near Mast Landing belonged to the Thomas family. Here, Everett Thomas, a shoe factory worker at A.W. Shaw, is shown with his family.

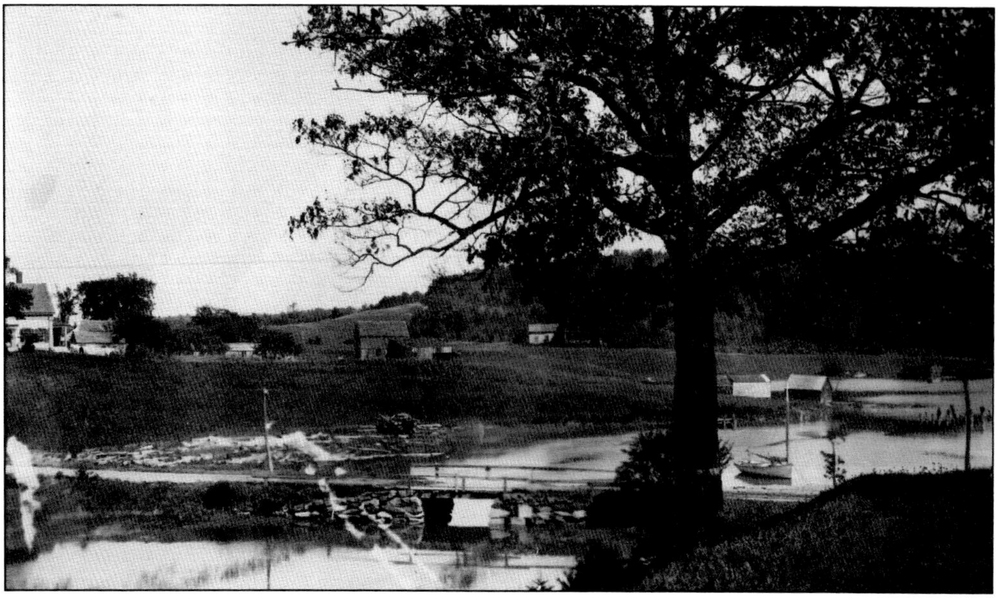

Before the coming of the railroad to Freeport in 1849, Porter's Landing Village was the port for Freeport Center. In 1770 a road was constructed from the landing inland to Durham to move freight. The village was then called "Bartol's Point Landing" for trader George Bartol who came here before the Revolution. Seward Porter and his family then came in 1782 and ran a shipyard, eventually selling their holdings in the early 1830s to Rufus Soule who proceeded to build as many as one hundred ships here. This is a view of the old shipyard site at the Landing prior to 1920.

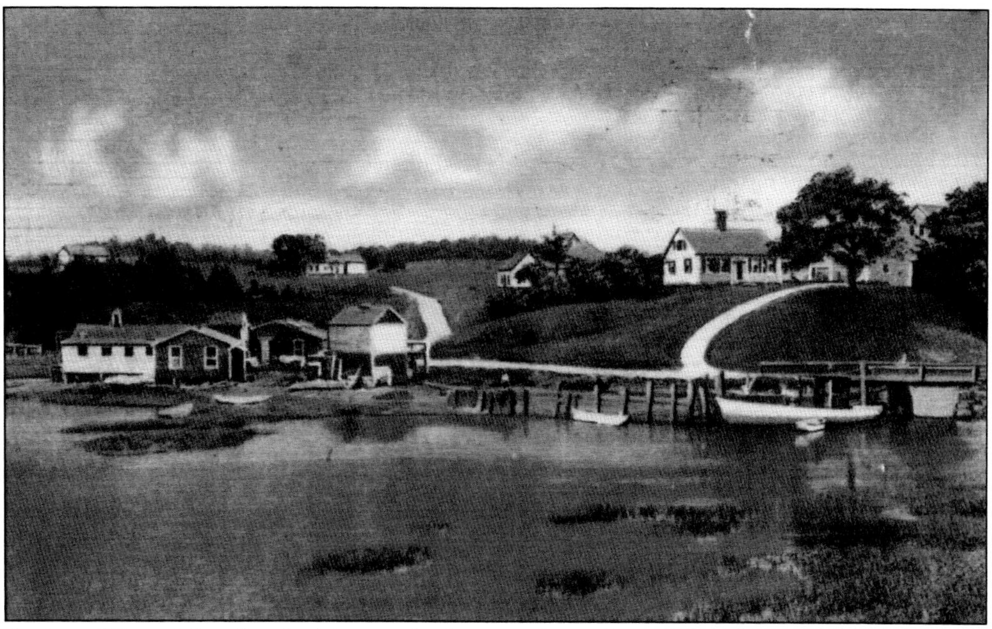

A view of Porter's Landing looking south, showing the crab meat factory then in operation.

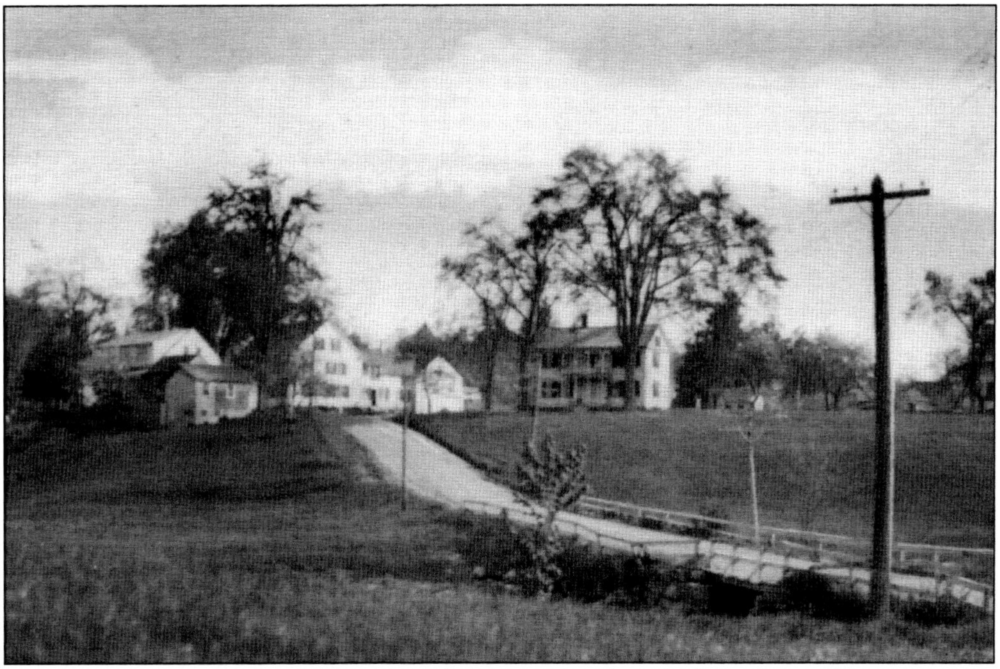

Early twentieth-century photographs of Porter's Landing Village show the community in summertime and wintertime. Many of the houses, which still stand today, were built by shipbuilders, sea captains, and traders prior to 1860.

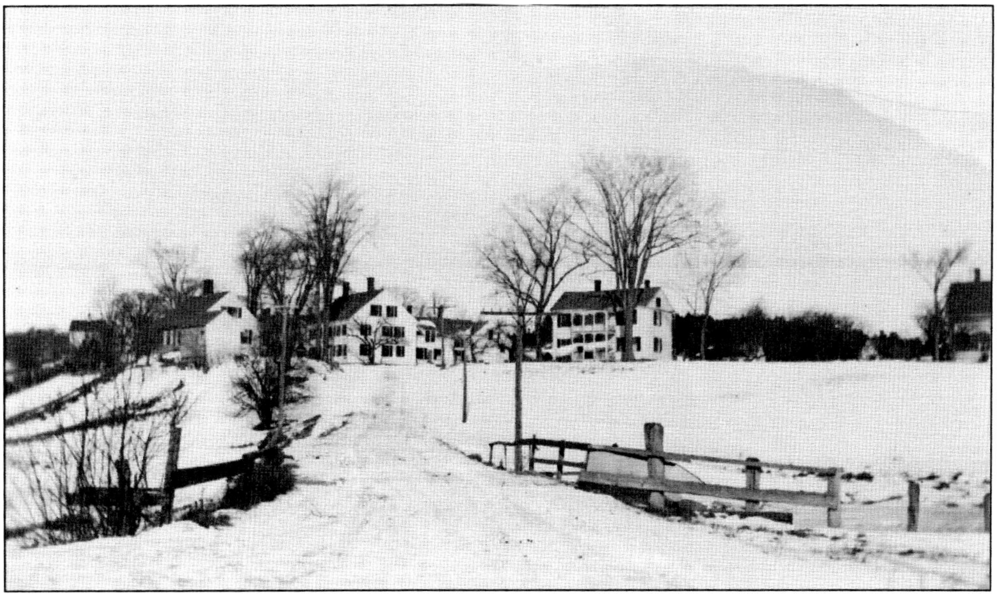

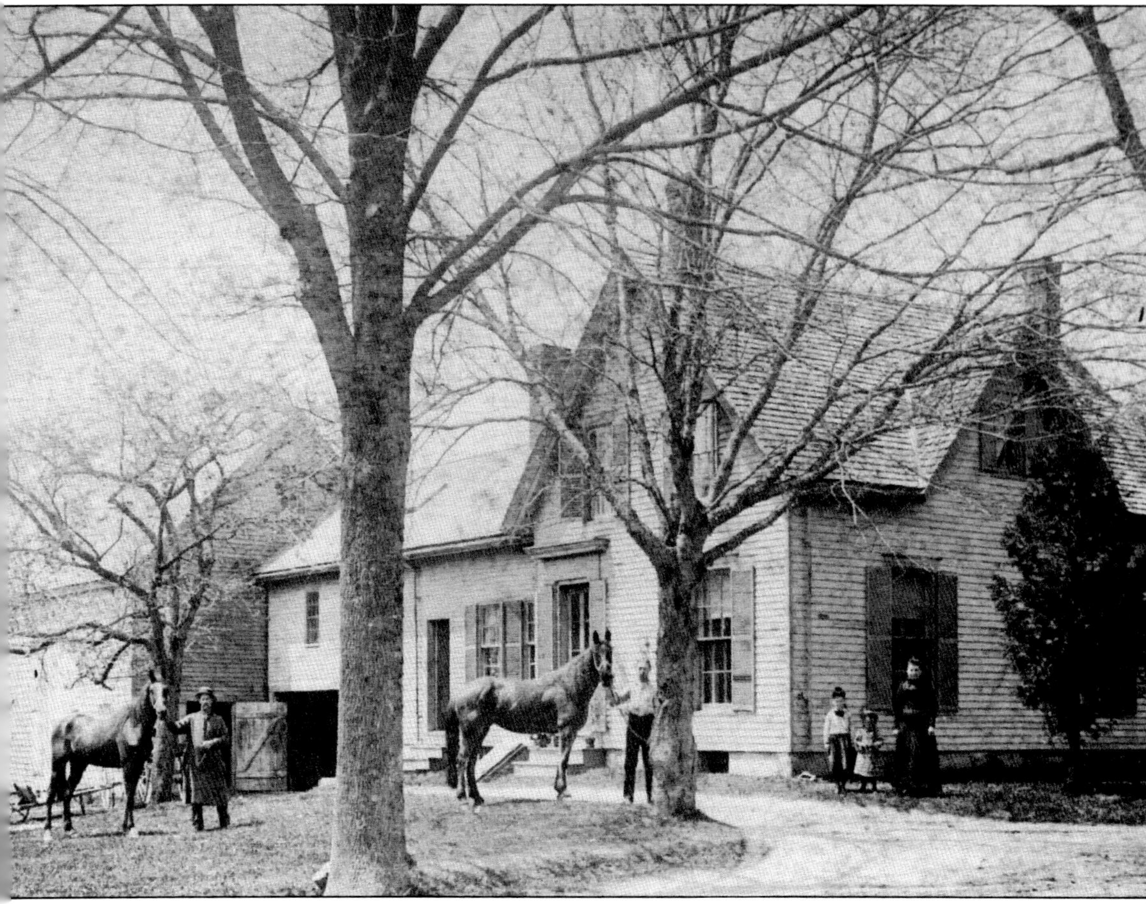

Charles Henry Pettengill, identified in 1857 as a "lumber dealer," purchased this farm on South Street in 1844 from his father, Jason. Seen in this *c.* 1890 photograph in front of the house are Charles Henry's son, Daniel Lane Pettengill (holding a horse), with his wife, Gertrude, and their first two children, Thora and Jason. To the left is Daniel's brother George Pettengill, holding another horse. The original barn seen in this photograph was replaced in 1895 with a large Victorian gabled barn still used today.

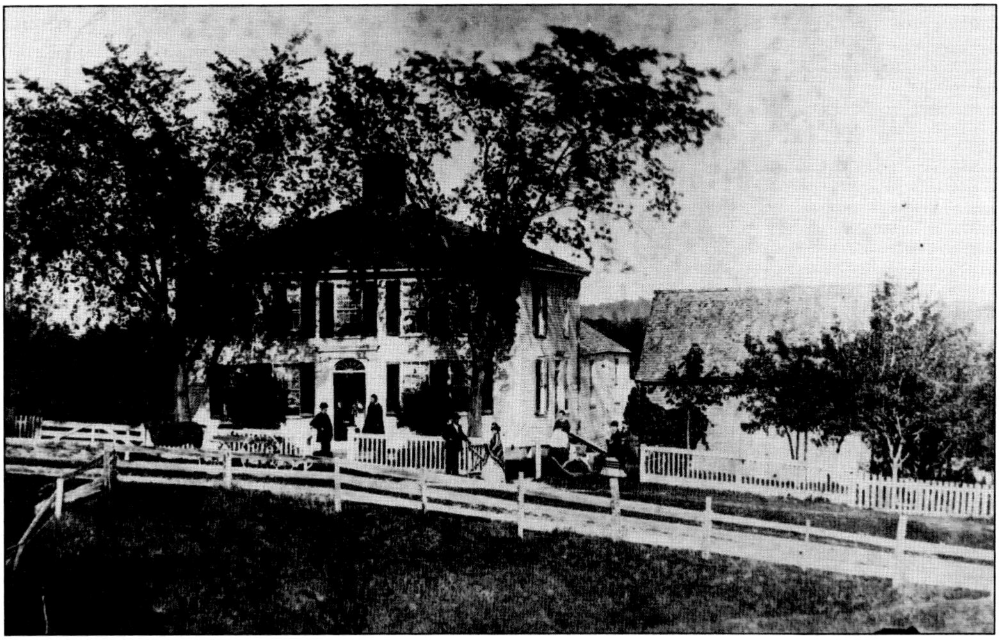

An early photograph shows a house on South Street in Porter's Landing, built in 1801 by Jeremiah Coffin. His daughter Louisa married Thomas Chase in 1825 and the newlyweds moved into the house with her parents and later inherited it in 1839. Thus it became known as the Chase House and was home to Thomas and Louisa's seven sons.

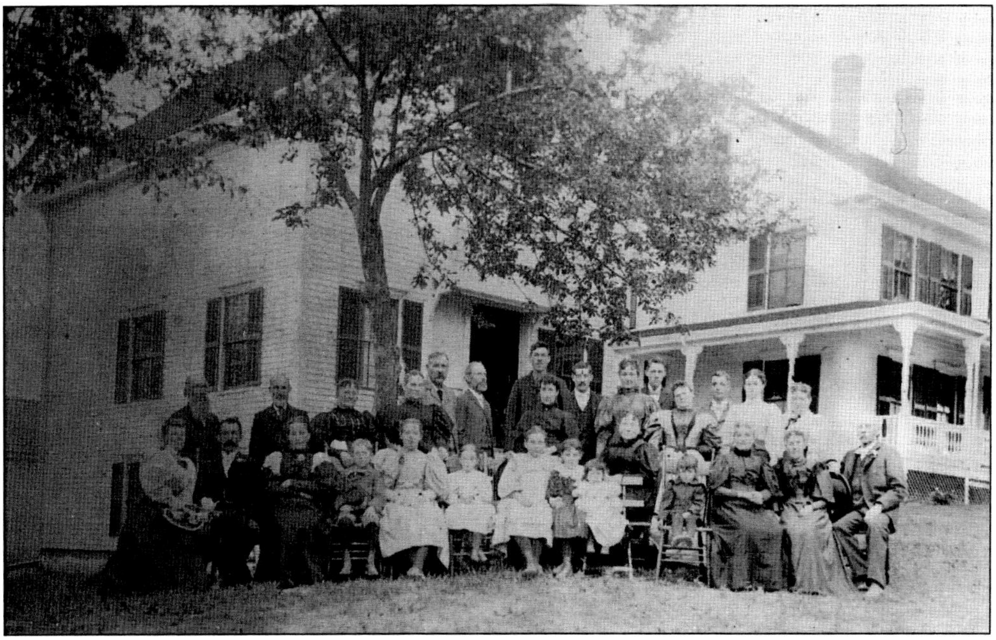

The extended Chase family gathered on the lawn of the Anderson-Chase House in Porter's Landing for this photograph, c. 1900. Edward Chase came back to Freeport from California in 1895 and purchased the old Anderson House on South Street, across from his parents' house (the Coffin-Chase House). He has been identified as the man on the extreme right of this photograph.

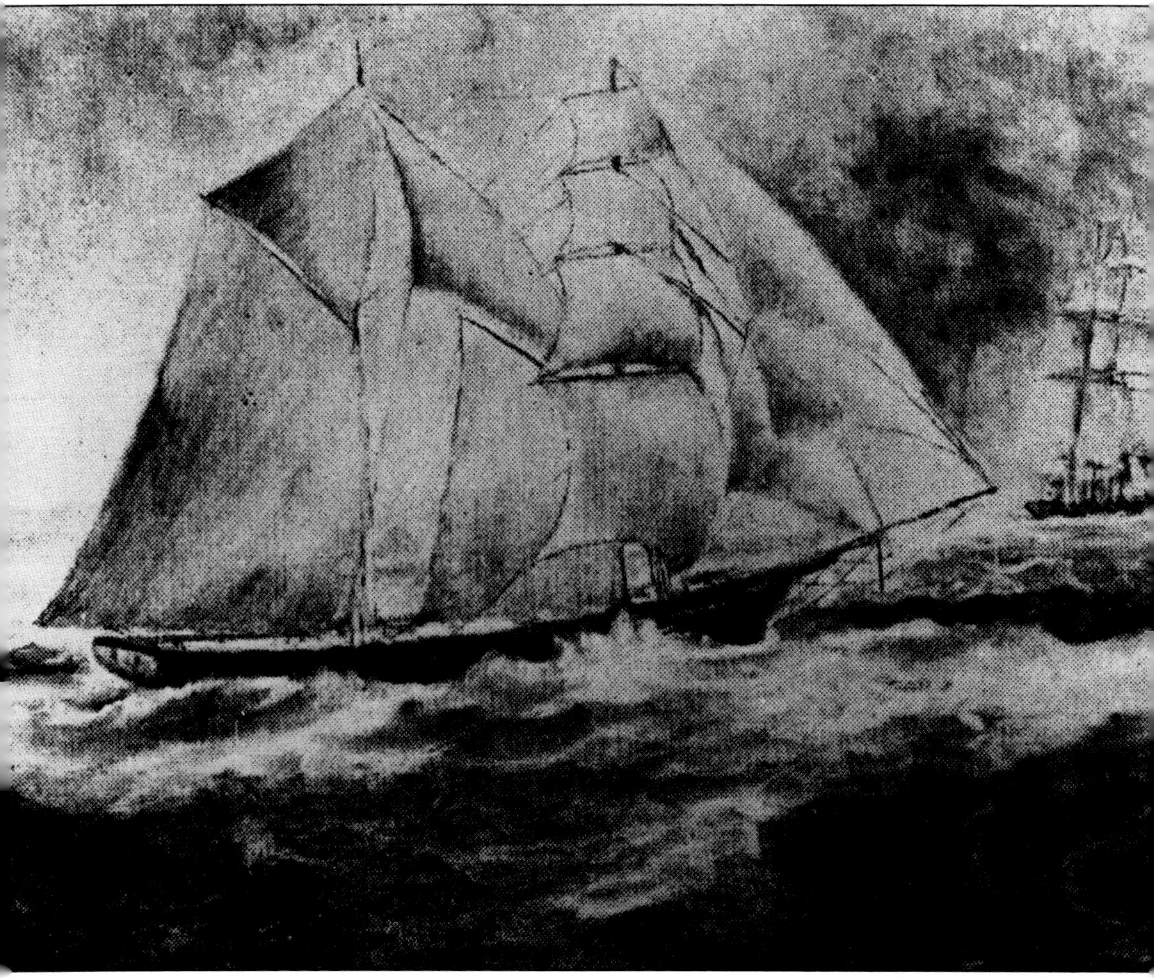

Upon the arrival of Seward Porter in 1782, the Porters began building a number of vessels here, the most famous being the armed privateer *Dash*, built in 1813 by Master James Brewer for the Porters. During the War of 1812 she captured fifteen prizes but was finally lost in 1815 with sixty young crewmen aboard, including Captain John Porter and his brothers Ebenezer and Jeremiah. Several other Porter vessels were built in the yard before Rufus Soule purchased it in 1834.

Five

South Freeport and Bustins Island

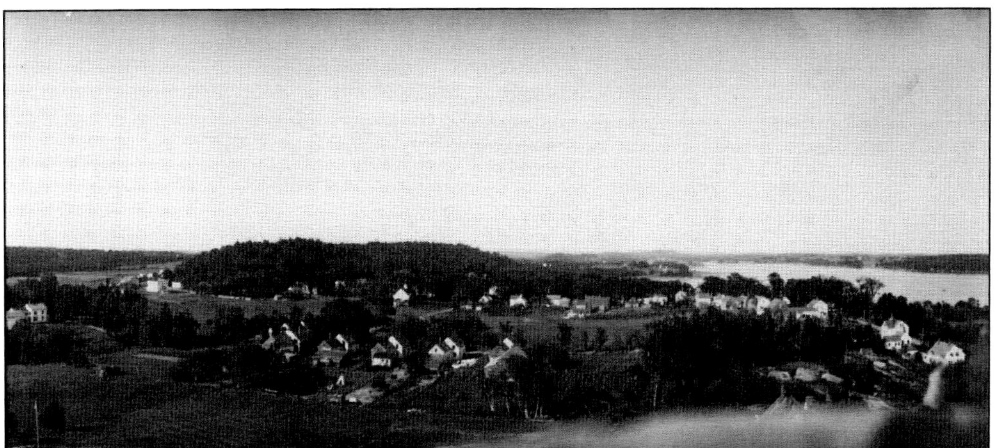

South Freeport village is seen here from Casco Castle around the turn of the century.

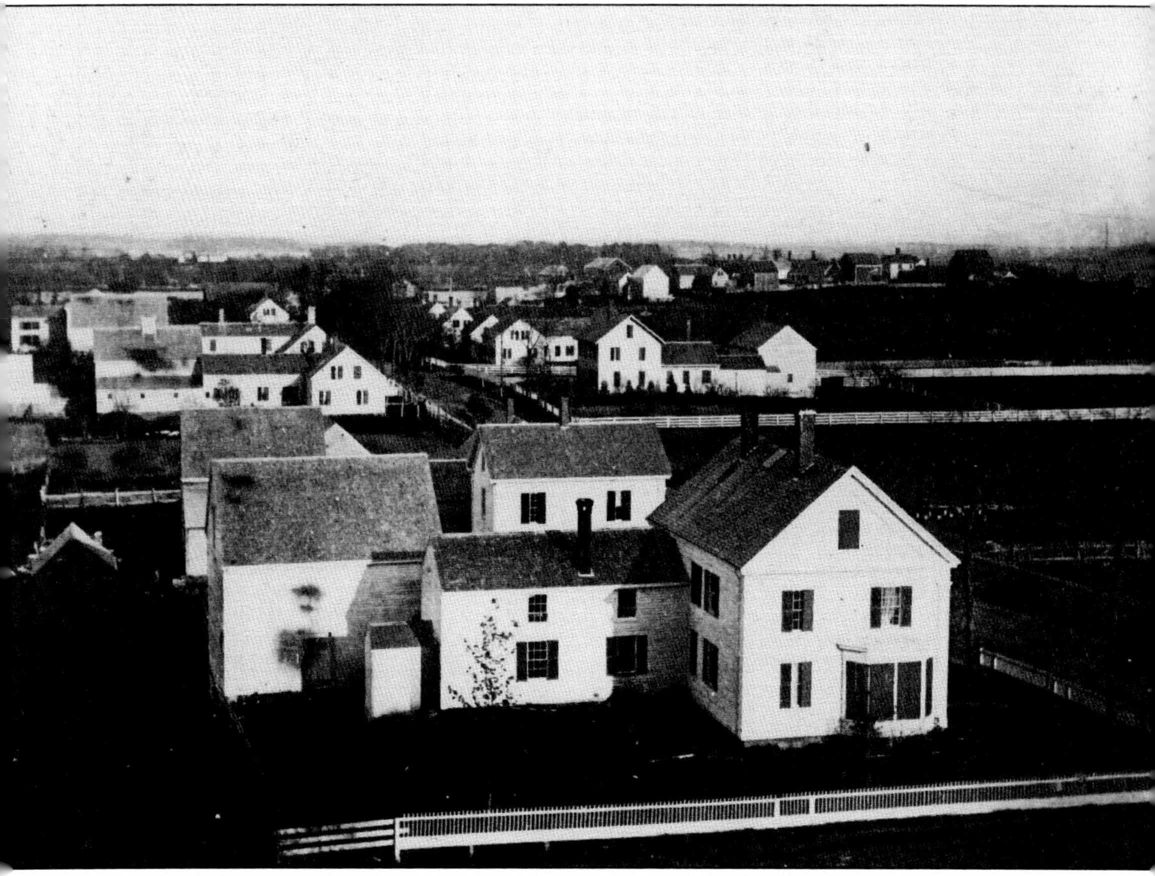

Originally known as Strout's Point, South Freeport had shipbuilding, fishing, and farming for its principal industries. Most of the commerce was by water and until the 1830s there was only one public road to Freeport village. In the mid-1800s, shipbuilding brought many craftsmen associated with the industry to settle here. The Soules and the Blisses were major shipbuilders and further upriver, the Talbot and Cushing-Briggs yards launched a total of nine sailing vessels in 1854. South Freeport's shipbuilding activities continued through World War I and World War II and at the turn of the century the village also became a tourist destination with the opening of Casco Castle. Today, although the Castle has burned and shipbuilding is gone, South Freeport is still much like it was in this 1870 photograph.

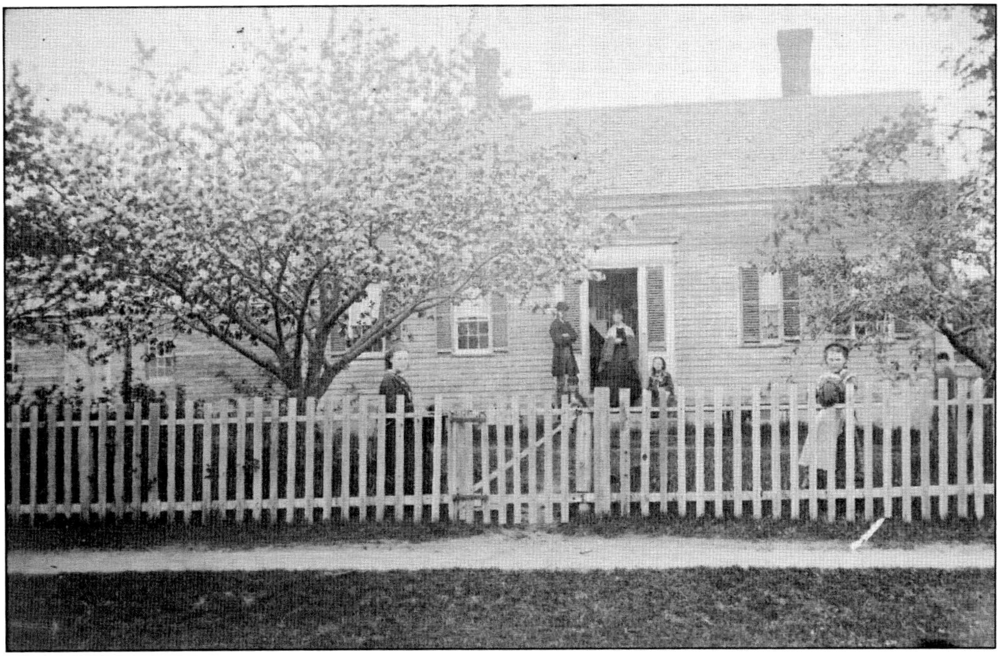

In 1857, at the corner of Pine Street and South Freeport Road, stood the home of George W. Randall, a "House and Ship Joiner," who designed and built several houses in Freeport prior to the Civil War. During the war he served in the Union Army and rose through the ranks to become brigadier general. After the war he worked as an architect in the south and as supervisor of U.S. Government quarries. The G.A.R. post in Freeport is named for him.

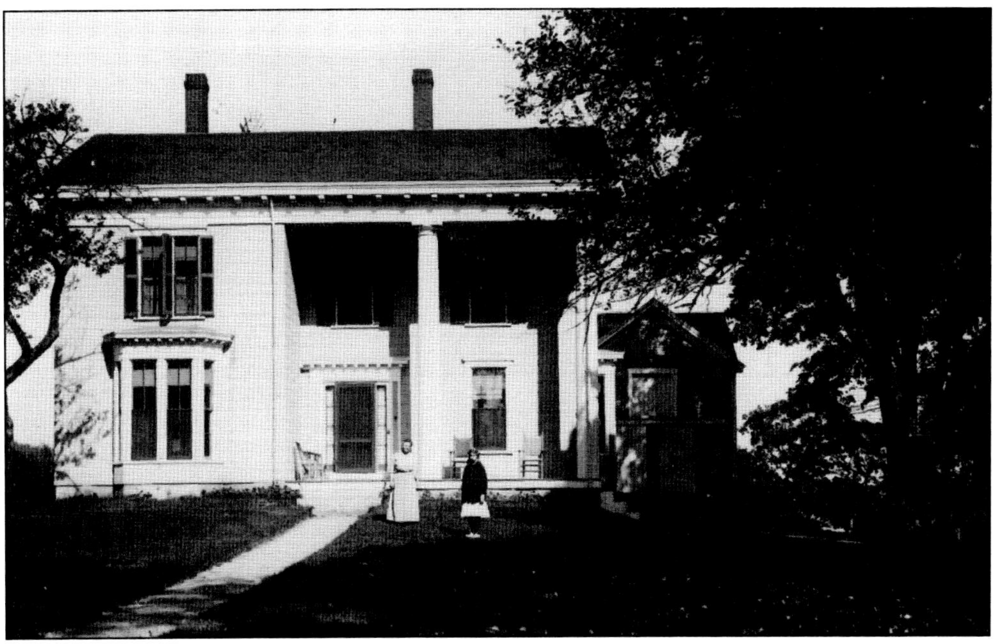

One the houses designed by George W. Randall was "Elm Lea," built *c.* 1854 for Ambrose Curtis, a South Freeport shipbuilder.

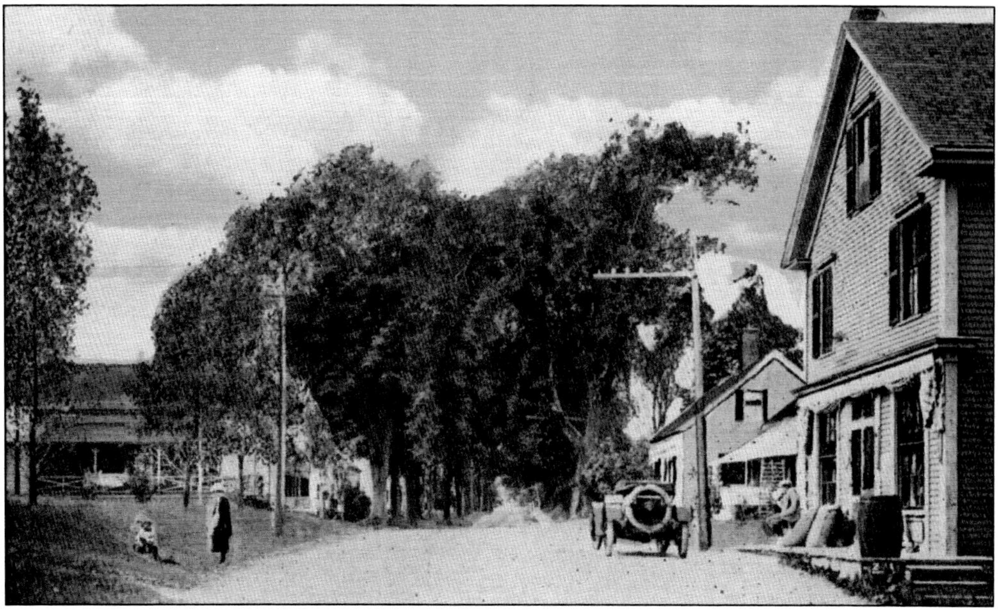

A view of Main Street in South Freeport looks west, away from the water, and shows the general store and post office, the first building on the right, which was run by E.S. Butler.

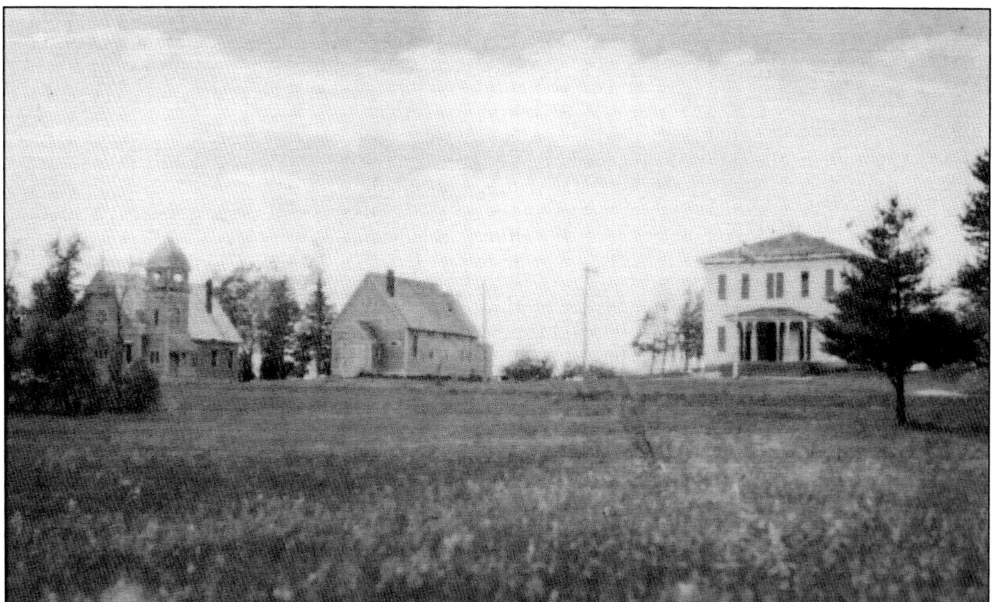

A postcard shows the South Freeport Congregational Church and vestry, and the South Freeport Grammar School. The Queen Anne-style church, built in 1884, is distinctive for its bell tower, shingles, and porch. The vestry, which was built in 1898, is now connected to the church.

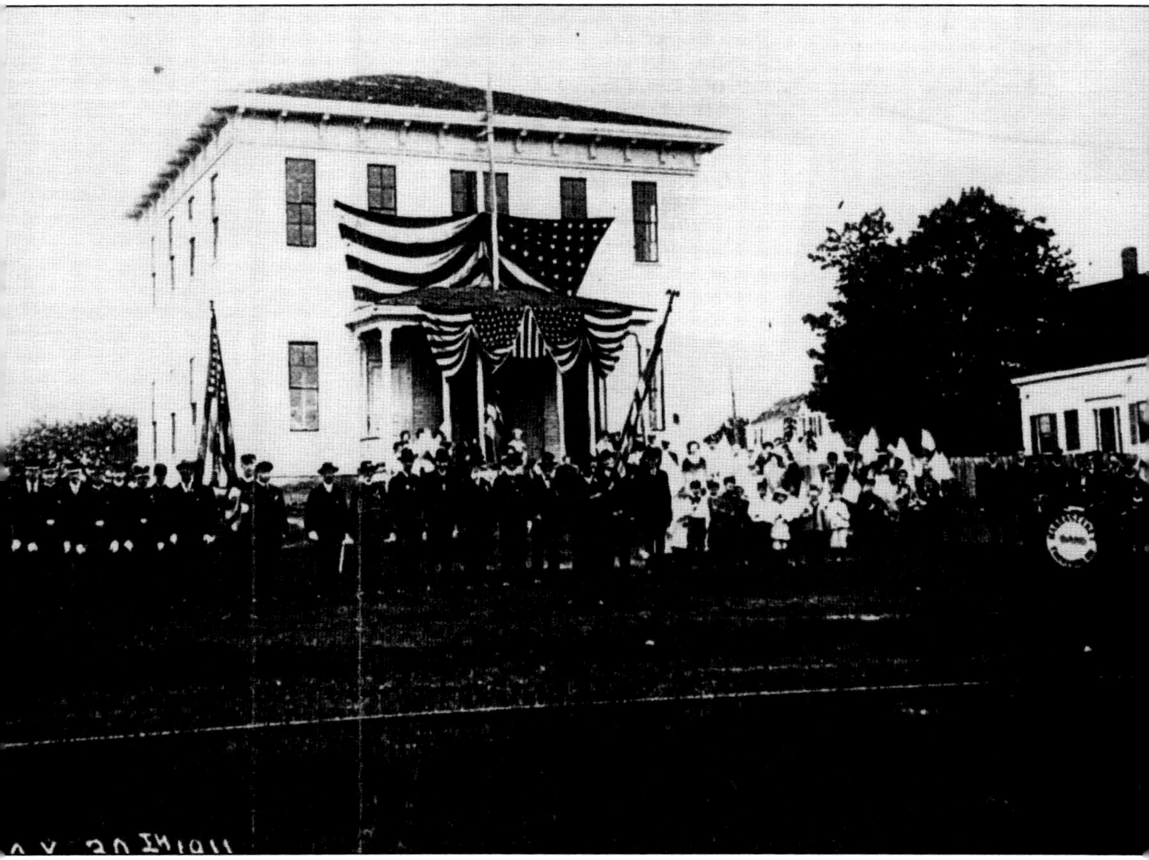

The South Freeport Grammar School celebrated Memorial Day 1911 with the Harraseeket Band (on the right) and a gathering of school children and veterans (on the left). This Italianate building, built 1867, was torn down in 1956. The trolley tracks which were laid along the road in 1902 can be seen in the foreground.

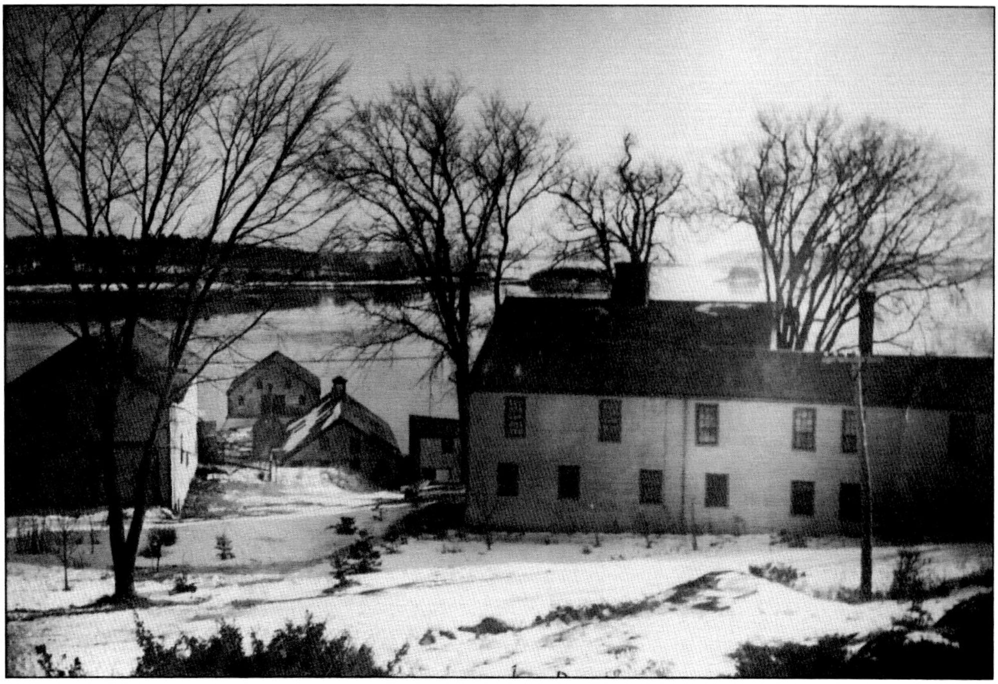

From the hill above Dixon's wharf, the view shows the Harraseeket River and harbor entrance by Wolfe's Neck and Pound of Tea Island, *c.* 1900. The canning factory on the wharf opened in 1876 and closed in 1900. The firm of William K. Lewis & Bros. ran the factory, which canned clams, fish, and lobsters, as well as corn from local farms. The large center-chimney house with ell in the foreground belonged to Charles Dixon at the turn of the century and burned in 1907.

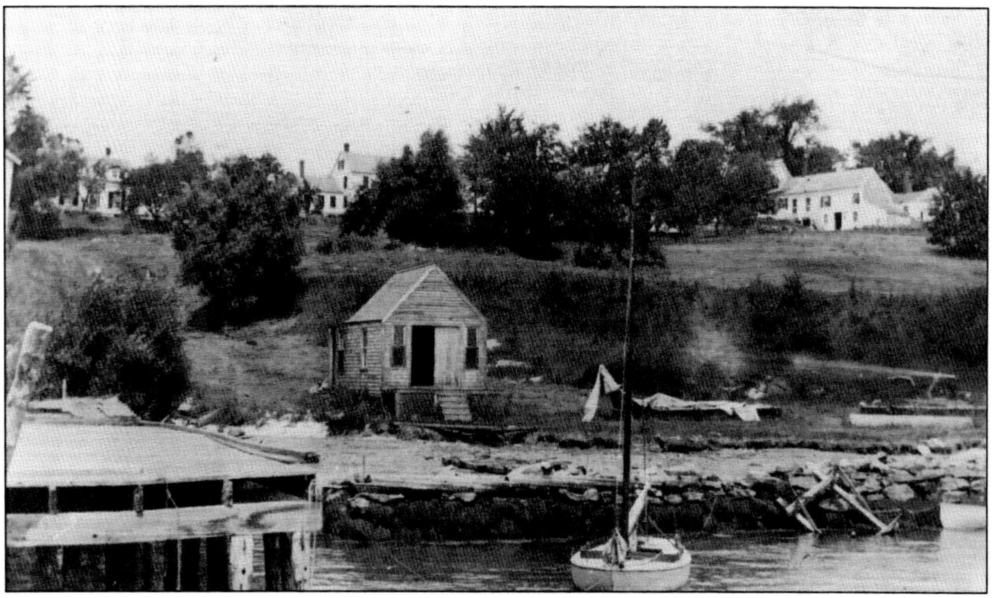

A view of Dixon's Wharf looks towards South Freeport village.

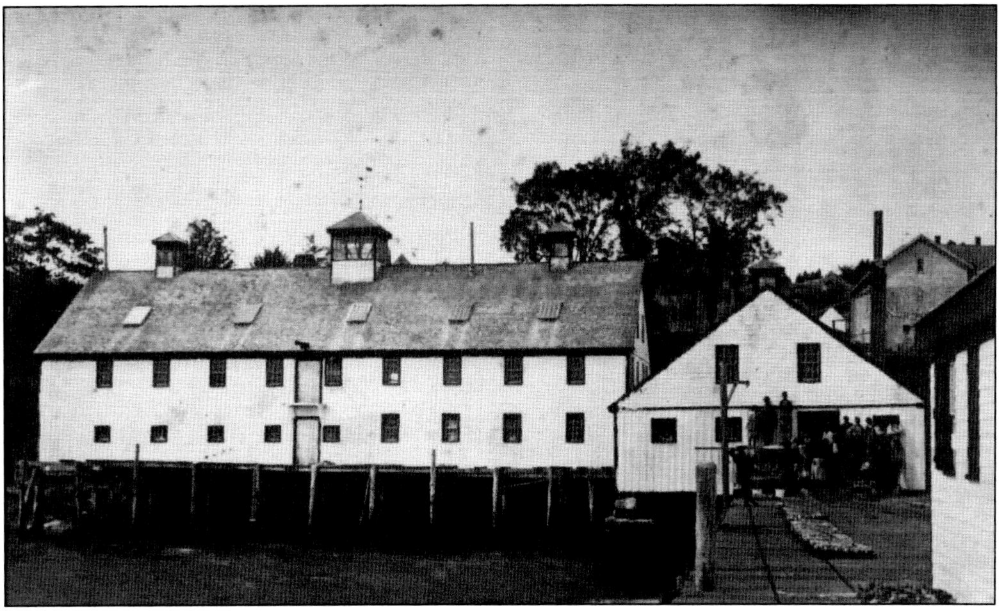
Another view of Dixon's wharf shows the canning factory, *c*. 1920.

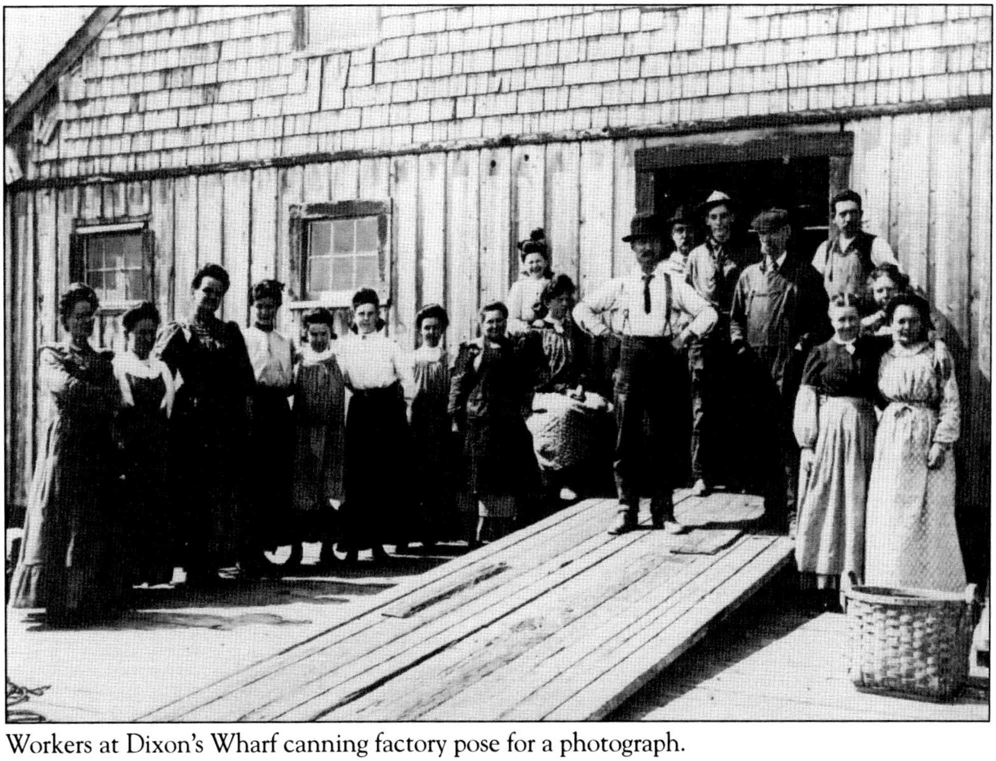
Workers at Dixon's Wharf canning factory pose for a photograph.

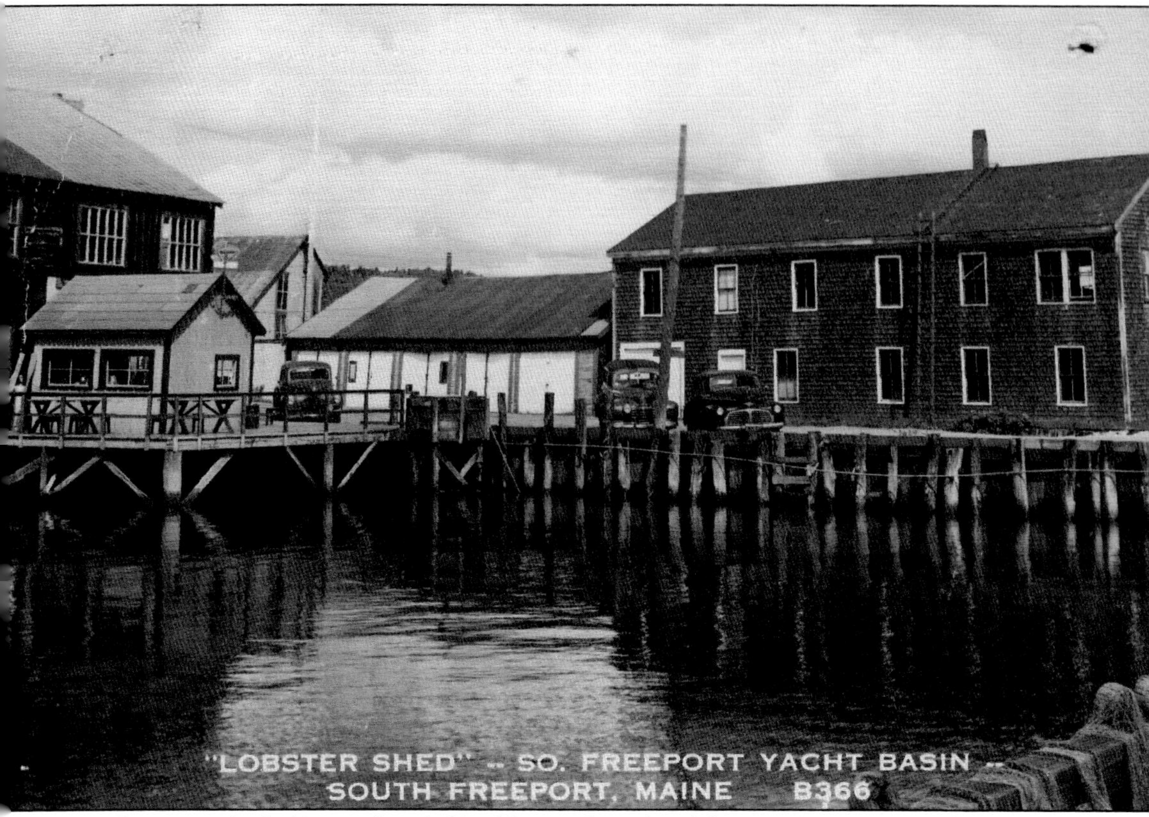

The two-and-a-half-story shingled building at the right of this c.1950 view is the oldest building remaining on the waterfront today, built c. 1831 when Union Wharf was sold to the Strout's Point Wharf Company. The large building on the left was built c.1870 by the Soule Yard run by the brothers Enos, Henchman, and Clement Soule. The small lobster shack and dock on the left is a precursor of today's Harraseeket Lunch and Lobster Company.

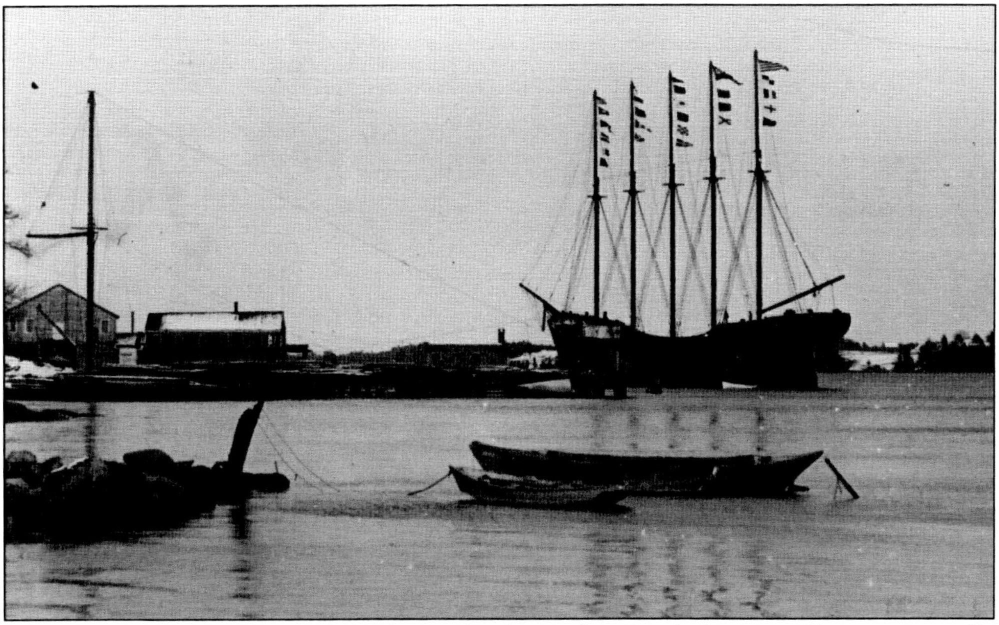

The schooner *Sintram* was built at the Soule Shipyard in South Freeport. She was originally designed as a Ferris-type steamer for the war effort in 1917 and 1918, for the purpose of delivering supplies to Europe. Still unfinished at the war's end, the ship was redesigned and converted to a five-masted schooner which was launched in December 1920. Her career was short, and within a year she sank after a collision.

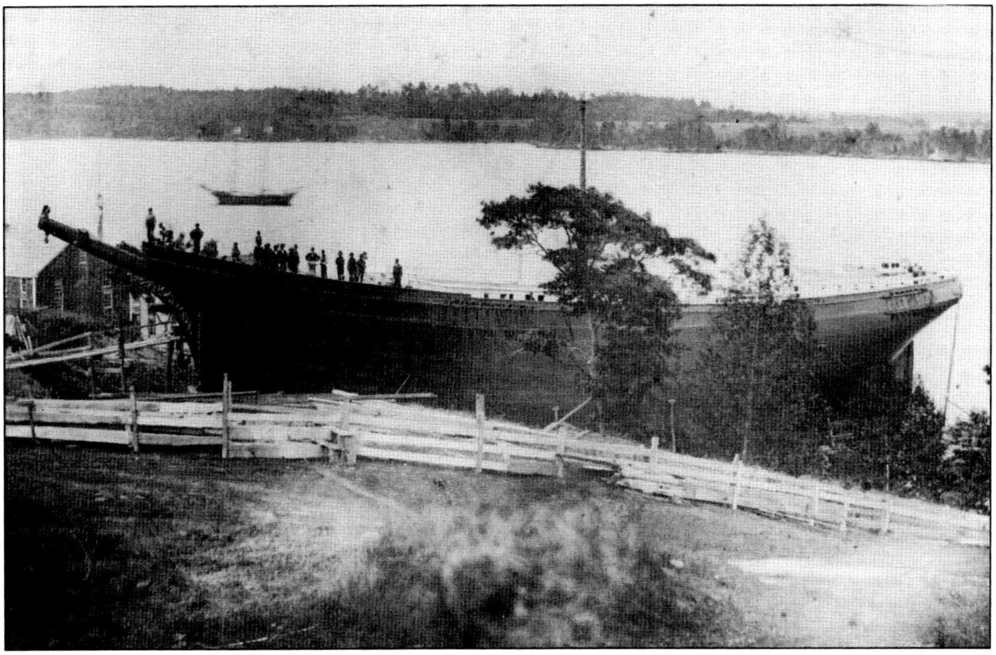

The *Tam O'Shanter II*, built in the Soule Yard in 1875, was popularly described as "the clipper of the fleet." The *Tam* was a Cape Horner and made ten voyages between North Atlantic ports and San Francisco. She later sailed the Pacific, making journeys to the Far East and Japan. She was lost in the Gaspar Straits in 1899.

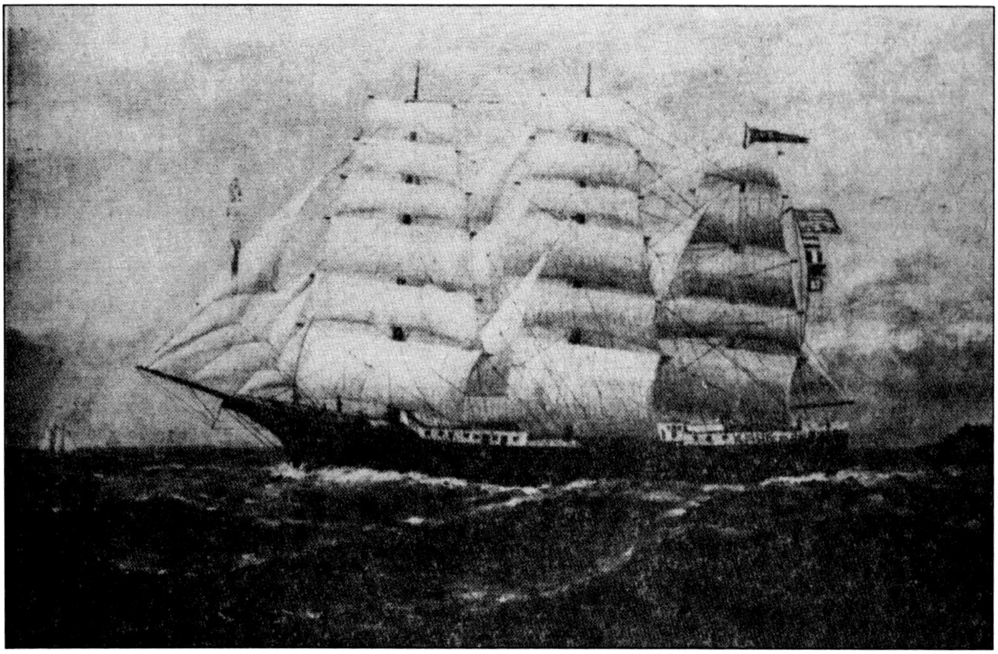

The ship *John A. Briggs*, launched at the Cushing and Briggs yard in September 1878 was the largest ship built at Freeport. Rufus Soule Randall, a part-owner, was her first captain. Among those present at the launch was President James A. Garfield. Stores and schools were closed that day, and 7,000 persons crowded the Harraseeket River for the great event.

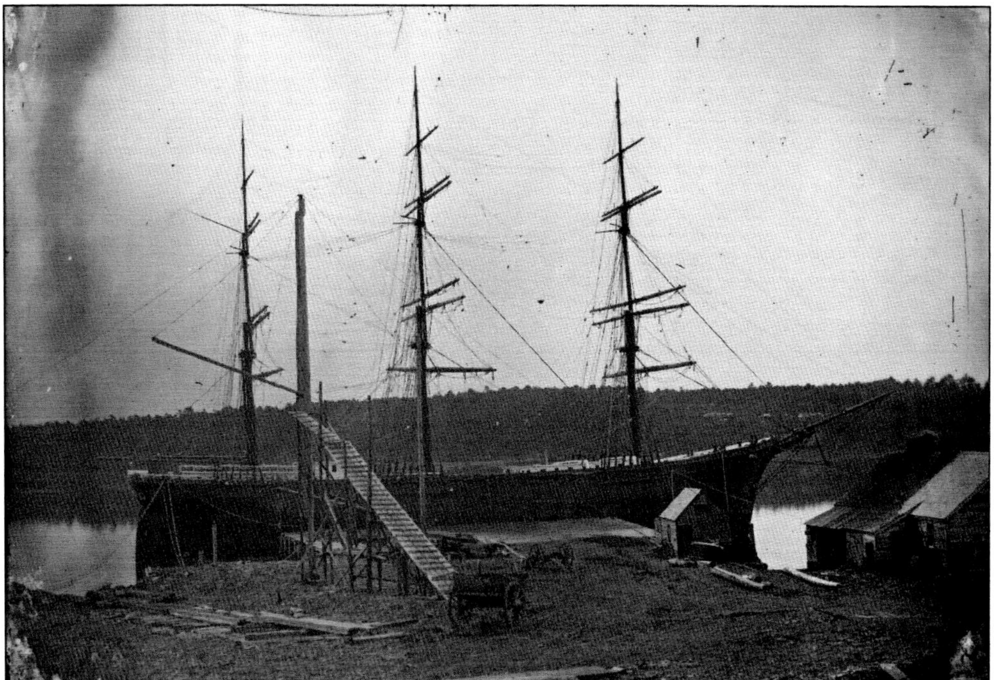

Another Cushing and Briggs ship, the *Wilna*, was launched in 1880. The *Wilna* was the last ship built in that shipyard.

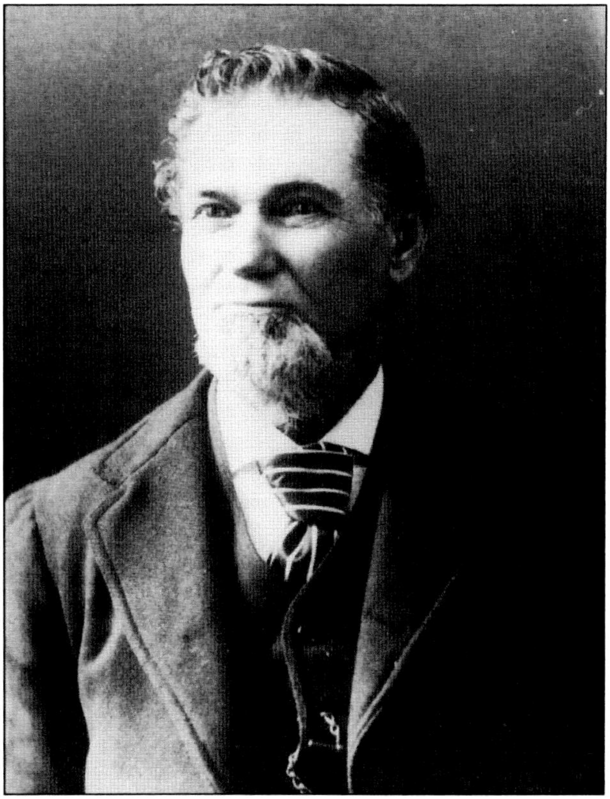

Emery Jones (1827–1908) was Freeport's most famous figurehead carver. His residence and shop were in South Freeport. There he carved many figureheads, name boards, stars, eagles, and whatever ornaments the builder or ship owner desired. The picture below shows the *George R. Skolfield* figurehead in his shop c. 1885. This figurehead is now in the Mariner's Museum in Newport News, Virginia.

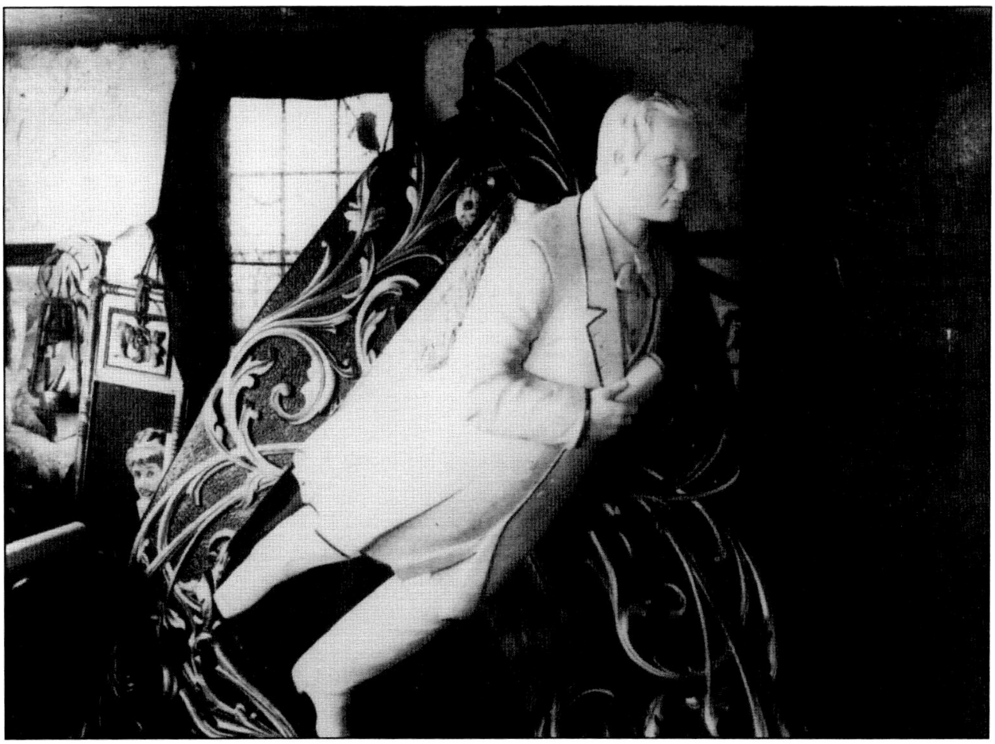

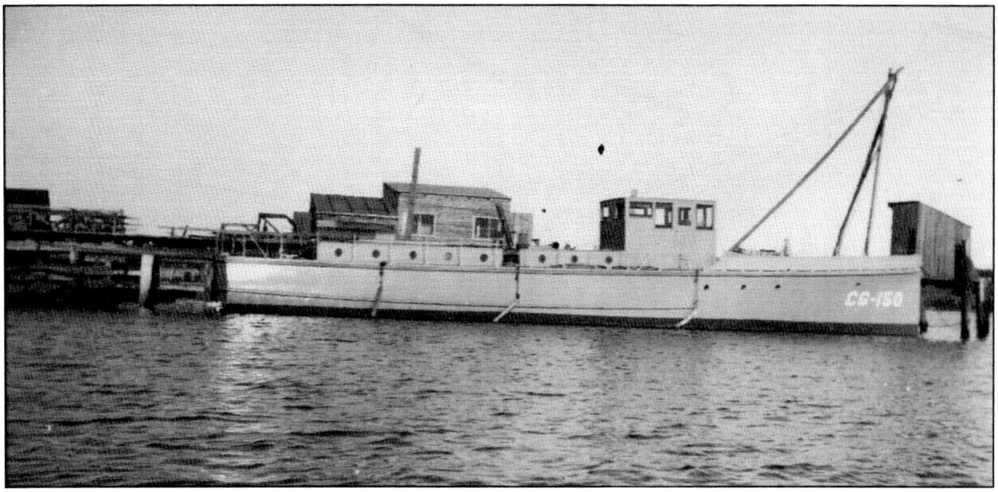

This rum chaser was built at the Soule yard in November 1924. Contracts for government rum chasers (called "fast lobster boats" and used to combat smuggling during prohibition days) were obtained along with some fishing boat and yacht orders before the Soule Yard closed in the mid-1920s.

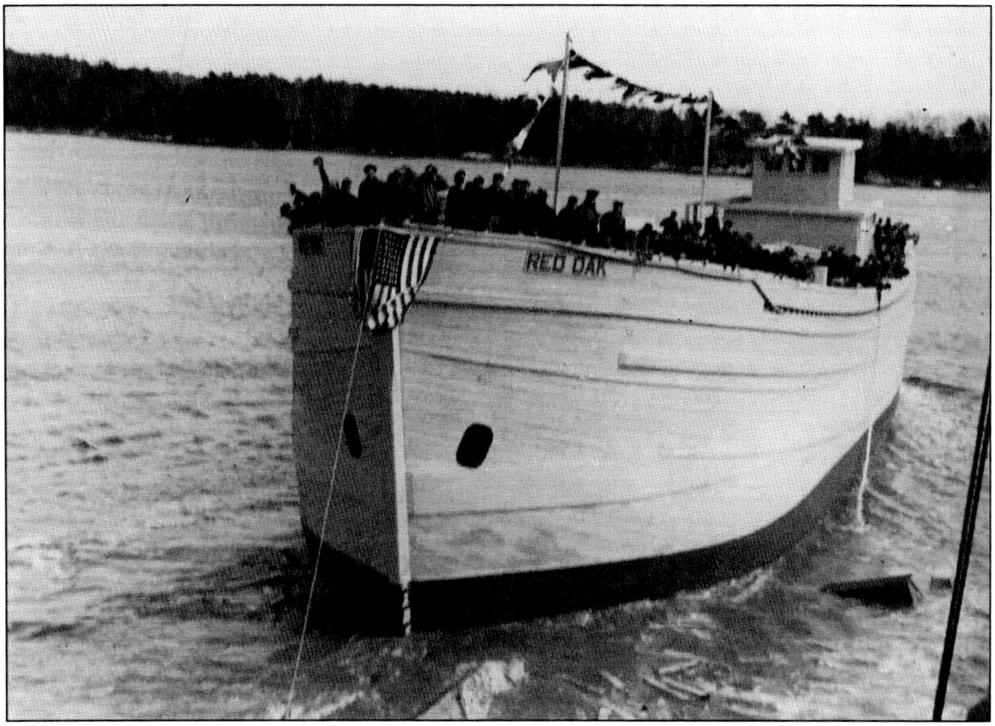

The Second World War gave brief new life to wooden ships, which were immune to magnetic mines, in the form of the Red Oak Barges. In June of 1942 the Casco Shipbuilding Company secured a contract from the government to build five barges and leased most of the shipyard property in South Freeport. The first barge, the *Red Oak I*, was launched in April of 1942 and the second, *Red Oak II* on June 23. Two more barges were completed before the Maritime Commission canceled their contract for the fifth barge, which was then dynamited and destroyed.

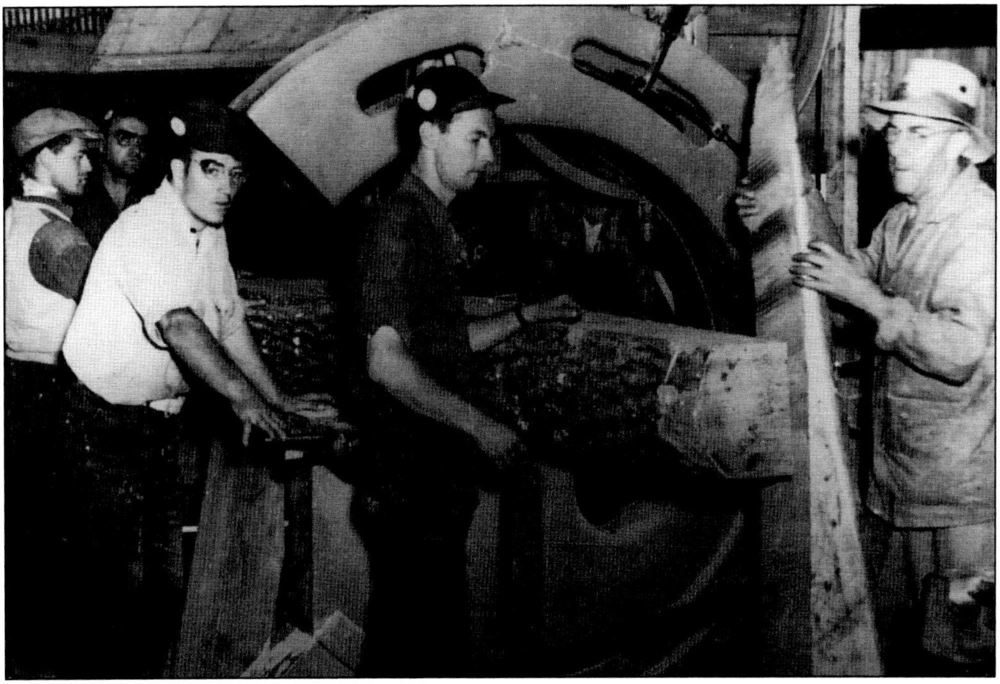

These two photographs show the building of the Red Oak barges at the Casco Shipbuilding Company. The barges proved to be more expensive to build than projected and the company was forced to close.

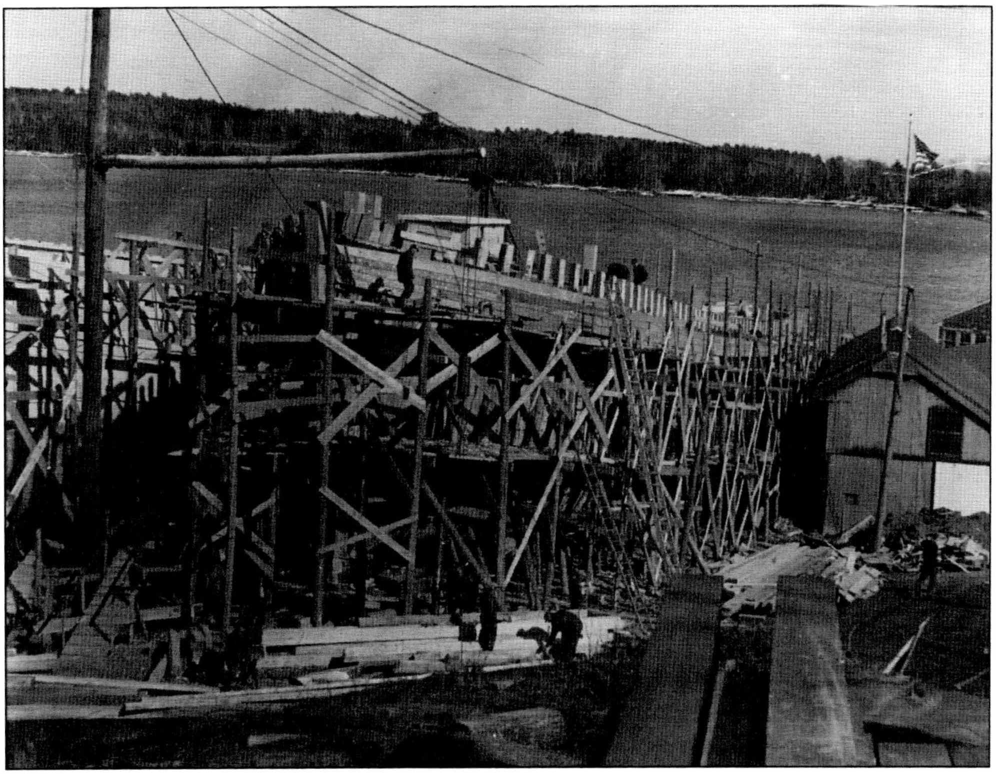

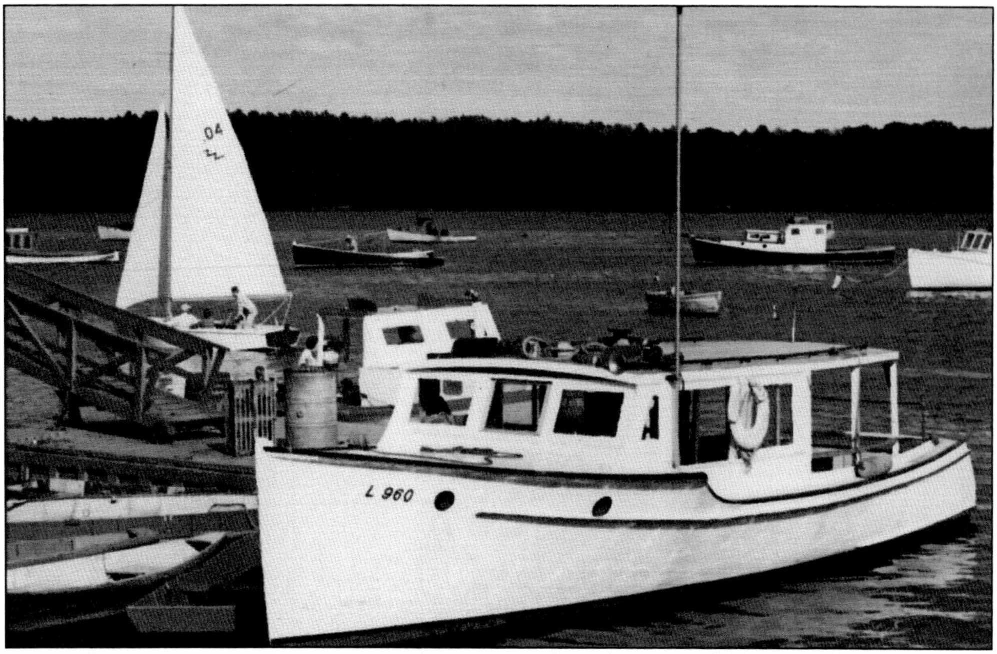

Bustins Island, a summer colony, is reached by this ferry from South Freeport. Over the years, Bustins Island has been a close-knit community with some eighty summer cottages, a store, a restaurant and, for a time, a boys' camp run by Captain (later Admiral) Donald MacMillan. Archie Ross has ferried families to Bustins for over fifty years.

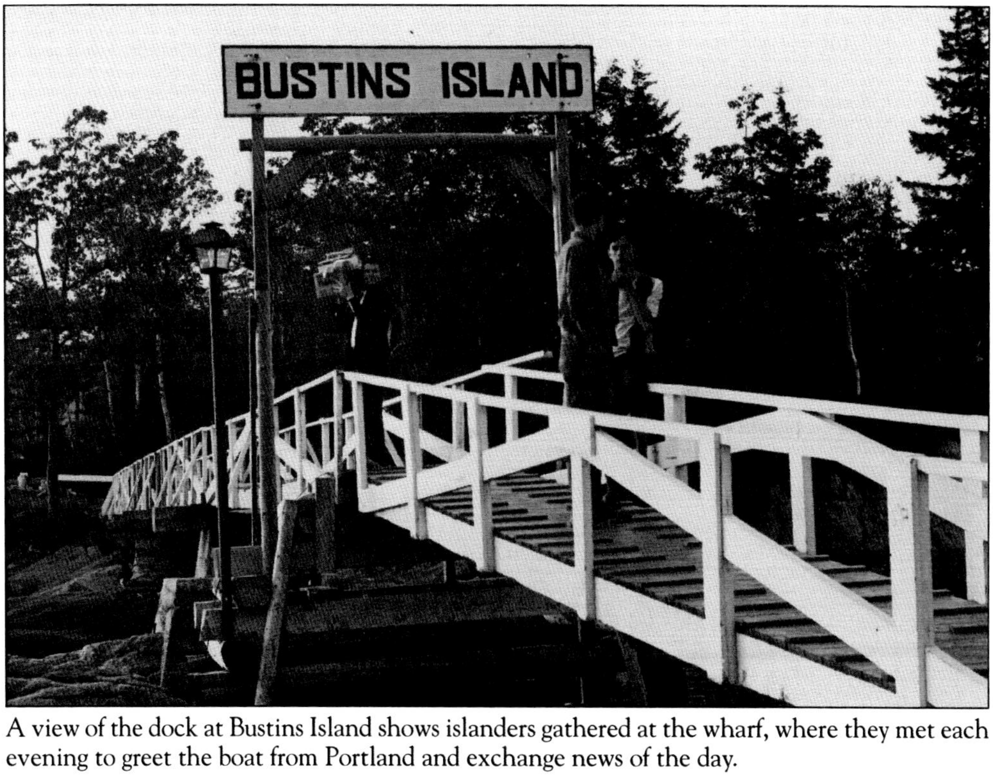

A view of the dock at Bustins Island shows islanders gathered at the wharf, where they met each evening to greet the boat from Portland and exchange news of the day.

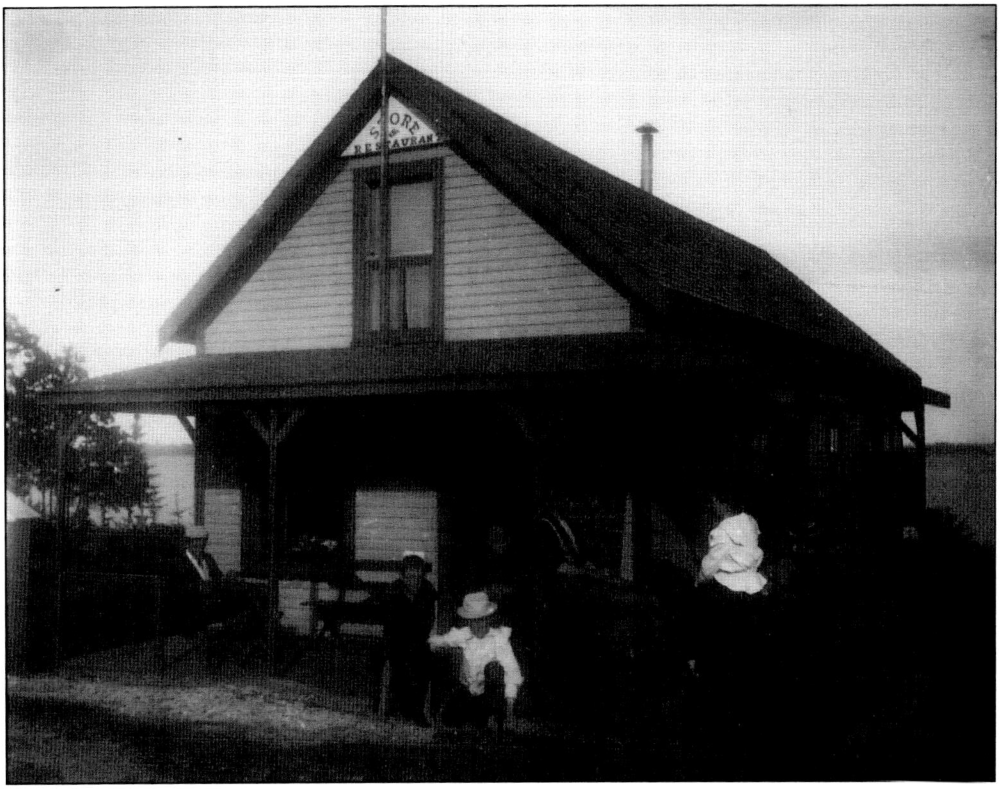

The store on Bustins Island was erected by William G. Merrill in 1895 and featured a deep porch across the front. In 1900 the Merrills sold the store to Fred Wilson, who added a kitchen and enlarged the front of the store to accommodate a small restaurant.

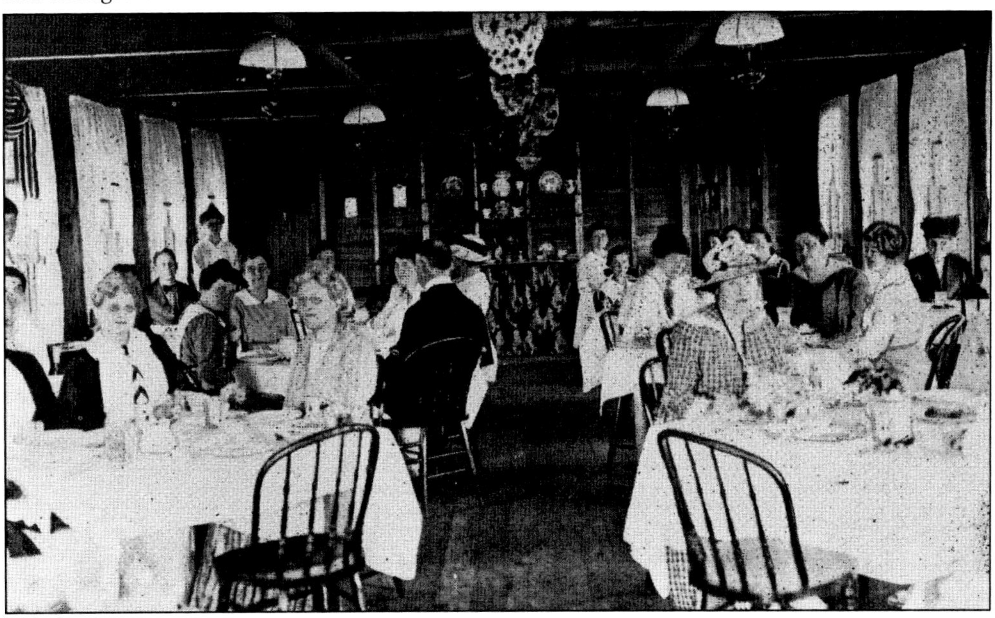

In 1916 the store was sold to Mr. Herbert Cole, who converted it to an establishment called Ships Inn. This interior picture was taken in the dining room in the 1920s.

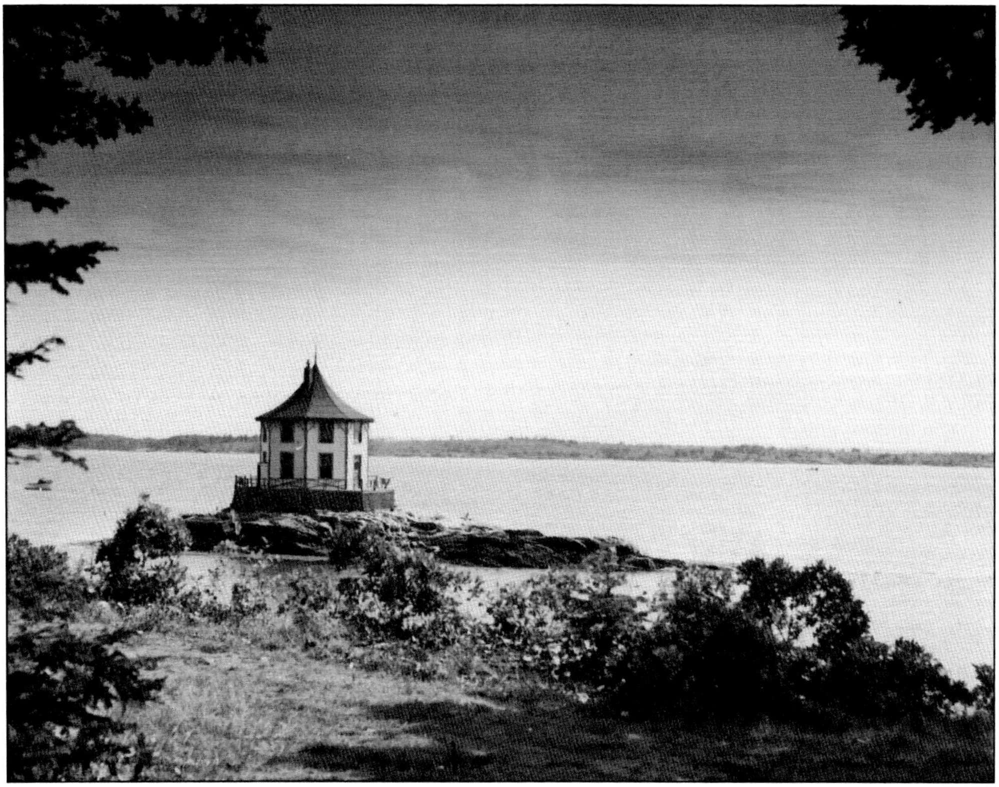

One of the most novel and picturesque cottages on Bustins Island was "the Nubble," built on a rocky ledge in 1909 by Arthur Reynolds of Freeport. This two-story building is octagonal, with a conical roof through which a chimney projects. At low tide "the Nubble" can still be reached by walking across the flats, but at high tide it is surrounded by water.

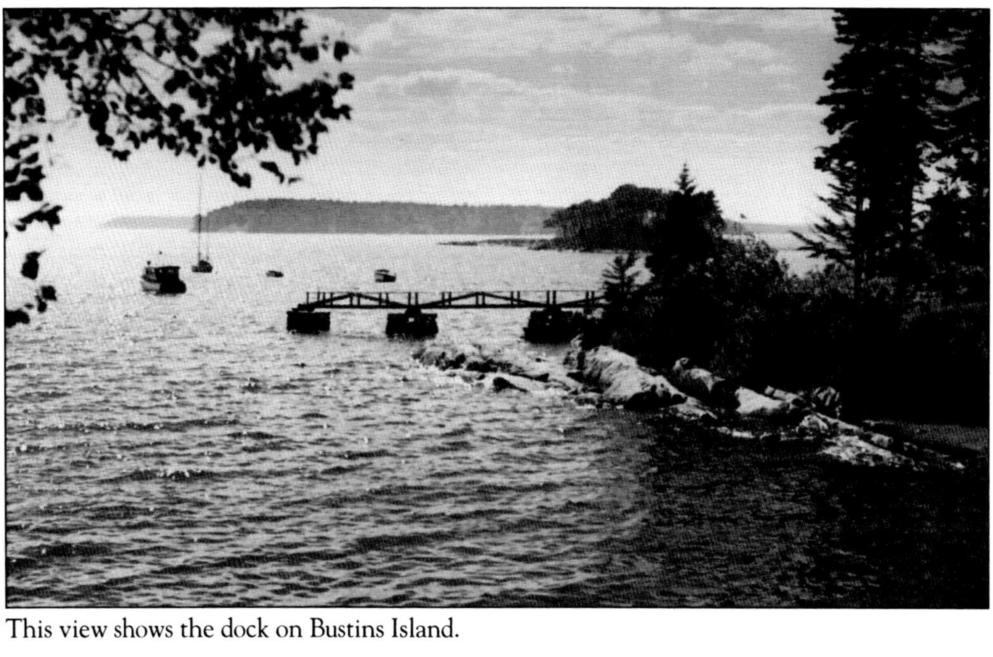

This view shows the dock on Bustins Island.

Six

People and Organizations

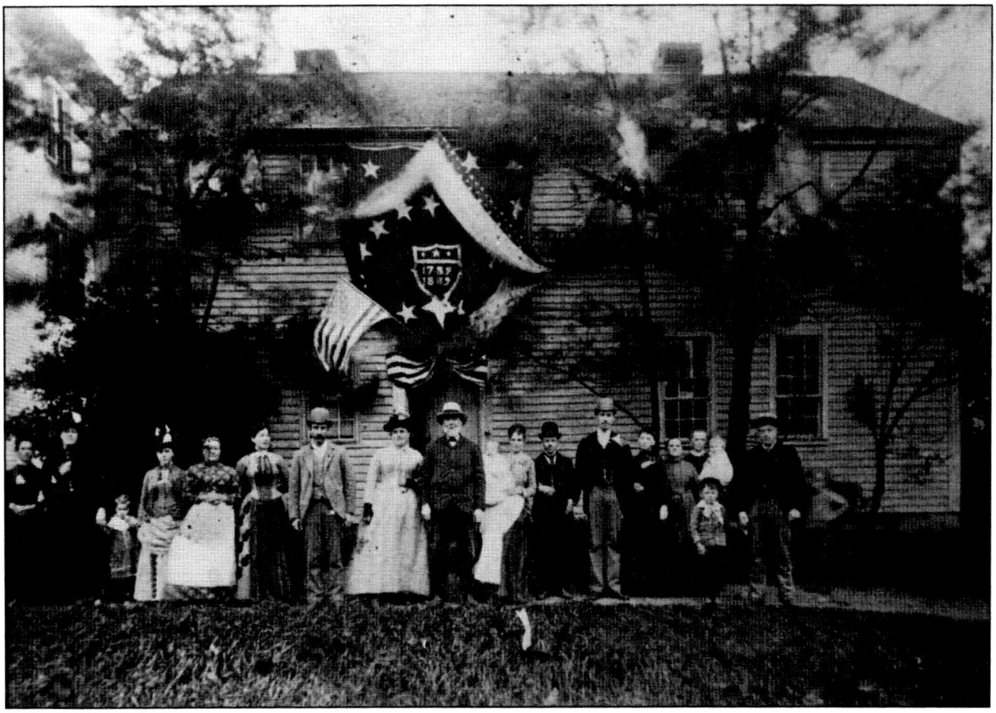

This old saltbox house, located on Bow Street, was the home of sign painter William Curtis. Here Mr. Curtis is shown on the front steps with his family celebrating Freeport's centennial in 1889.

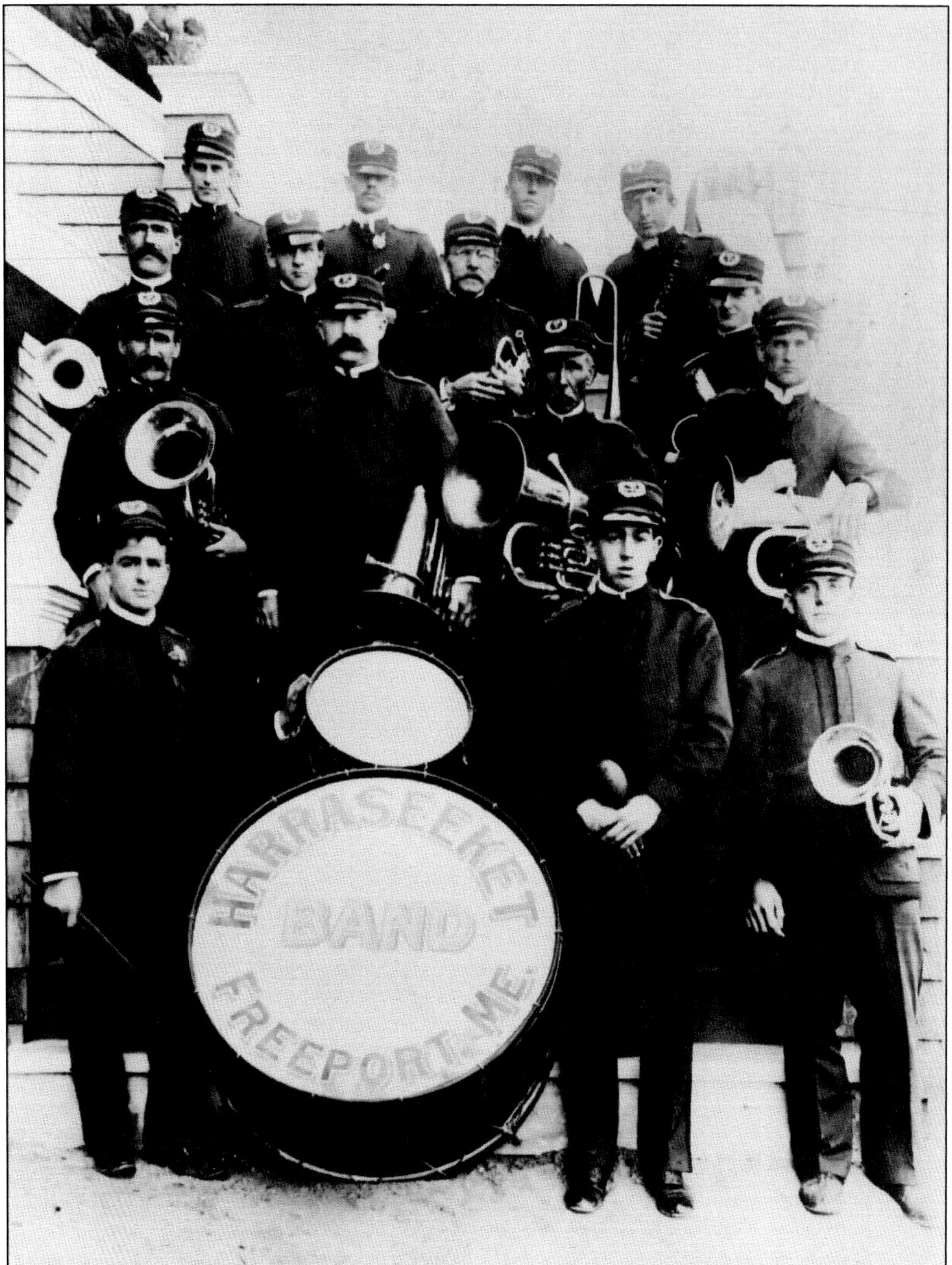

A prominent organization in the history of Freeport was the Harraseeket Band, first organized in 1880. Nearly every musical person in Freeport and Pownal belonged to the band, which paraded through the village each Memorial Day and at each Merchants' Picnic. E.B. Mallet with his high drum-major hat made quite an impression on the school children when he led the band into marching formation.

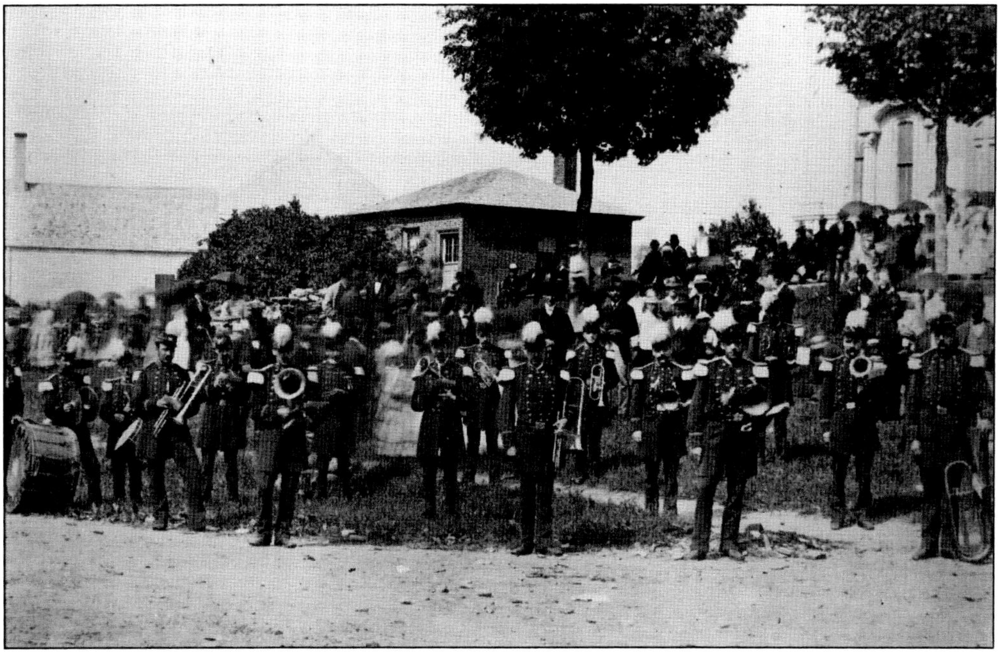

The Harraseeket Band is shown here in front of the former First Congregational Church before it burned in 1894.

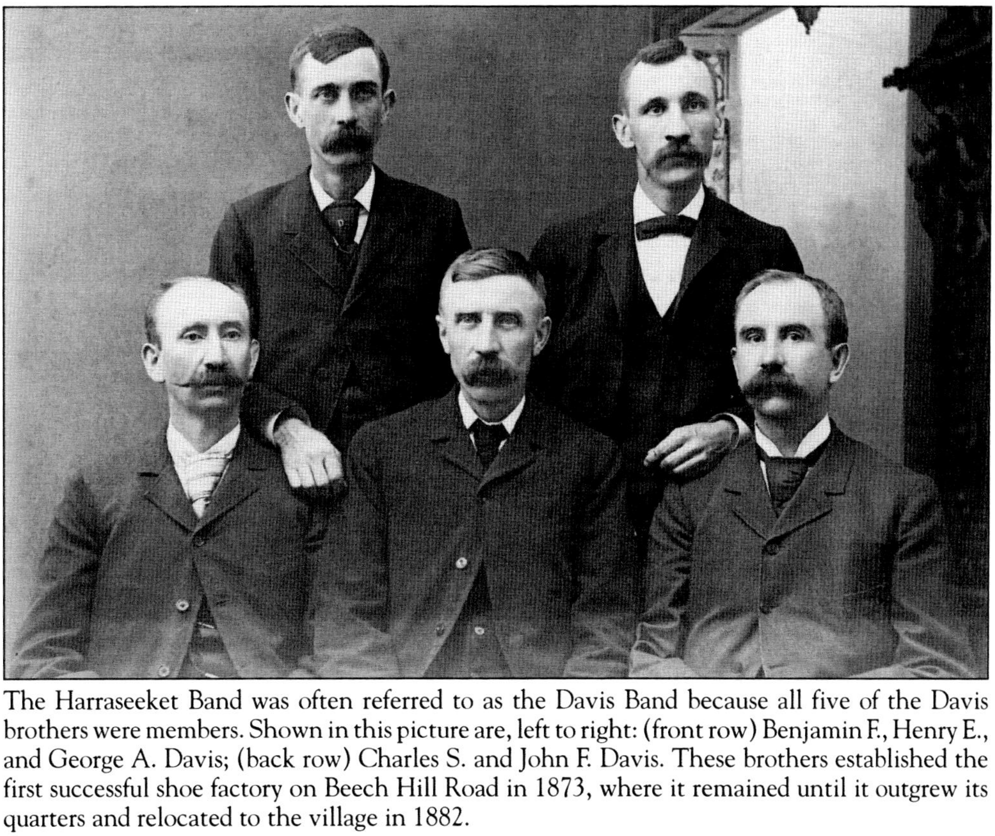

The Harraseeket Band was often referred to as the Davis Band because all five of the Davis brothers were members. Shown in this picture are, left to right: (front row) Benjamin F., Henry E., and George A. Davis; (back row) Charles S. and John F. Davis. These brothers established the first successful shoe factory on Beech Hill Road in 1873, where it remained until it outgrew its quarters and relocated to the village in 1882.

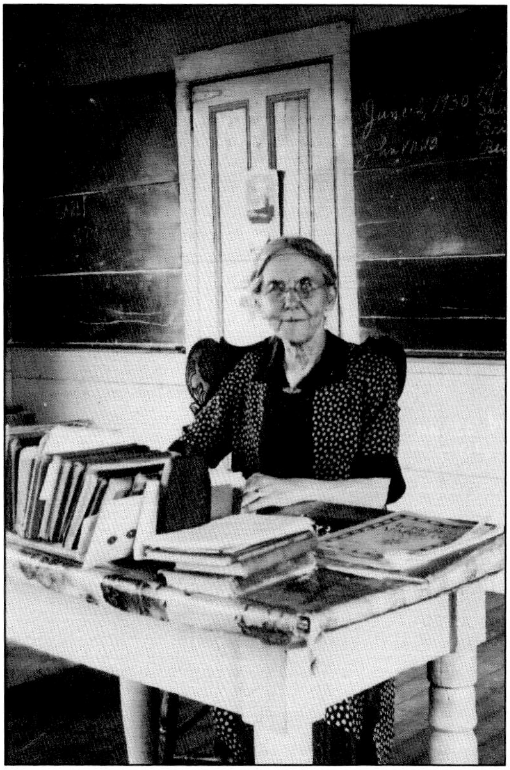

Fannie Mitchell sits quietly at her desk at the Porter's Landing School in 1930.

A group of children posed for this picture at the Maple Avenue School, c.1915.

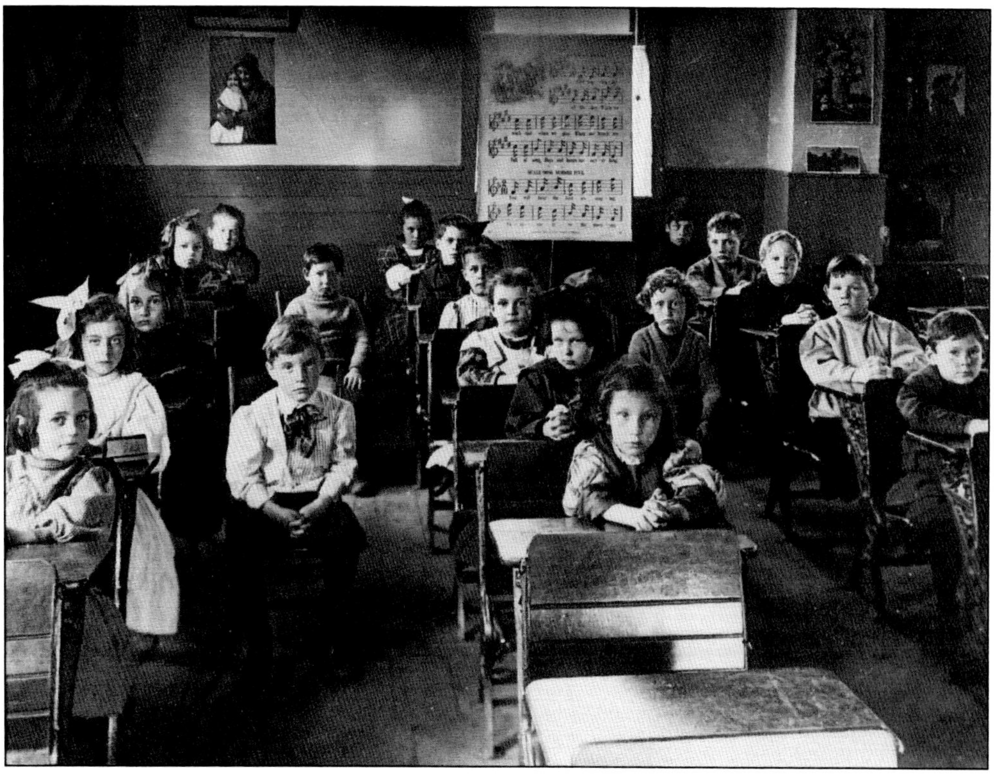

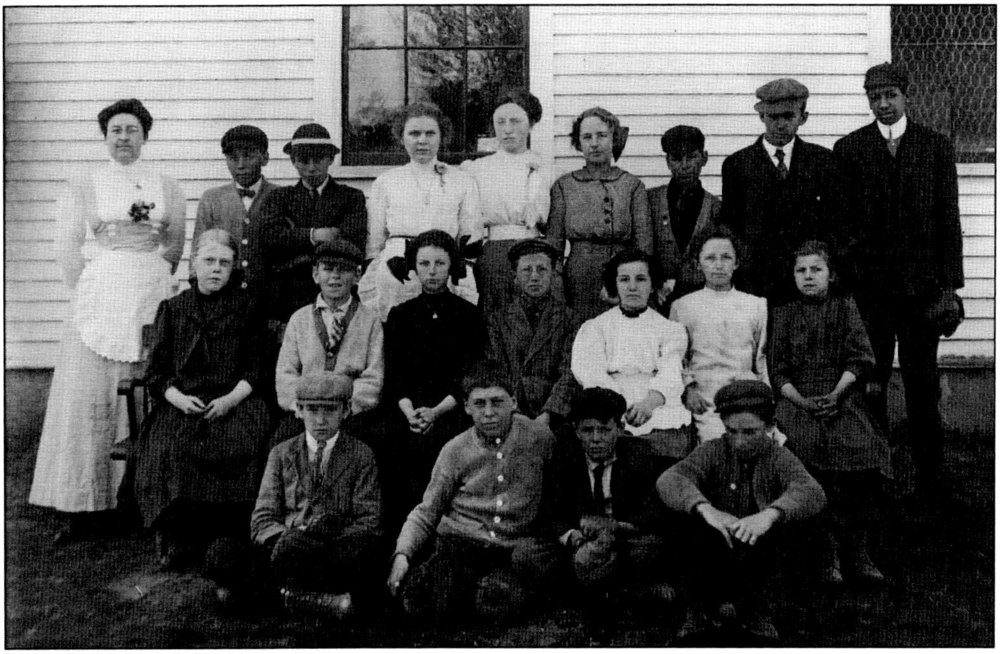

A 1912 picture of the South Freeport Grammar School shows Stephen Spottswood on the far right. Spottswood grew up to become bishop of the African Methodist Episcopal Zion Church in 1952 and chairman of the board of the NAACP from 1961 until his death in 1974.

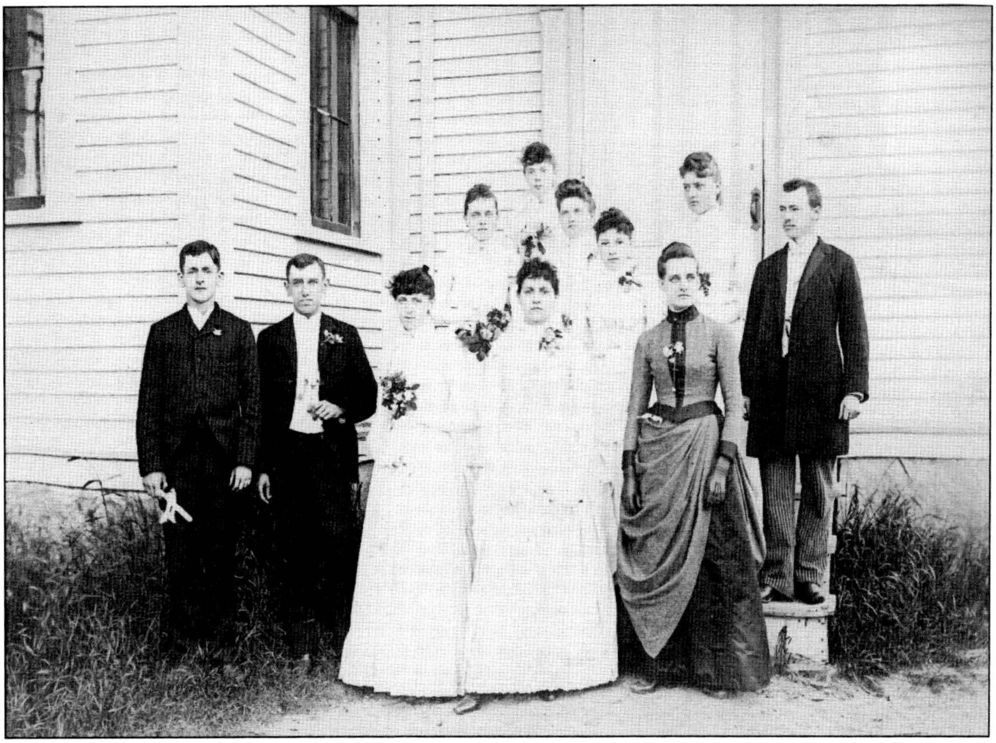

A graduating class of Freeport High School poses for the camera, c. 1890.

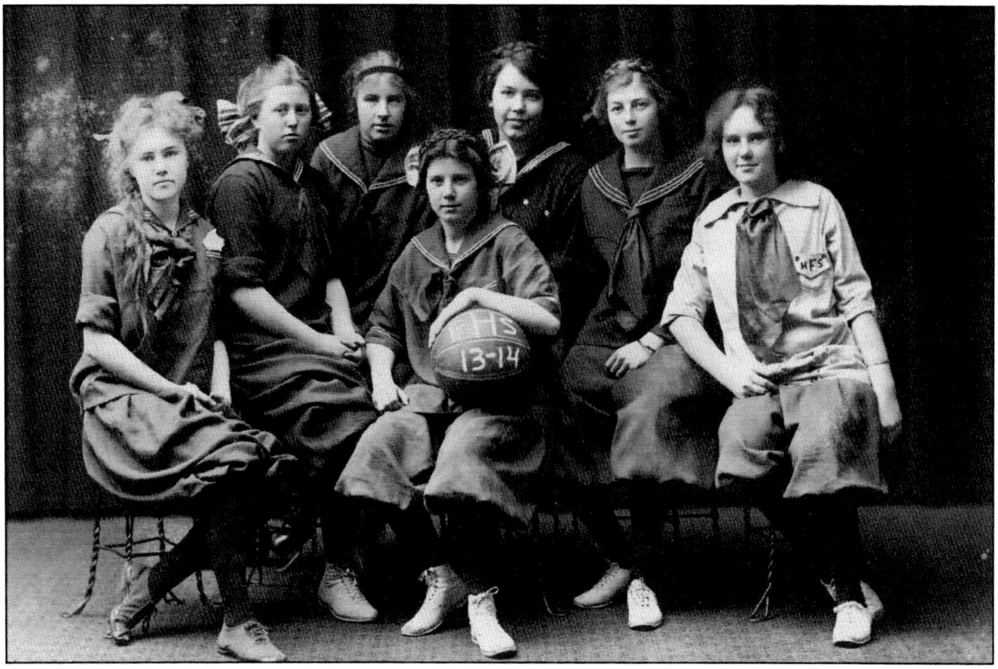

The Freeport High School girls basketball team in 1914 included players Maud Merrill, May Fogg, Louise Varney, Myra Brown, Marion Chase, Evelyn Groves, and Mabel Loring (in front with the ball).

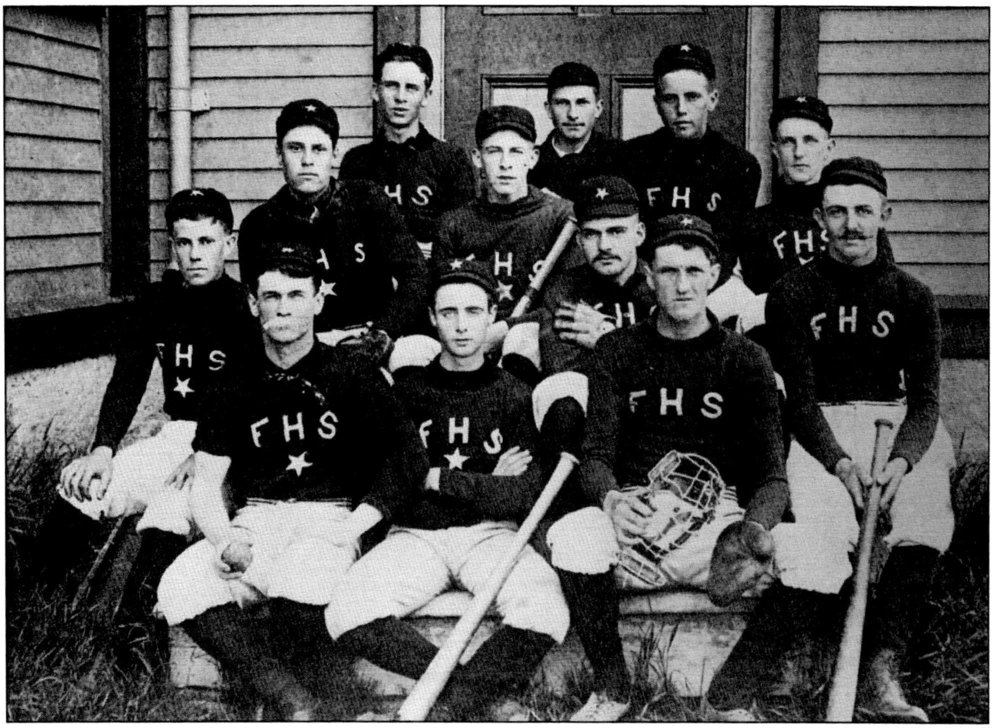

A few of the men have been identified in this 1887 picture of the Freeport High School baseball team. Levi Patterson, Donald MacMillan, and Benjamin Coffin are in the front row.

The four baseball players in this 1902 photograph are as follows: George Dennison, John Coombs, Carl Mitchell, and Ralph Curtis. John "Colby Jack" Coombs went on to pitch for the Philadelphia Athletics, Brooklyn Dodgers, and the Detroit Tigers.

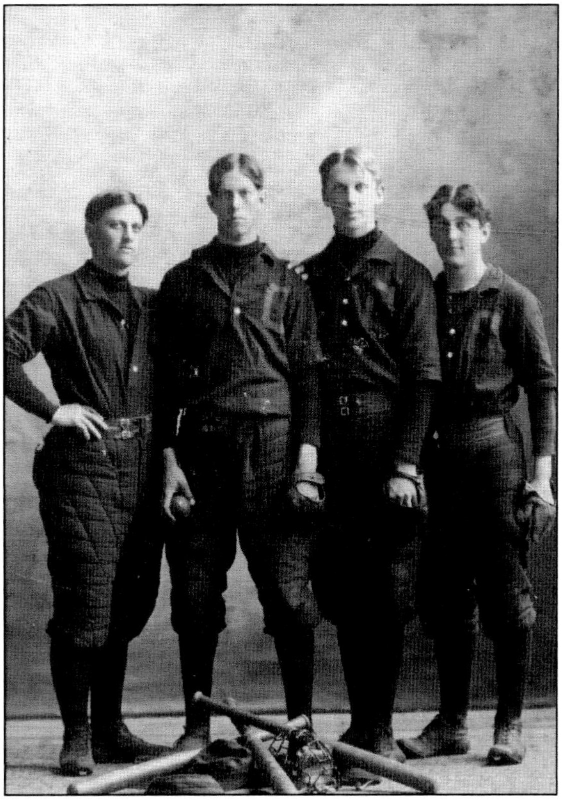

This is an early picture of the Town of Freeport baseball team.

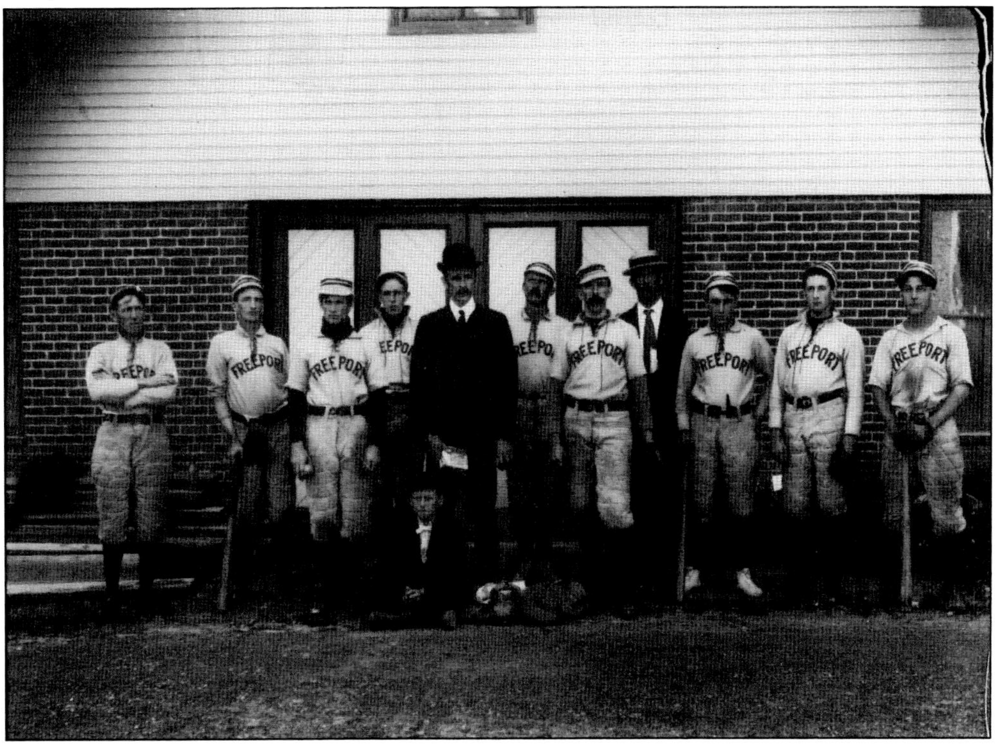

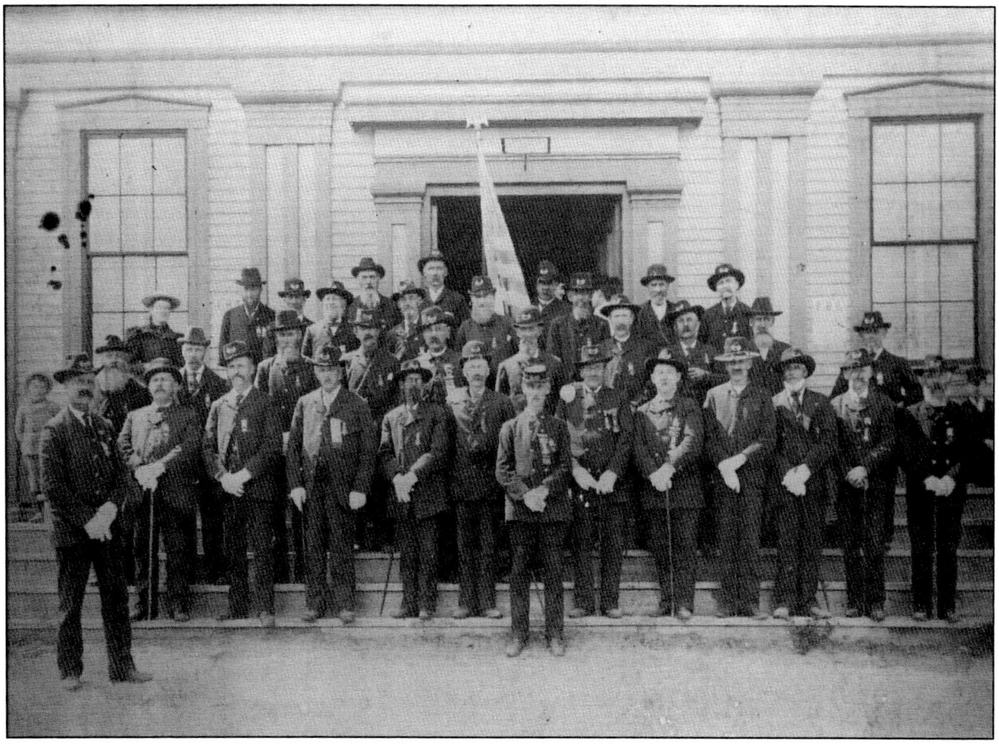

Many Freeport men took part in the Civil War. In 1889 this picture of the Civil War veterans was taken in front of the old town hall.

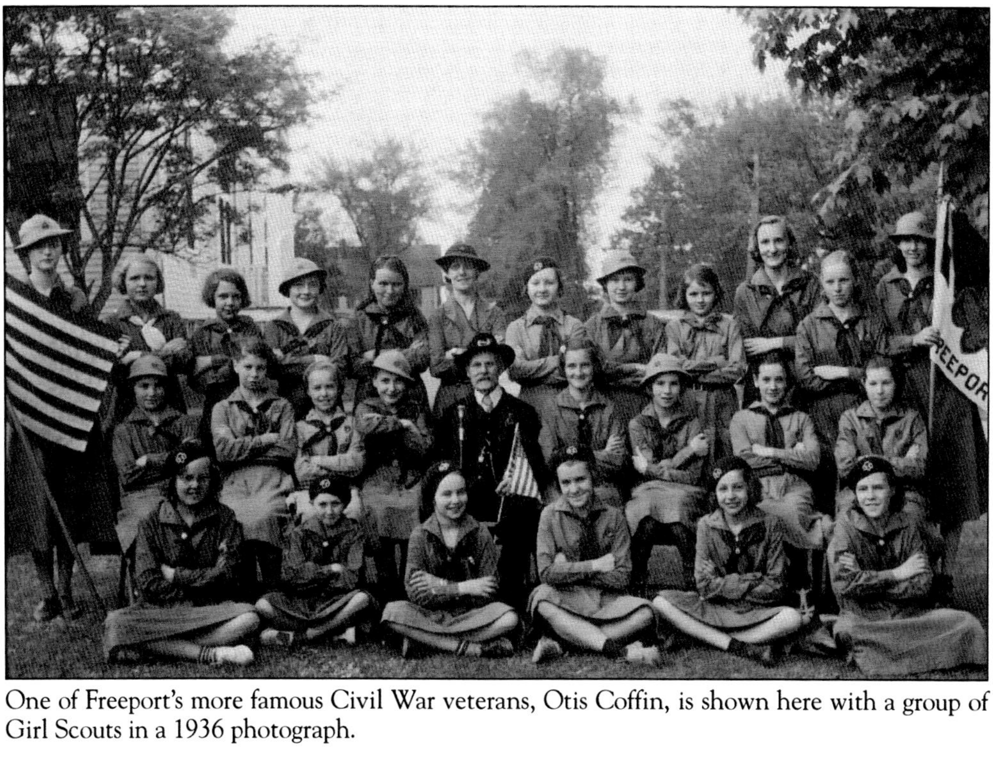

One of Freeport's more famous Civil War veterans, Otis Coffin, is shown here with a group of Girl Scouts in a 1936 photograph.

Otis Coffin, who lived to be one hundred, twice enlisted to fight in Maine Regiments during the Civil War and was an active member of the G.W. Randall Post of the G.A.R. At age ninety-seven he took a train to Columbus, Ohio, to attend the Diamond Jubilee Encampment and at age ninety-nine he attended the State Encampment in Belfast, Maine. This photograph shows him strewing flowers at the Soldiers and Sailors Monument on Memorial Day in 1943 at the age of ninety-nine.

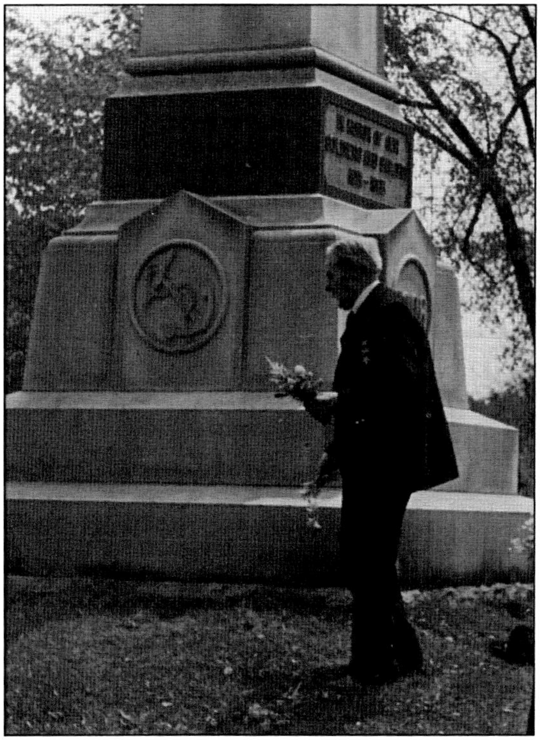

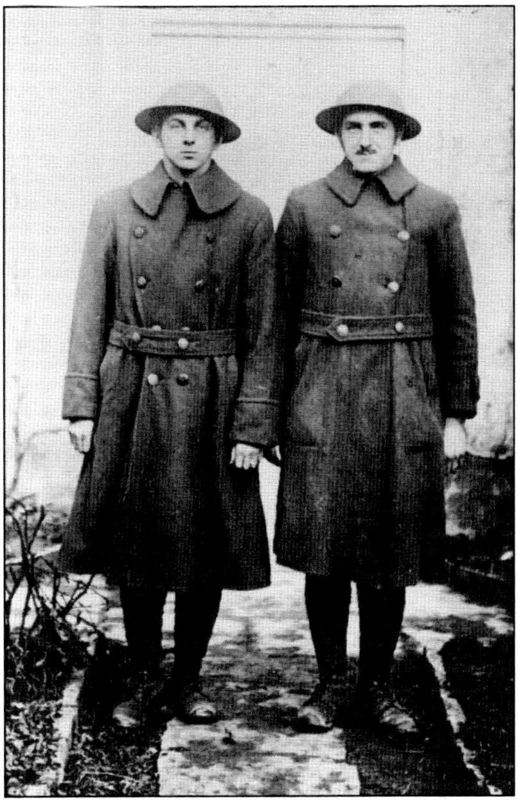

One of Freeport's World War I heroes was J. Arthur Stowell, who fought along with his brother, Raymond W. Stowell. J. Arthur "Artie" was killed in France while rescuing a wounded comrade in the midst of heavy fighting. For his valor, he was posthumously awarded medals from both the French and American governments. The American Legion Post in Freeport is named for him. Raymond (shown here on the left) survived the war and lived in Freeport until his death in 1963.

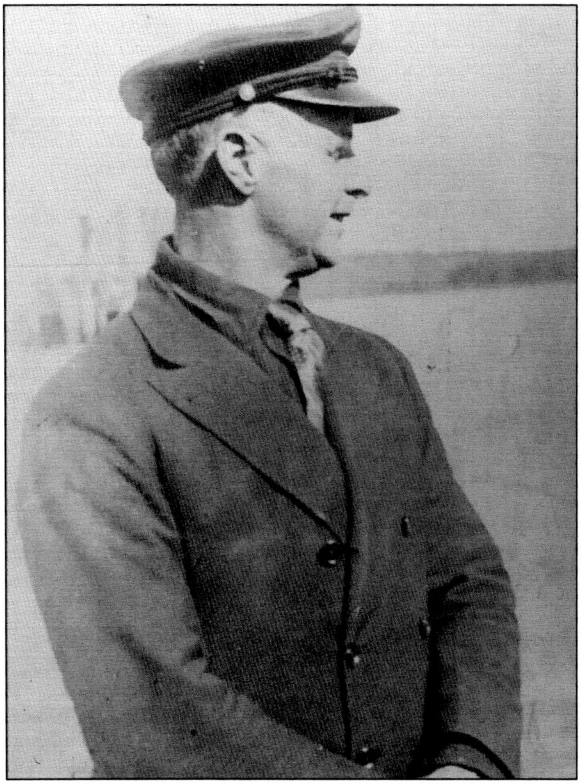

Donald MacMillan, who attended and taught at Freeport High School, was a member of the Peary expedition which discovered the North Pole in 1909. In his lifetime he made thirty trips northward on his schooner *Bowdoin* to do research. Captain "Mac," as he was affectionately called, was the first white man to reach many unexplored areas and provided much new information for maps of the Arctic. He died in 1970 at the age of ninety-five.

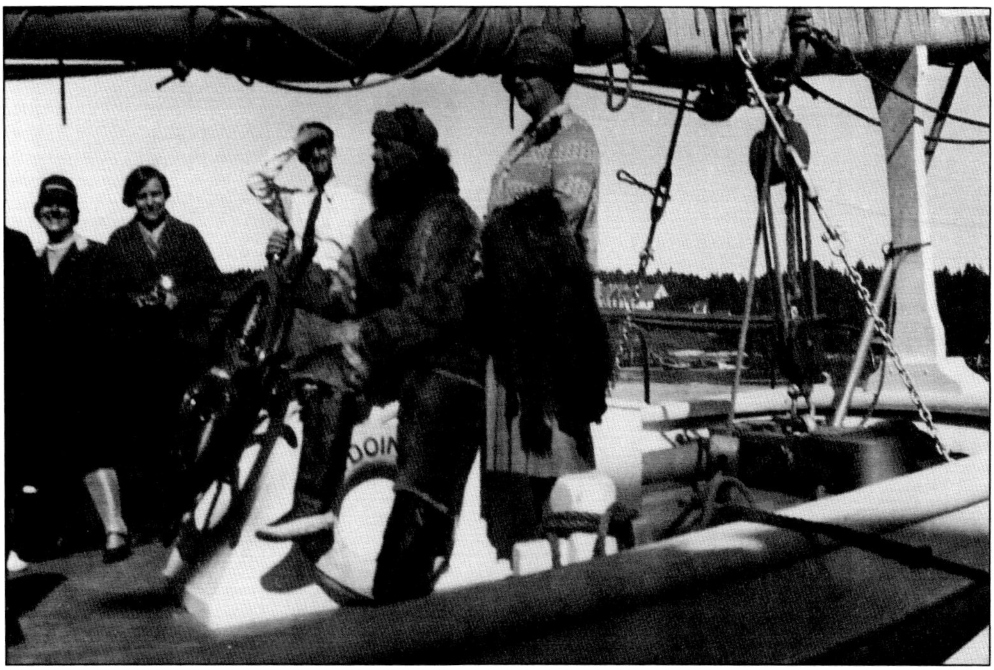

MacMillan, clothed in Arctic furs, is shown here on the *Bowdoin*. May Fogg, MacMillan's sister, is standing with a beautiful Arctic fur on her arm. Above Mrs. Fogg's head and to her left is the jury rig of the boom which was sprung during a bad squall coming down from Labrador.

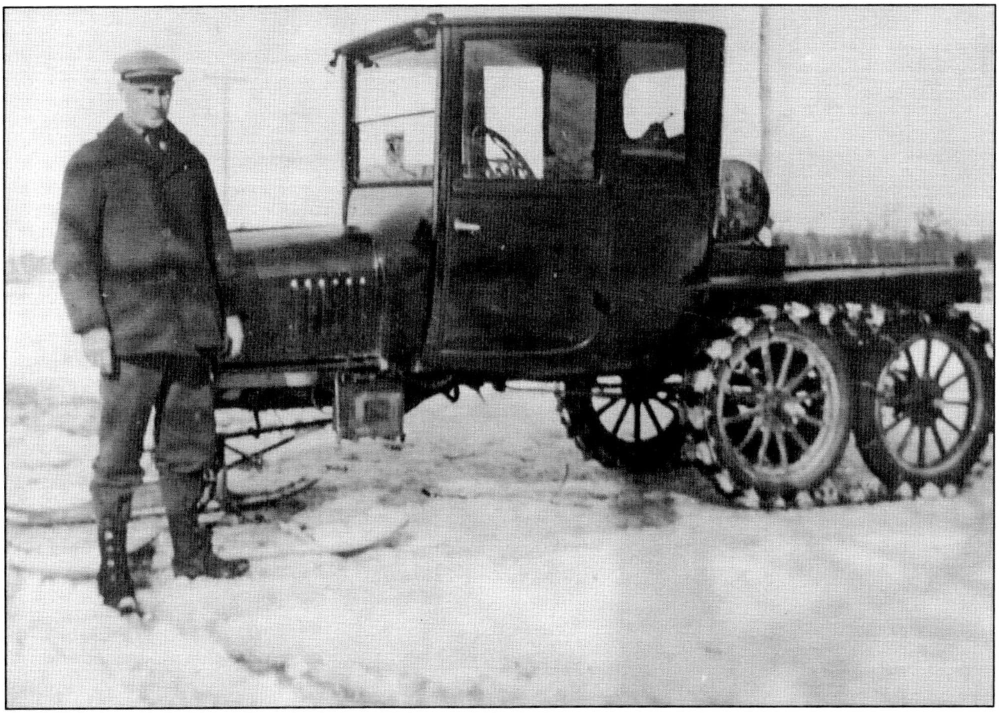

Dr. Arthur Gould was one of Freeport's physicians during the mid-1900s. Gould and his colleague Dr. Howard ran the Freeport Hospital from 1926 until the mid-1940s. Here Dr. Gould is shown with the Model -T that he had converted into a "snowcat" for winter rounds.

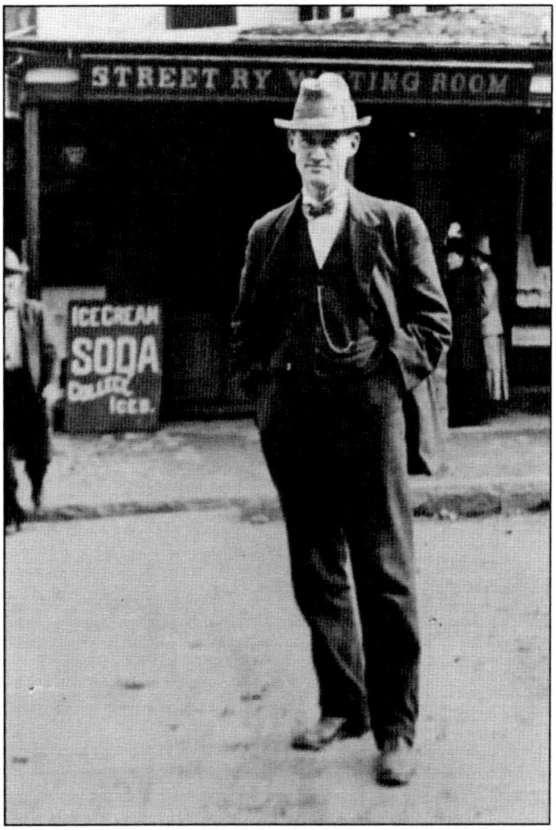

Winthrop C. Fogg is shown here in front of the Patterson Block. The *1912 Business Directory* lists Mr. Fogg as a druggist, in business on Main Street for twenty-seven years, and as postmaster. He died in 1917.

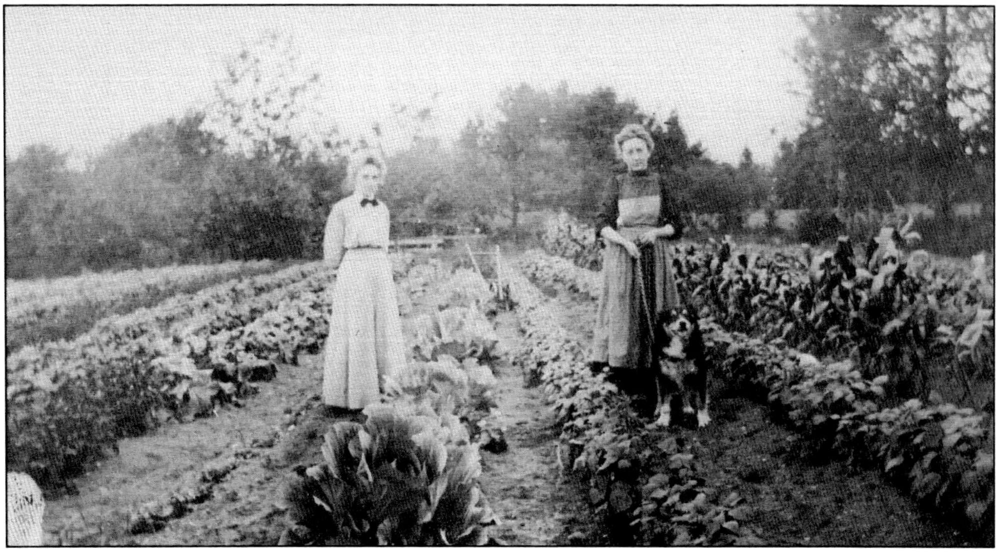

Minerva Gammon and her sister Mabel Gammon Ficket pose here in their garden on Pleasant Street.

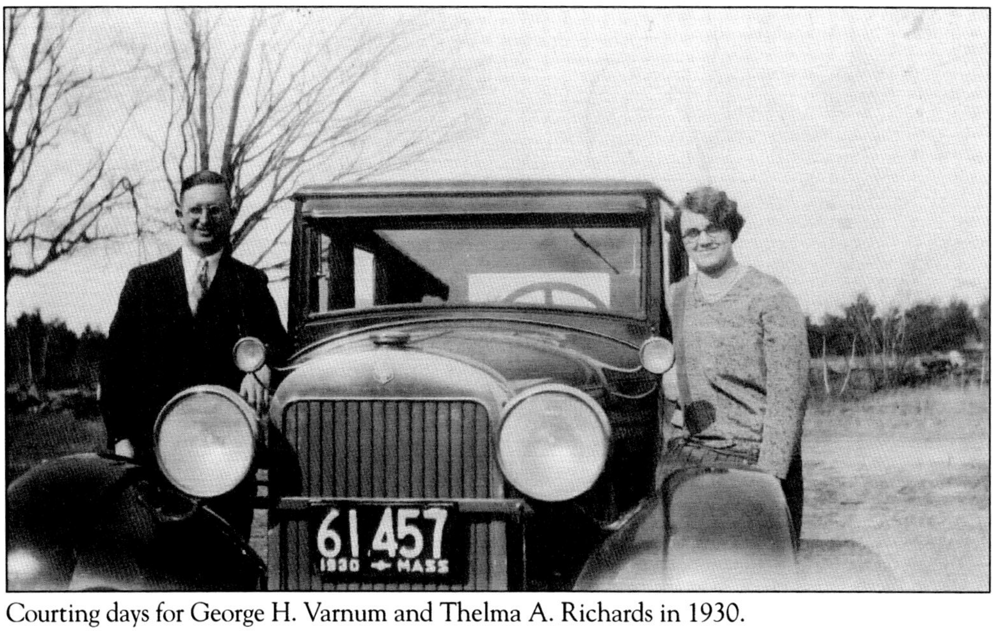

Courting days for George H. Varnum and Thelma A. Richards in 1930.

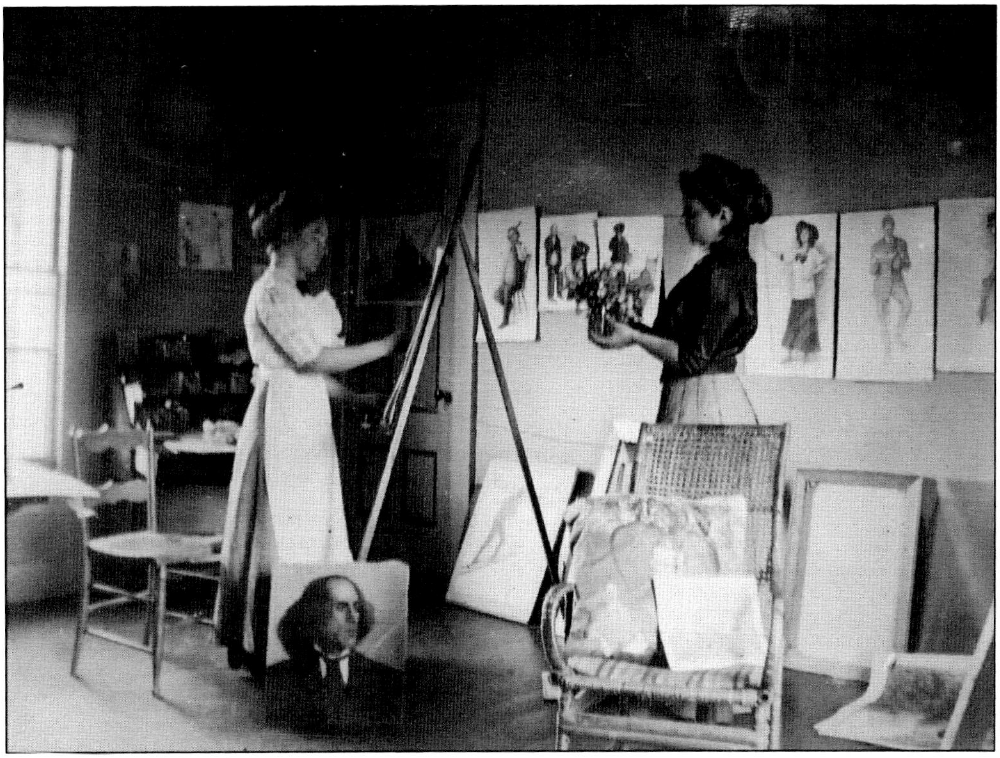

Helen K. Randall and Lillian Fogg often worked together in Helen's studio on Main Street. Helen, the daughter of Captain Rufus Soule Randall, was an accomplished artist and founder of the Freeport Art Club. After her death in 1976, her Main Street brick dwelling became the Freeport Historical Society.

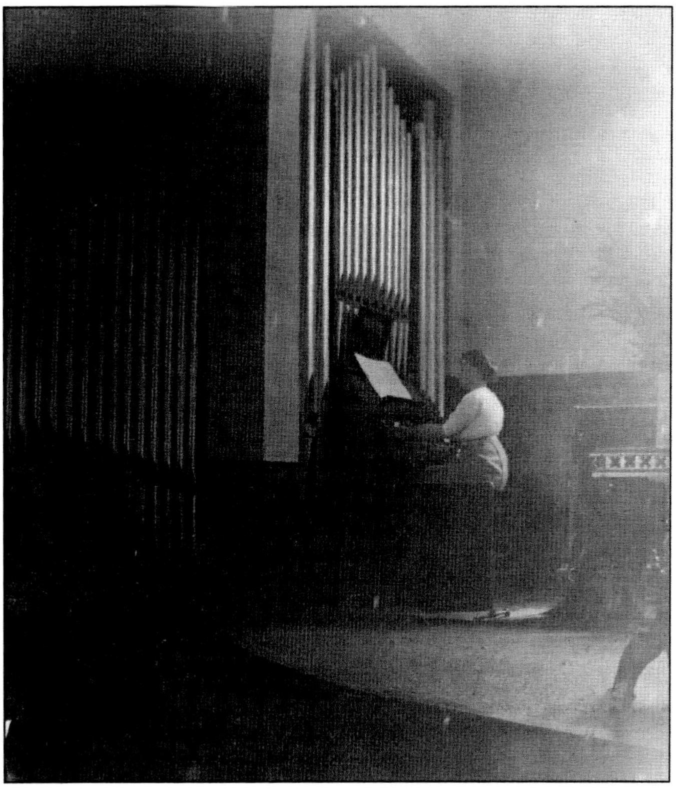

An interior view of the First Parish Congregational Church on Main Street shows Marguerita Soule at the organ.

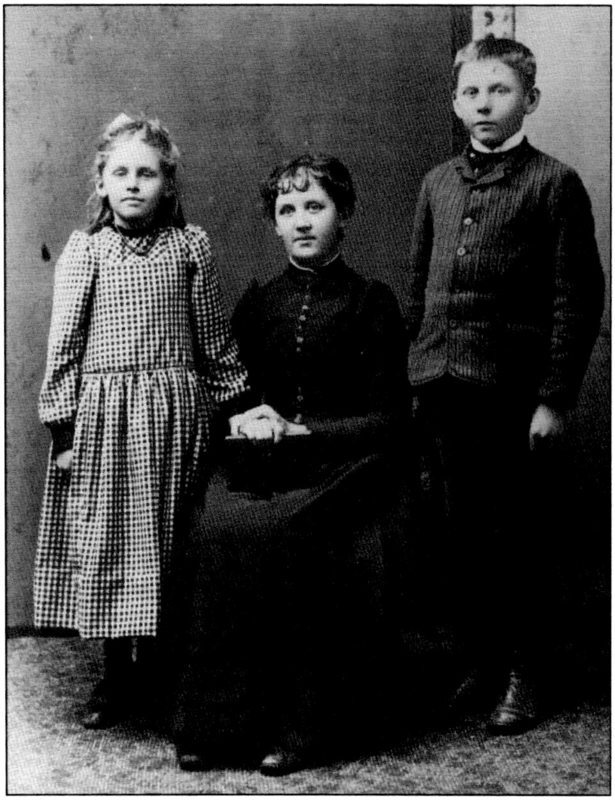

Mildred, Ethel, and Frank Pettengill, seen *c.* 1890, were the children of Wallace and Adelaide Pettengill. Two of the children, Mildred and Frank, lived on and worked the family farm and Mildred remained there without plumbing and electricity until 1965. The property was acquired by Mr. and Mrs. L.M.C. Smith and then given to the Freeport Historical Society.

Augustus Holbrook and Wallace Pettengill take a boat ride, as illustrated in this *c.* 1900 photograph.

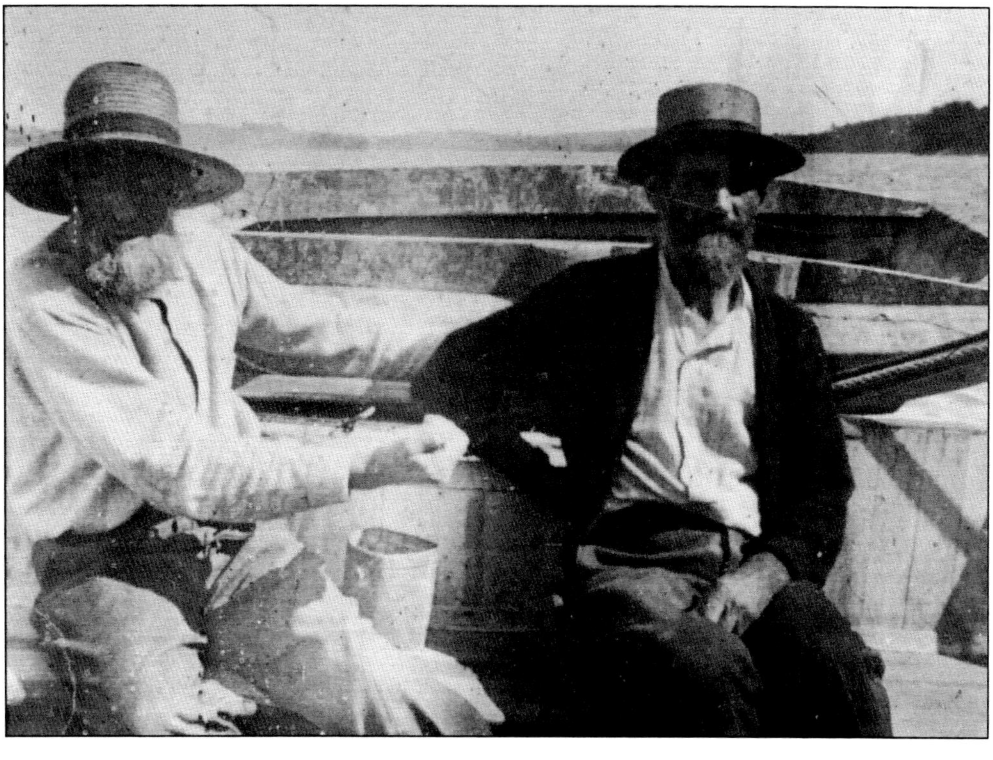

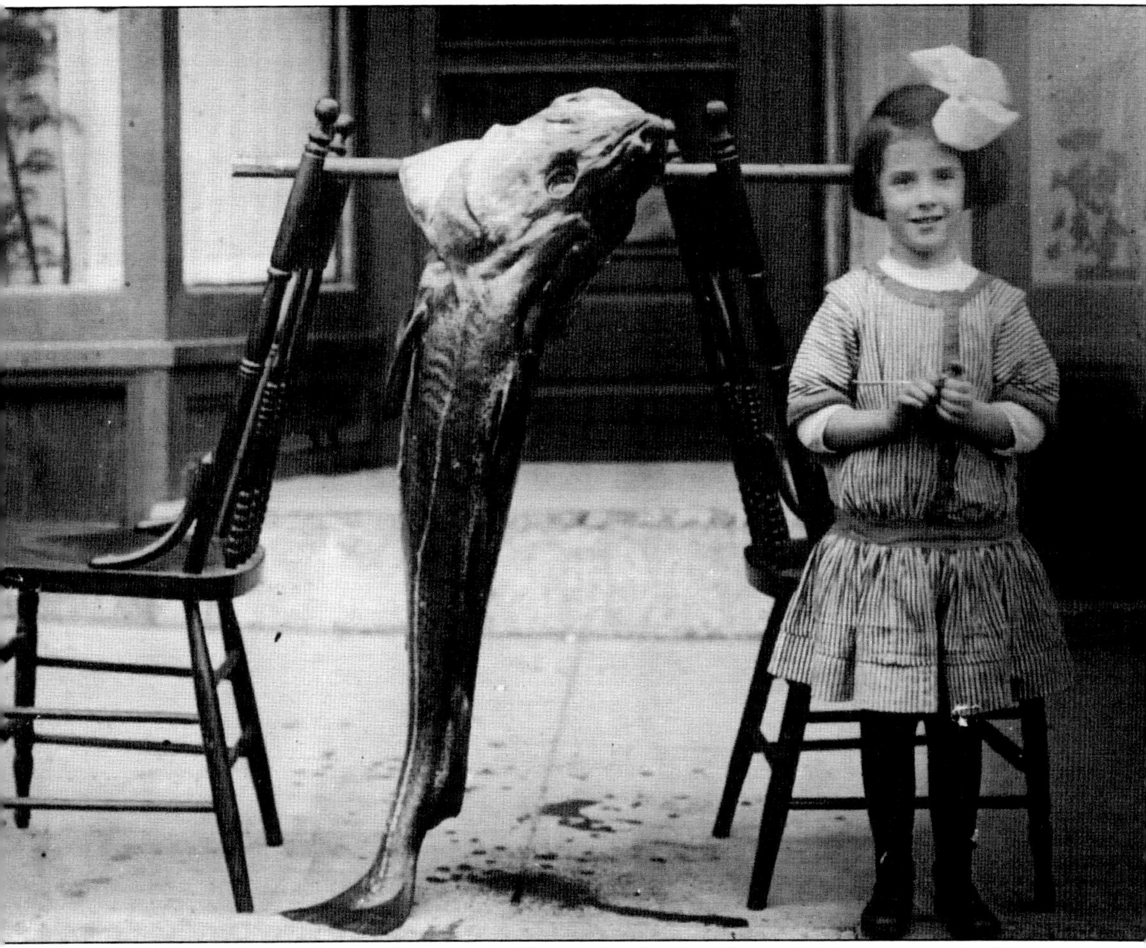

In 1913, Evelyn Kennedy stands in front of her father Luther Kennedy's business in the Davis Block. The codfish was said to have been at least one hundred years old.

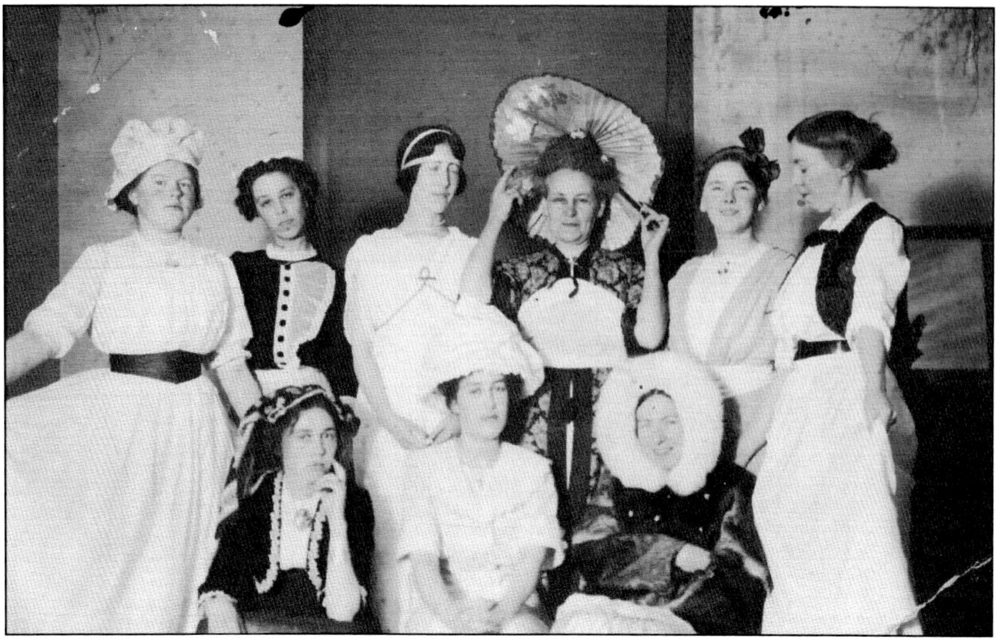

An "Around the World Supper" photograph taken at the First Congregational church captured participants, from left to right as follows: (front row) Anna Averilla, Delia Bowden, and Mildred Stowell; (back row) Marguerita Soule, Helen Strout, Pearl Libby, Mae True, Eldena Soule, and Agnes Dunning.

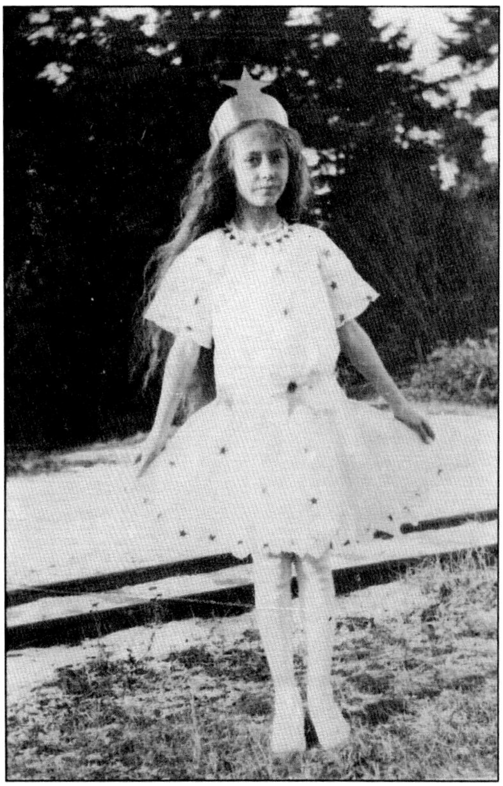

Young Harriet Lowell wears her "Falling Star" crepe paper costume in 1913.

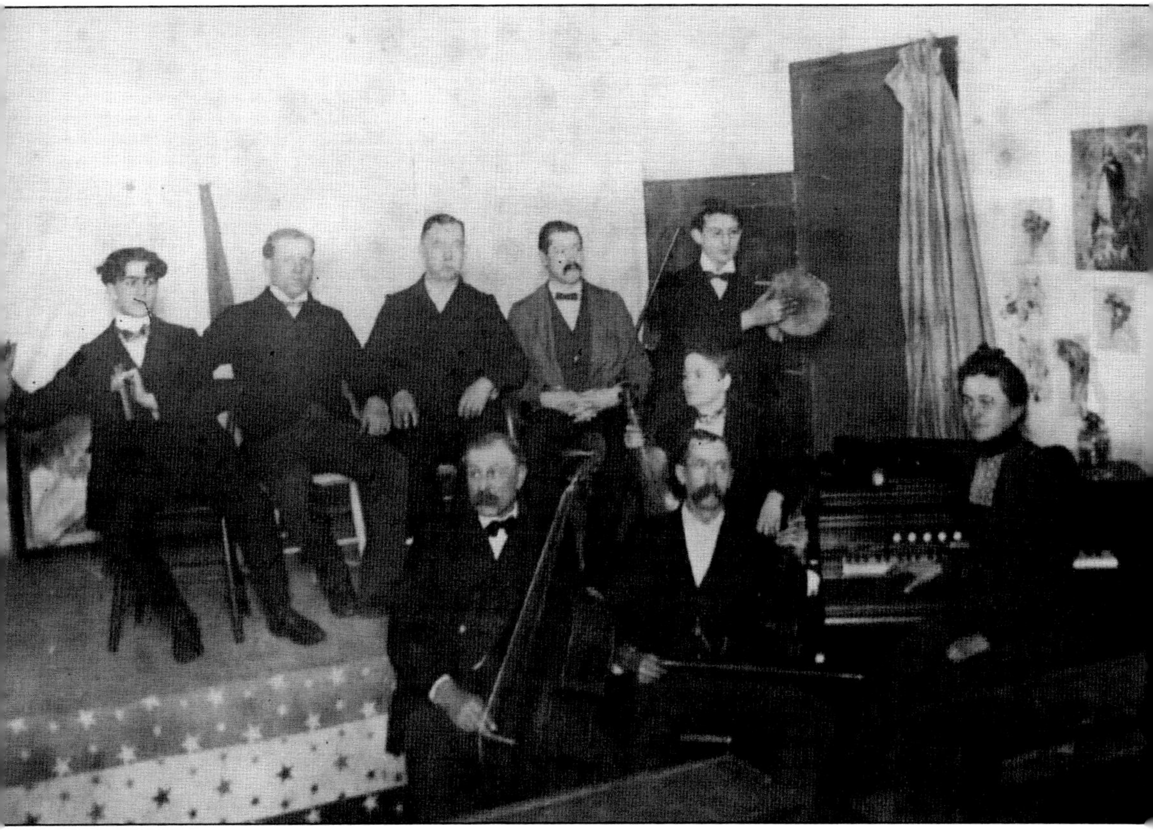

The Porter's Landing Minstrels included players, from left to right, as follows: (front row) Charles Chase, Marshall Bond, and Della Bryant; (back row) Clifton Bradbury, Willis Coffin, Andrew Bradbury, John Bryant, and Leonard Bradbury.

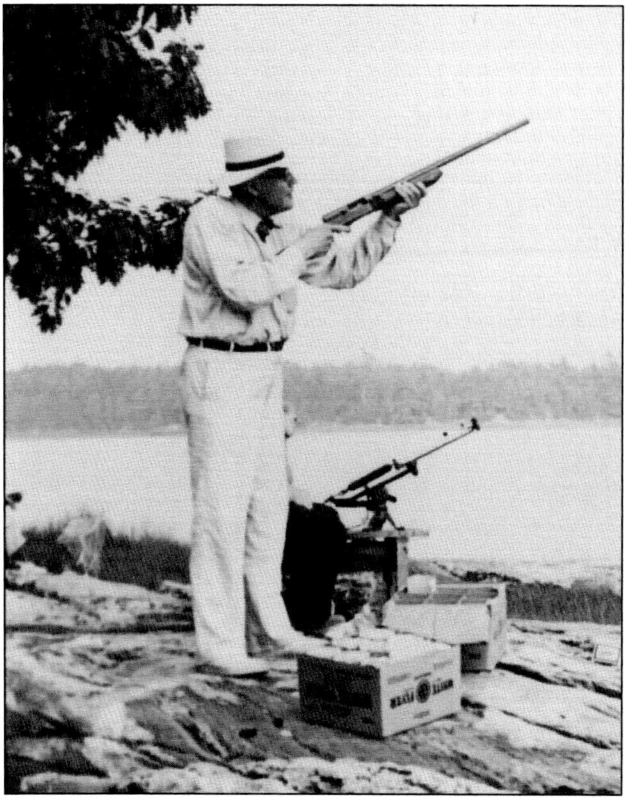

Freeport's most famous citizen, L.L. Bean, takes aim at the annual Employees Picnic.

Each year the businessmen in downtown Freeport attended the Merchants' Picnic.

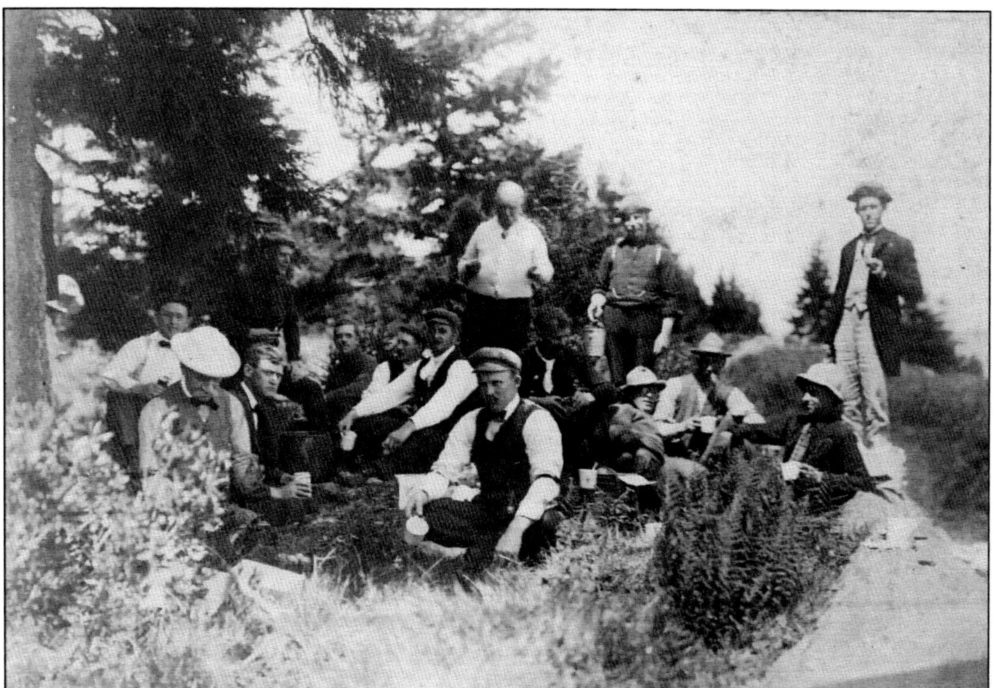

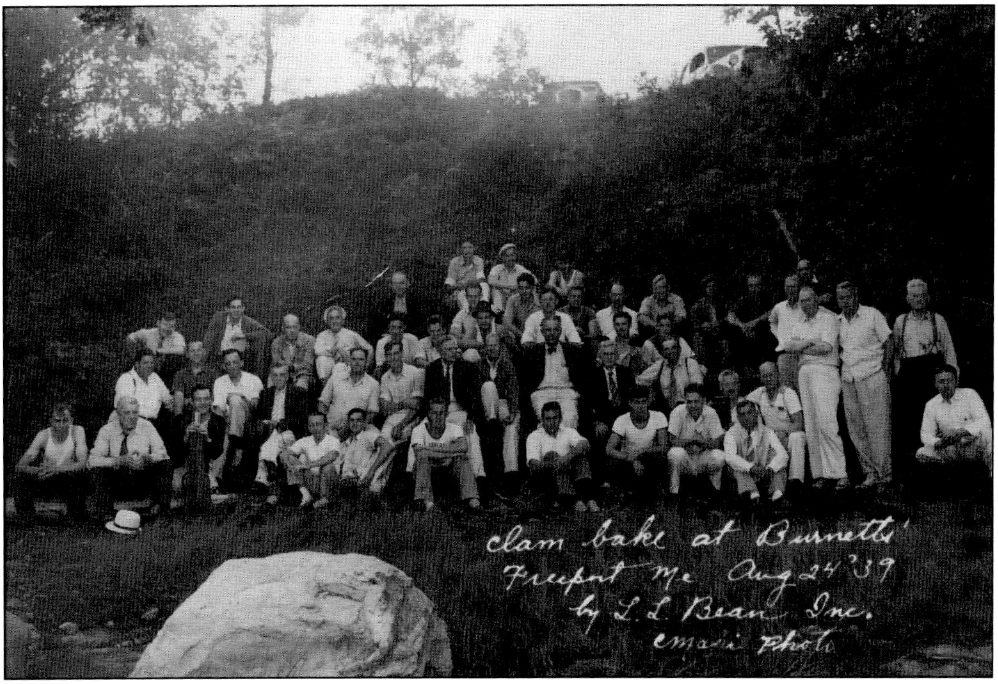

A picnic was a popular summertime activity in Freeport, as shown in this picture of a clambake given by L. L. Bean at Burnetts on Wolfe's Neck on August 24, 1939.

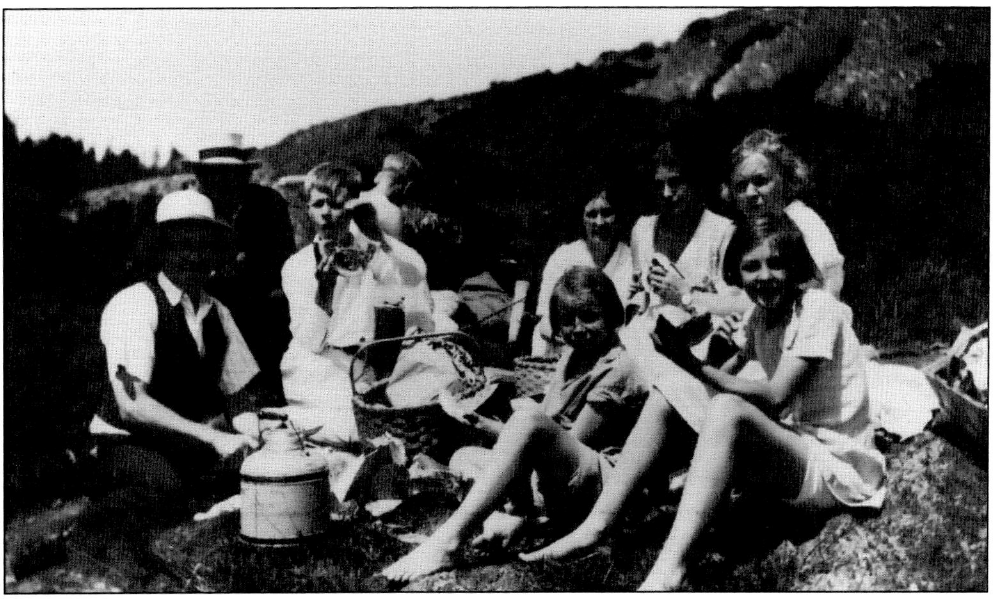

A photograph recalls a picnic with the Soule and Gould families.

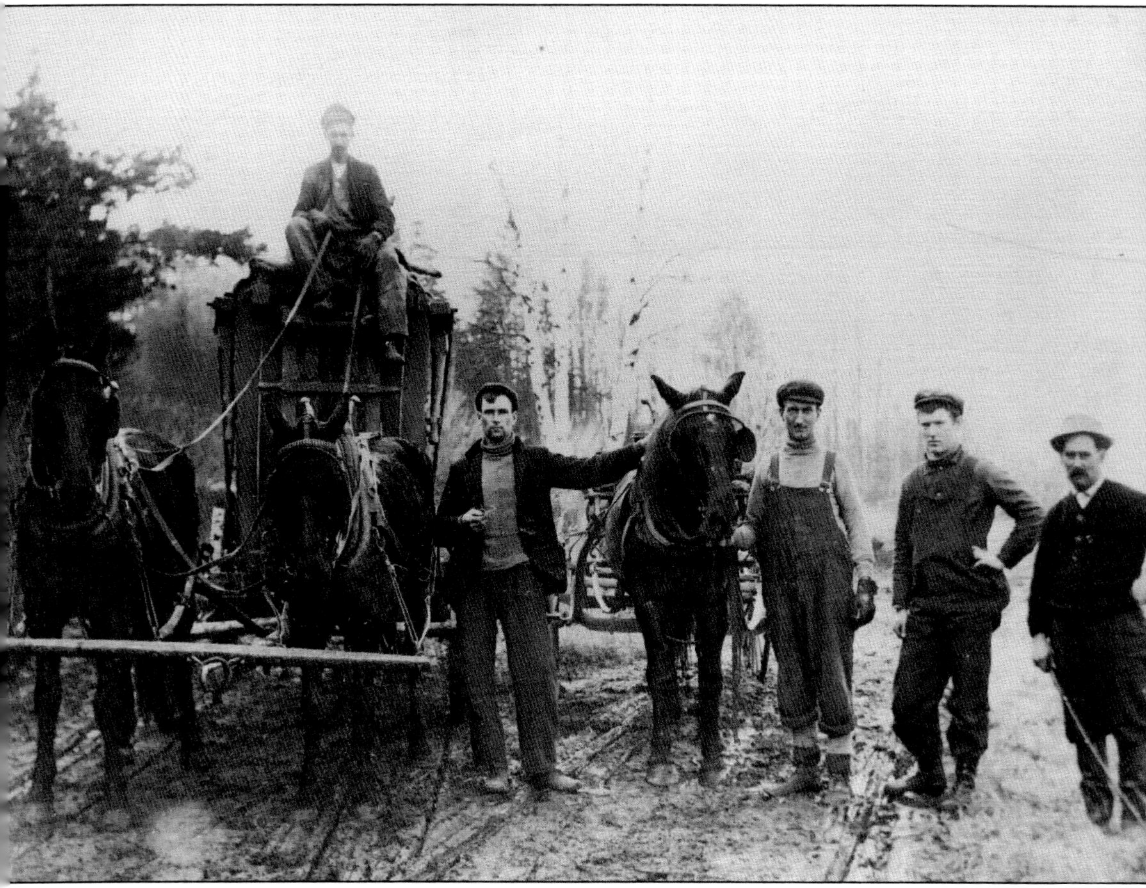

Haying was a summertime pursuit and hay was a profitable crop as well as a staple for a farmer's own immediate needs. Identified in this 1920 hay-press photograph are, from left to right, the following: Everett Byram, Victor Coffin, Atwood Brewer, Maurice Patterson, and Eddie Byram.

Seven

Tourism and Recreation

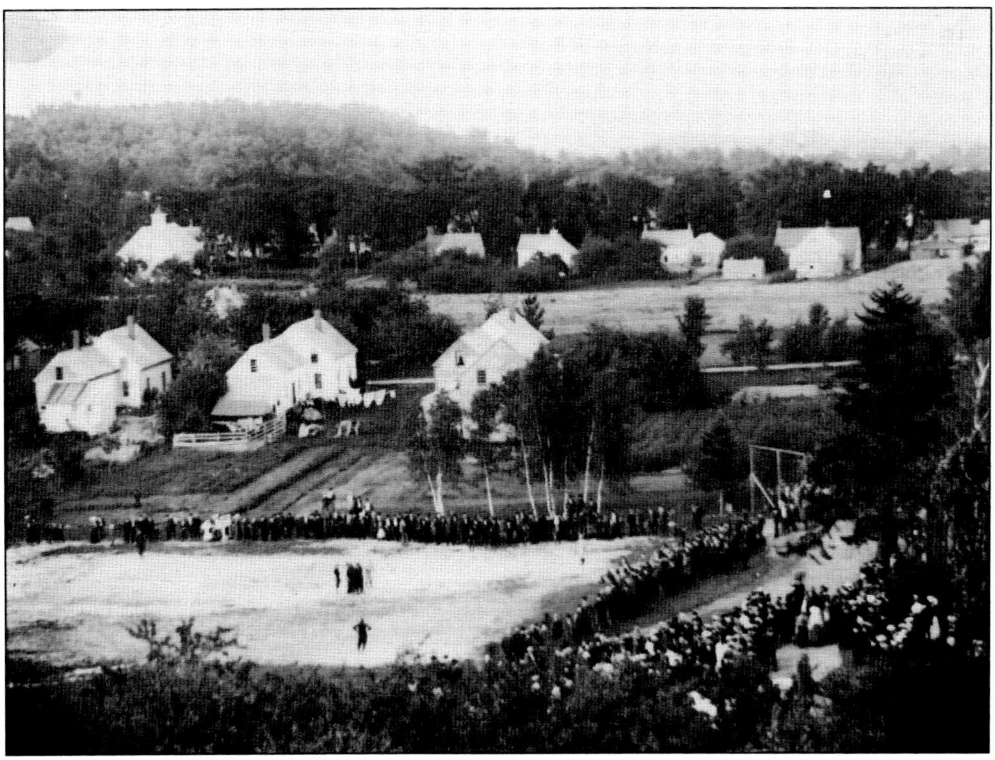

Baseball, always a popular form of summer recreation, was played on the ball field in South Freeport, c. 1905. This view is from Casco Castle looking toward Park Street.

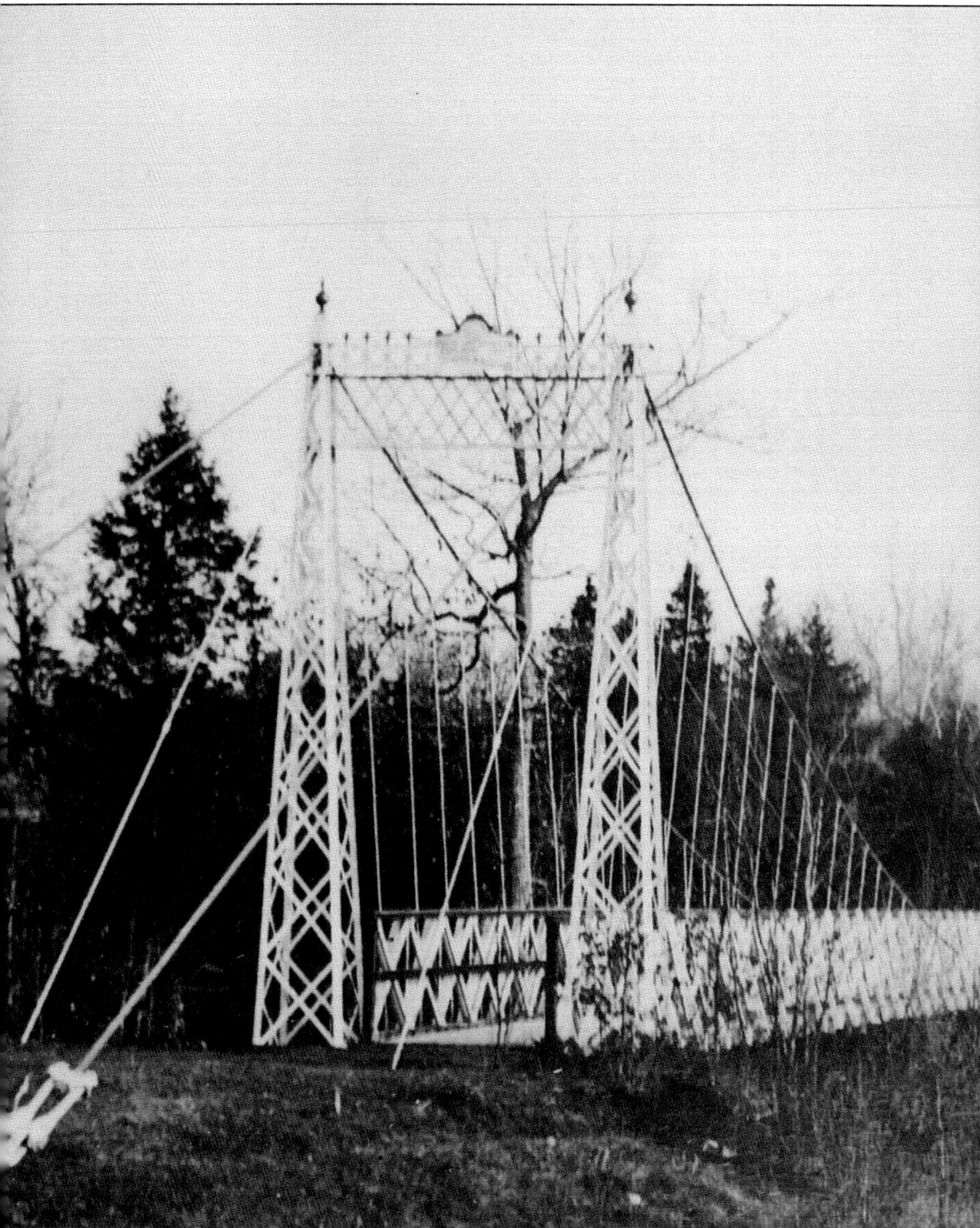

Casco Castle, built in 1903 by the owner of the Portland and Brunswick Street Railway, Amos Gerald, was a unique summer resort in South Freeport. People traveled by trolley and steamer to enjoy the hotel with its beautiful gardens, food, and comfortable accommodations. The

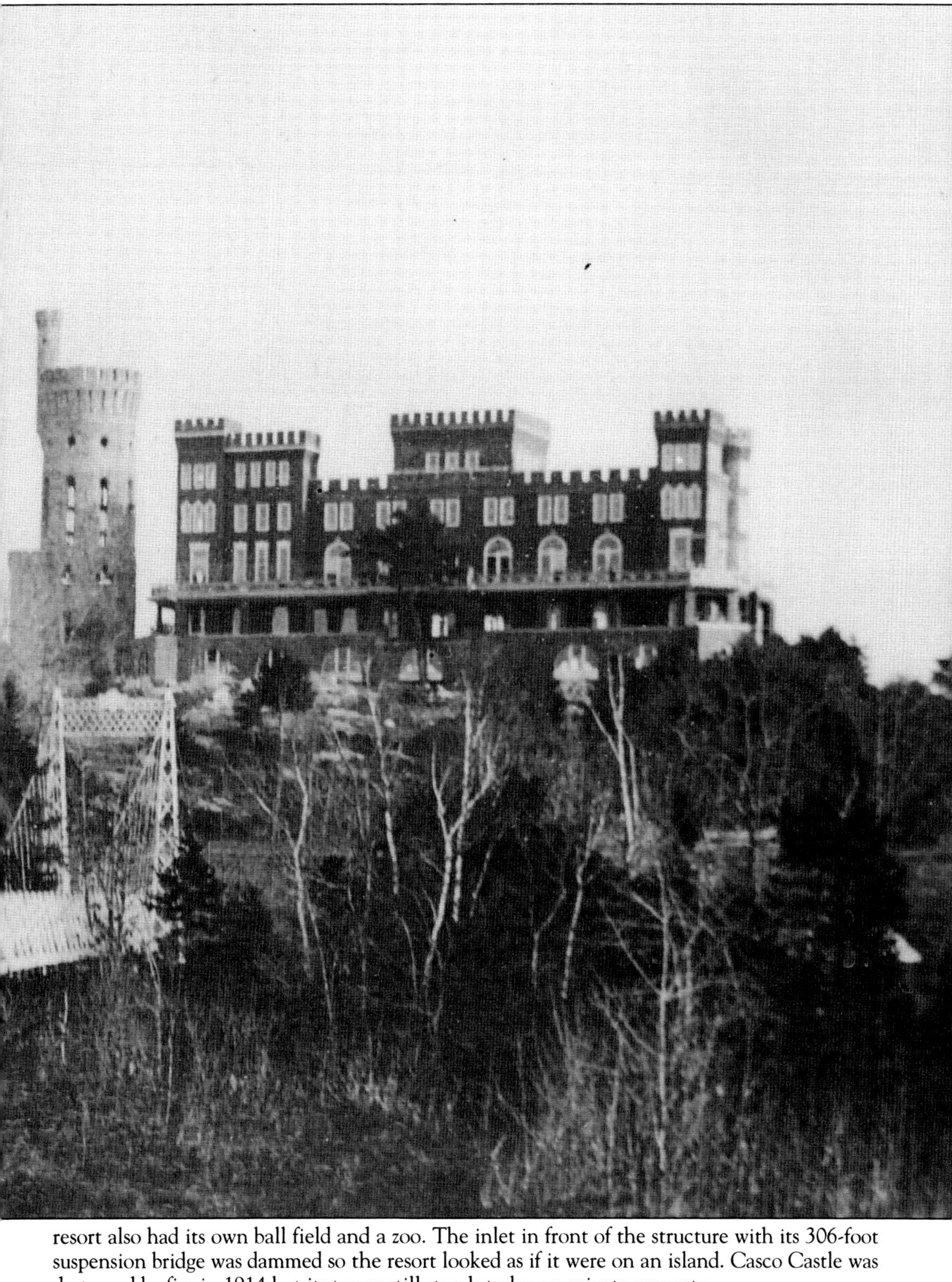

resort also had its own ball field and a zoo. The inlet in front of the structure with its 306-foot suspension bridge was dammed so the resort looked as if it were on an island. Casco Castle was destroyed by fire in 1914 but its tower still stands today on private property.

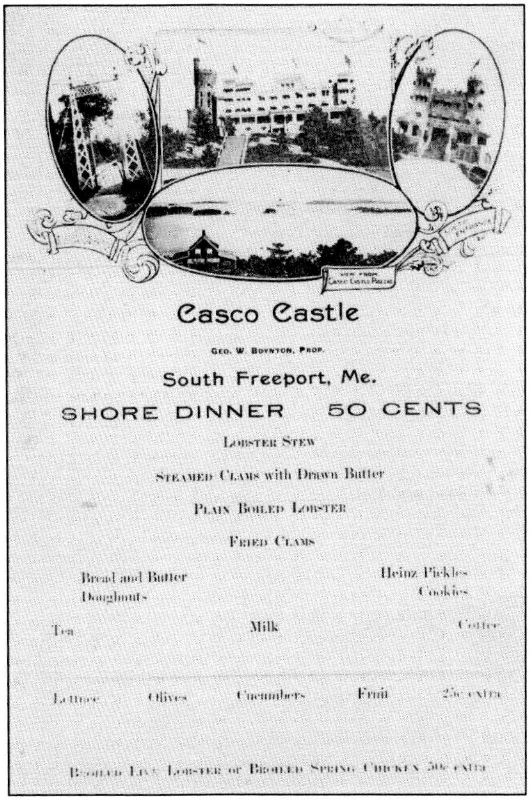

Casco Castle

Geo. W. Boynton, Prop.

South Freeport, Me.

SHORE DINNER 50 CENTS

Lobster Stew

Steamed Clams with Drawn Butter

Plain Boiled Lobster

Fried Clams

Bread and Butter
Doughnuts

Heinz Pickles
Cookies

Tea Milk Coffee

Lettuce Olives Cucumbers Fruit 25c extra

Broiled Live Lobster or Broiled Spring Chicken 50c extra

The menu of the Casco Castle dining room advertises a shore dinner complete with boiled lobster and clams for only 50¢!

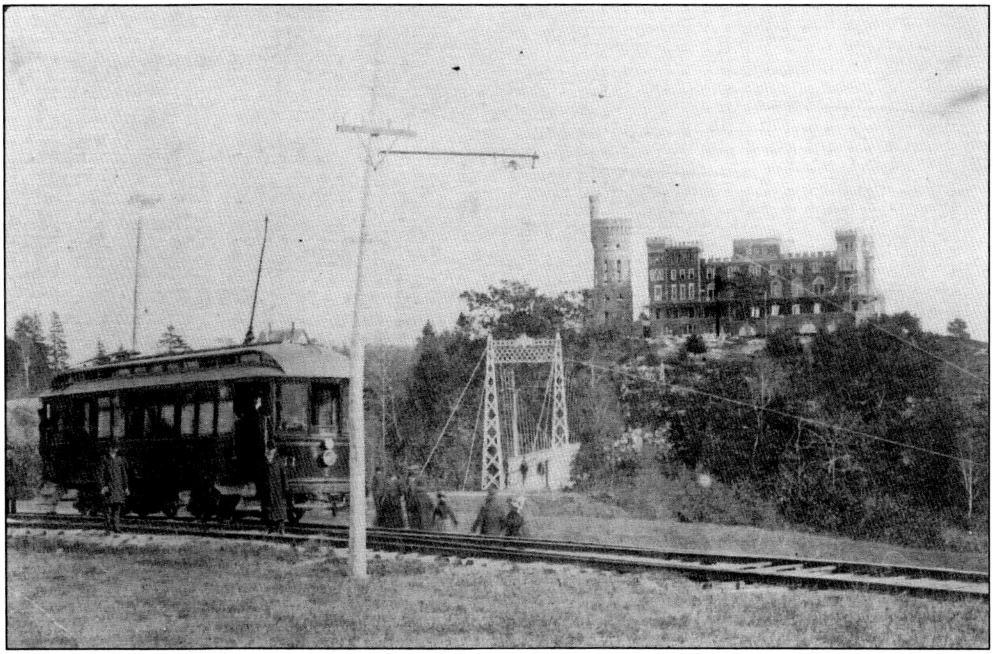

The ride on the trolley cars from Portland was well worth 20¢. The trolley car is dropping visitors off in front of the suspension bridge in this 1910 photograph. Children loved to run across the bridge; causing it to swing, and terrorizing other visitors.

The round tower at Casco Castle rises 185 feet above the high-tide mark. Until 1914 it served as a lighthouse at night. Captains welcomed this beacon and came to depend on it, missing it when the resort closed each fall.

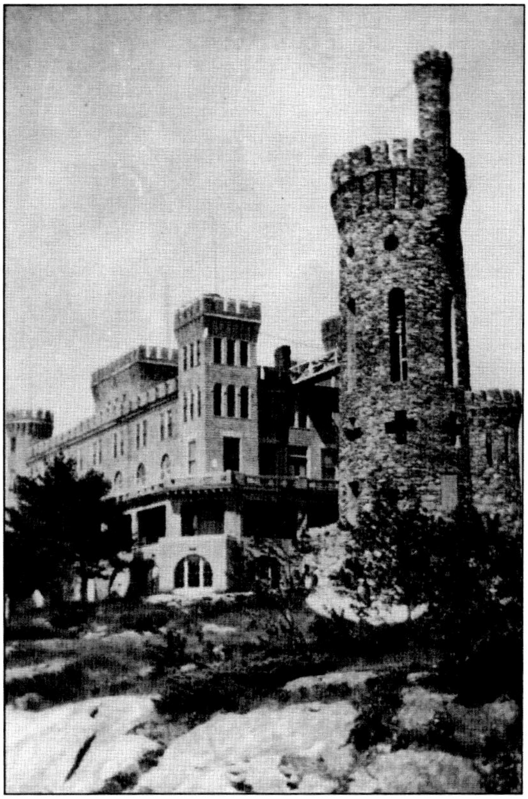

The zoo was one of the attractions of the Castle and it included bears, wolves, deer, monkeys, and Angus cattle, as well as buffalo. Newspapers reported that at one time some of the wolves escaped and frightened the neighborhood.

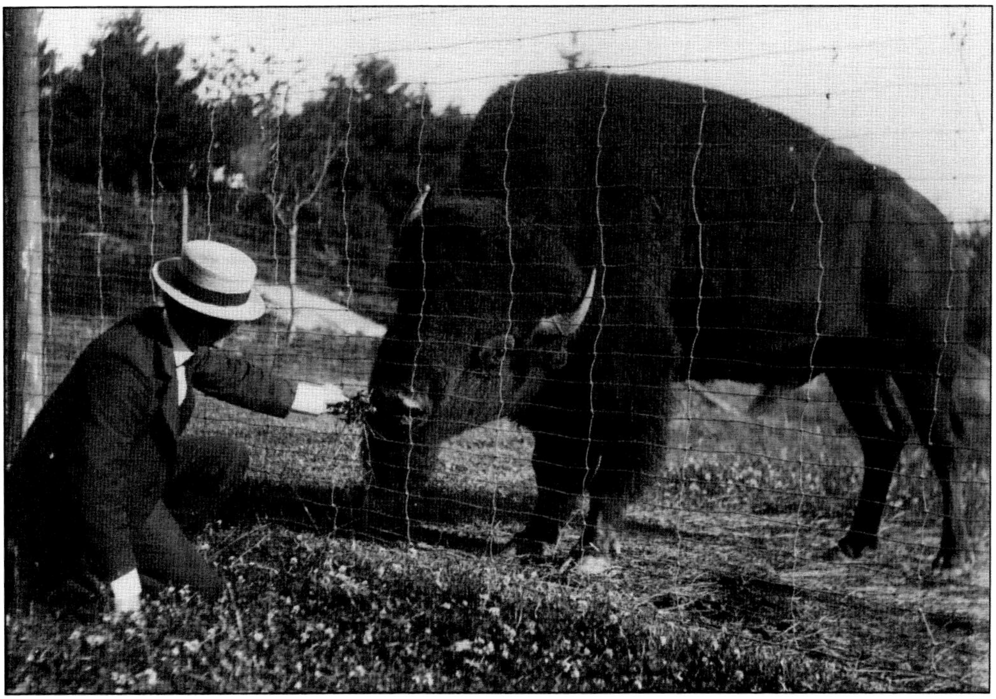

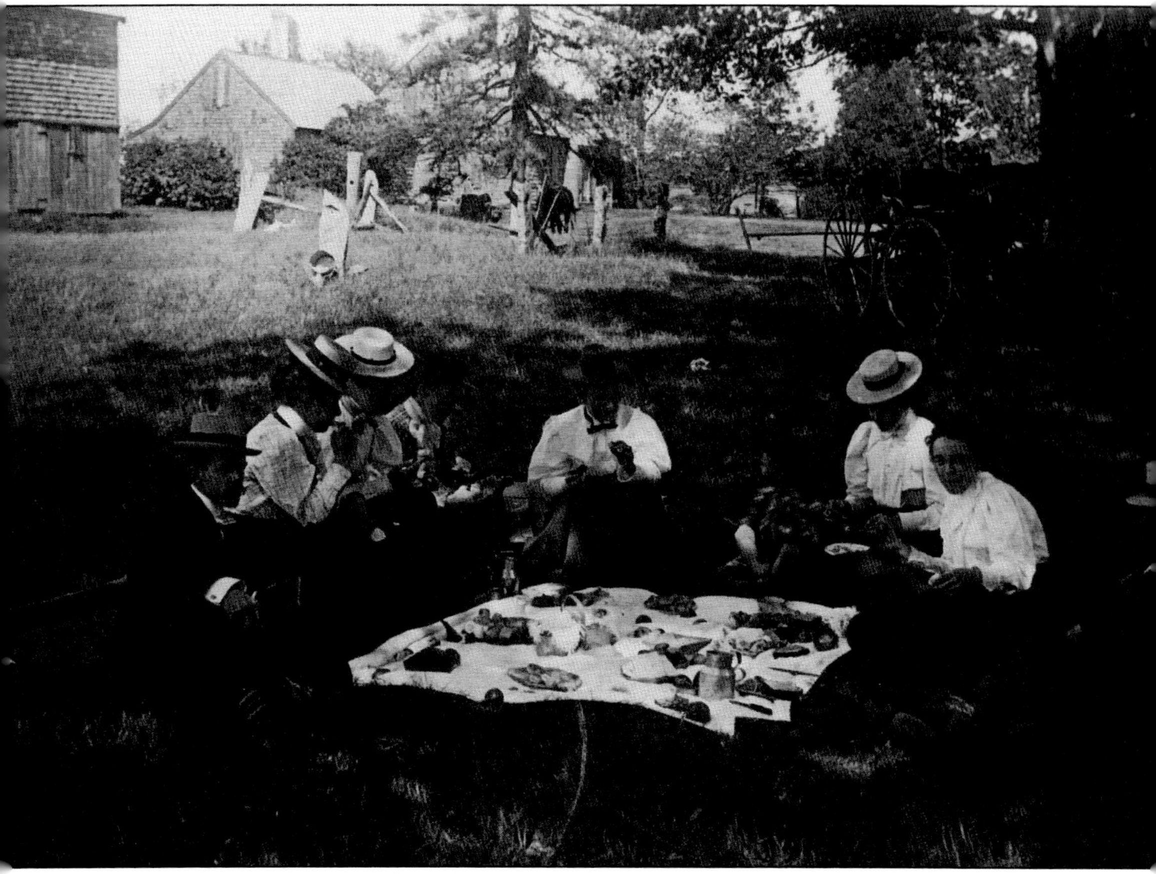

A picnic scene c. 1898 at the John Alvah Tuttle farm, now known as the Desert of Maine. Mr. Tuttle farmed this parcel of land which his grandfather, also John, had settled in the early 1800s, but the farm failed due to erosion caused by over grazing. Since the 1920s this area has been a major tourist attraction, first known as the Old Sand Farm and more recently, the Desert of Maine.

The Spring House at the Desert of Maine. This natural spring in the Desert once offered the thirsty visitor clear, clean ice-cold water but it is now buried by shifting and blowing sands.

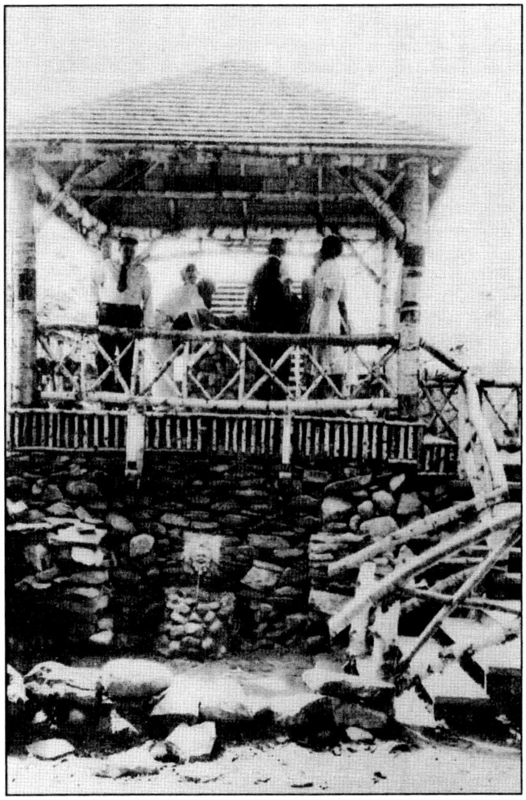

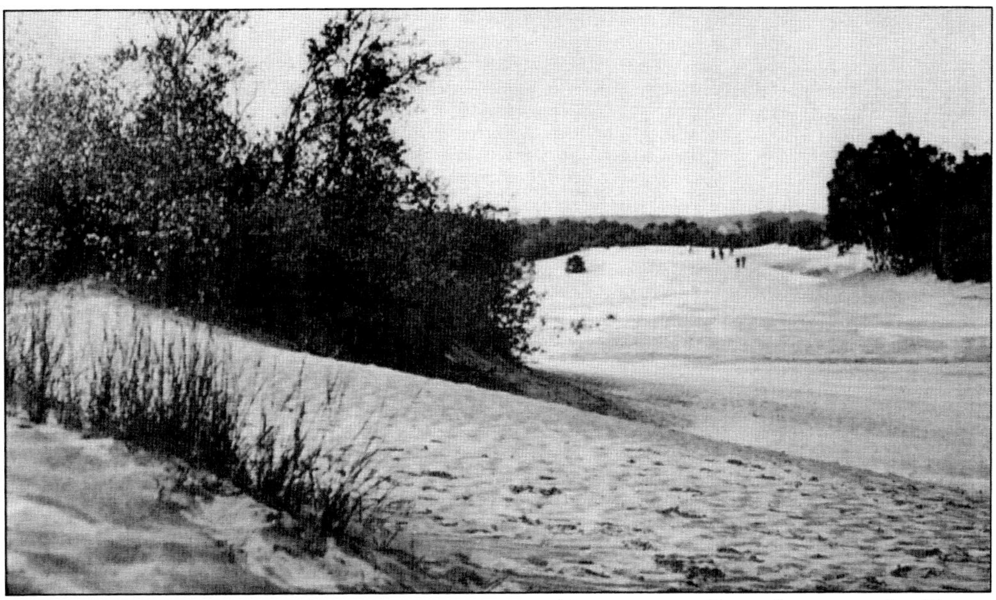

The sands of the Desert of Maine now cover a 40-acre area. Over the years the Desert advertisements have compared it with the Sahara, the Gobi, and the deserts of the western United States. The 1920s were the heyday of automobile camping, and the area was a mecca for tourists. Today's tour focuses more on history, environmental issues, and land use and still attracts 30 to 40,000 visitors each year.

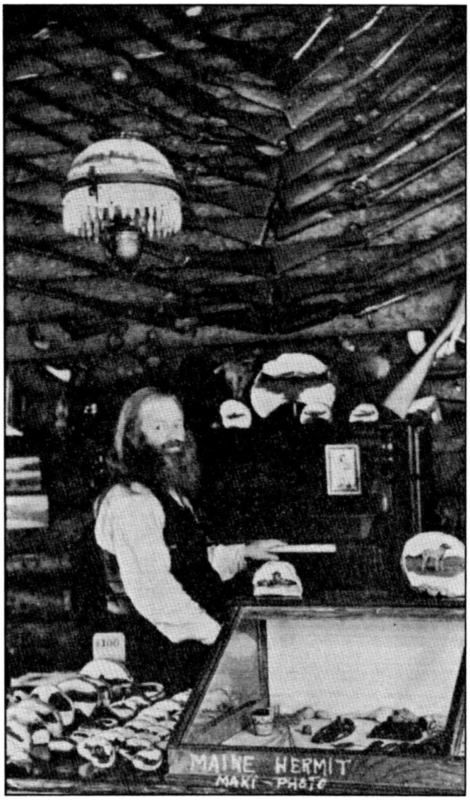

Charles Coffin was known as the "Hermit of the Maine Desert," a tourist attraction in the 1930s. He lived a short distance beyond the Desert of Maine and welcomed visitors to his home to chat and see his rare collection of antiques and curios, including his unique musical instrument made by combining two organs and a worn-out piano.

Be Sure and See -

The Maine Hermit

Located on the desert road

Freeport - - - Maine

This is your chance to visit with the man of many trades and vocations. The man that has made his own musical instrument—combining two organs and a piano into one and playing them in a most original manner.

Here you will see a collection of many strange and curious things; rifles dating from 1737 to 1918, with their history, a four-barreled pistol—the only one of its kind ever made, handcuffs made in 1836 that have a National history, poison daggers from Bombay, a Portuguese sword taken from the Malay pirates, the outfit of a Union soldier that was in three battles and who is still alive, the first pencil sharpener, and many other odd and curious things.

Here you will see wood carvings done with a jackknife and chisel, and many oil paintings, all done by the Hermit himself. Wooden scissors with no center pin, a genuine French box joint—one piece of wood that was worth writing up by Ripley in—

"Believe It or Not"

See the one cylinder car—the father of the present day Chrysler.

There is an admission fee of 15c and it will be well worth your time and money to stop in.

If not satisfied, money refunded.

Novelty Instruments — Vocal Work

Entertainment

FOR ALL VISITORS - ONE OR MORE

This advertisement for the Maine Hermit enticed many visitors to visit his home making him the most-talked-of, the most-written-of, and the most-photographed man in town at that time.

Allen's Lookout on the Desert Road was a tourist destination in the 1940s where visitors could climb the 135 steps and get views not only of the Desert of Maine but of the White Mountains and the Maine countryside as well.

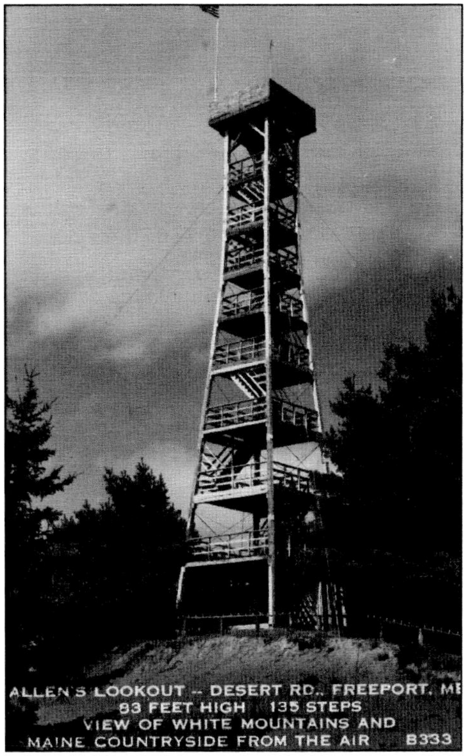

The store at the base of Allen's Lookout was a place where visitors could stop for snacks and information.

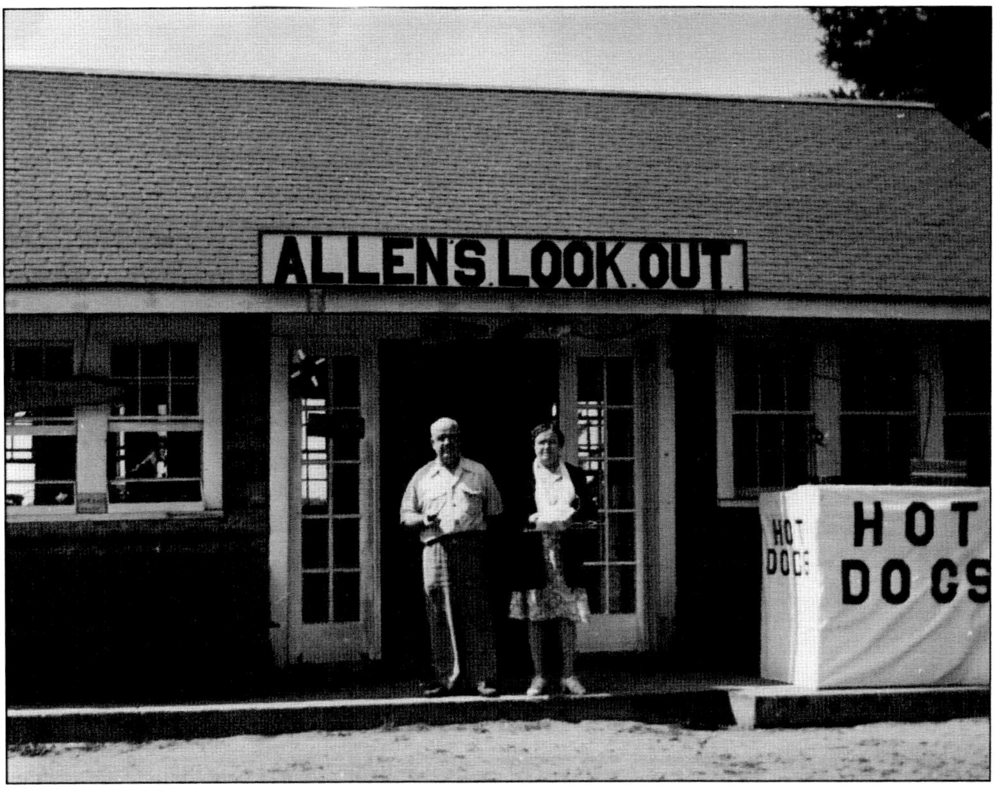

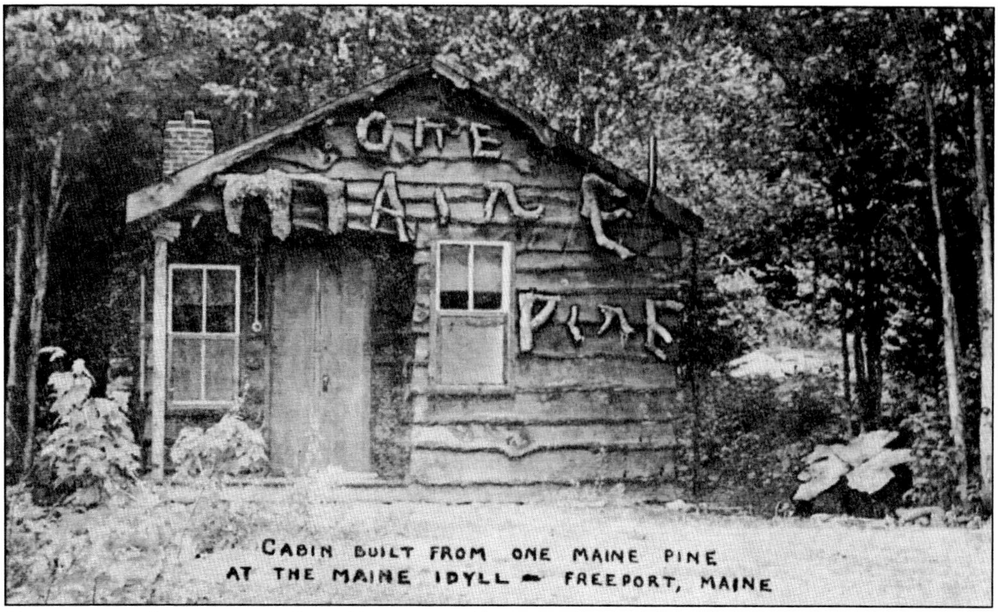

Summer motels sprang up along Route 1 in Freeport during the 1920s as more tourists drove north in their new automobiles. In those days it took nearly fourteen hours to get from Boston to Bar Harbor. The Maine Idyll, just north of Freeport Square, was just one of the cabin colonies that welcomed the weary travelers. It is still in business today and run by the same family, the Marstallers.

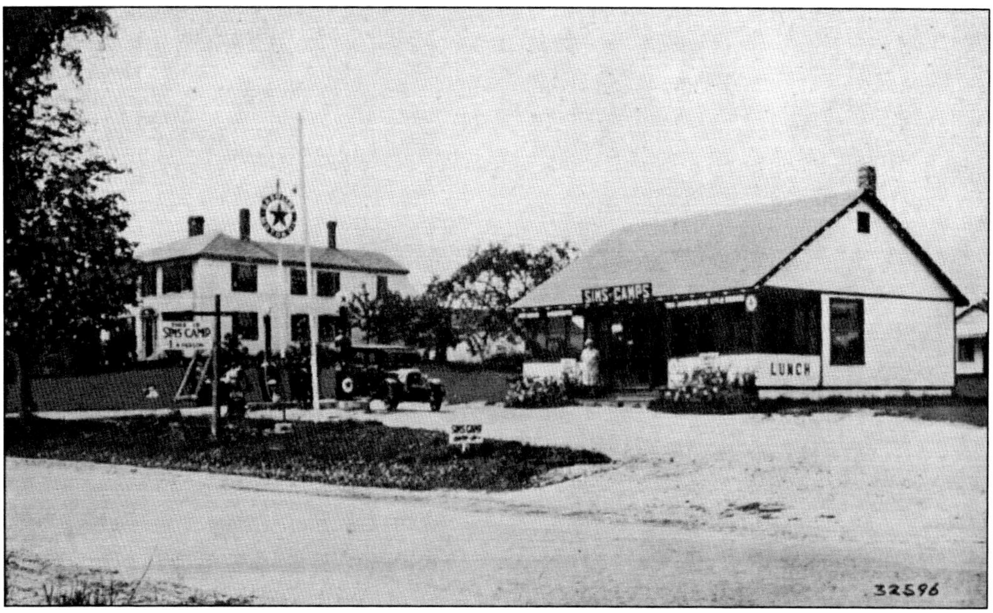

Sims Camps was located on Route 1 south of Freeport and boasted running water in each camp, toilets, electric lights, and home-cooked meals served by Mrs. Sims.

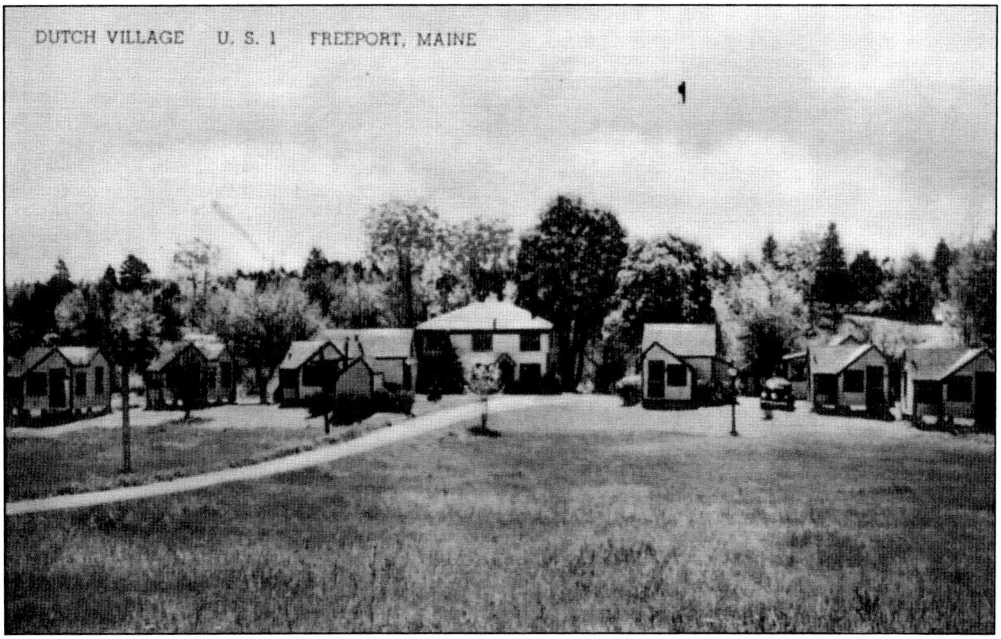

Dutch Village, shown here c.1940, is still in business today. It is located just south of Pine Street on Route 1.

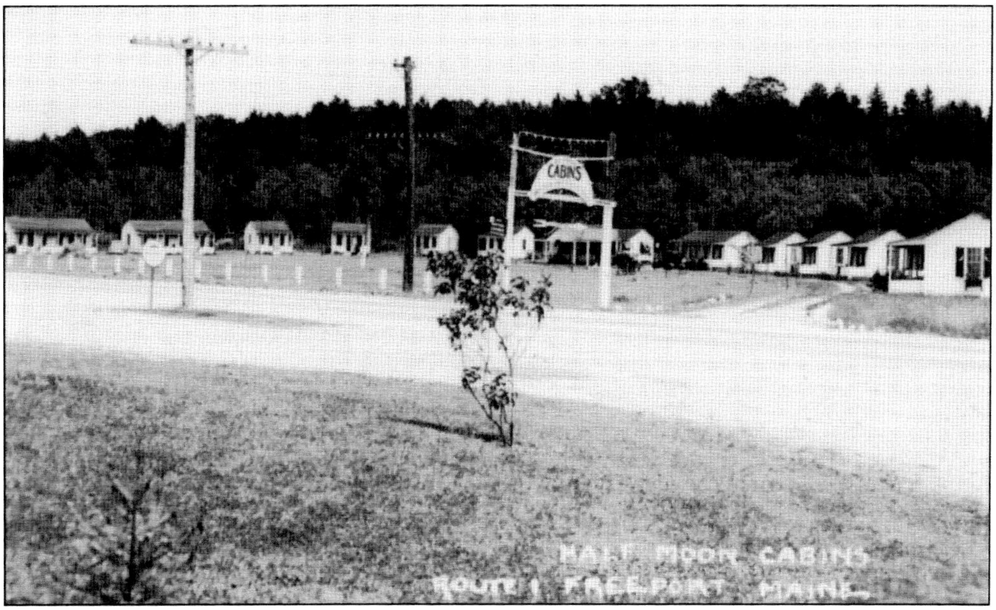

Half Moon Motor Courts was yet another haven for summer visitors. The motel opened in 1920 and had fourteen cabins. Its neon sign became a local landmark. After the interstate highway was built, Route 1 businesses declined and some, like Half Moon Motor Court, were forced to close.

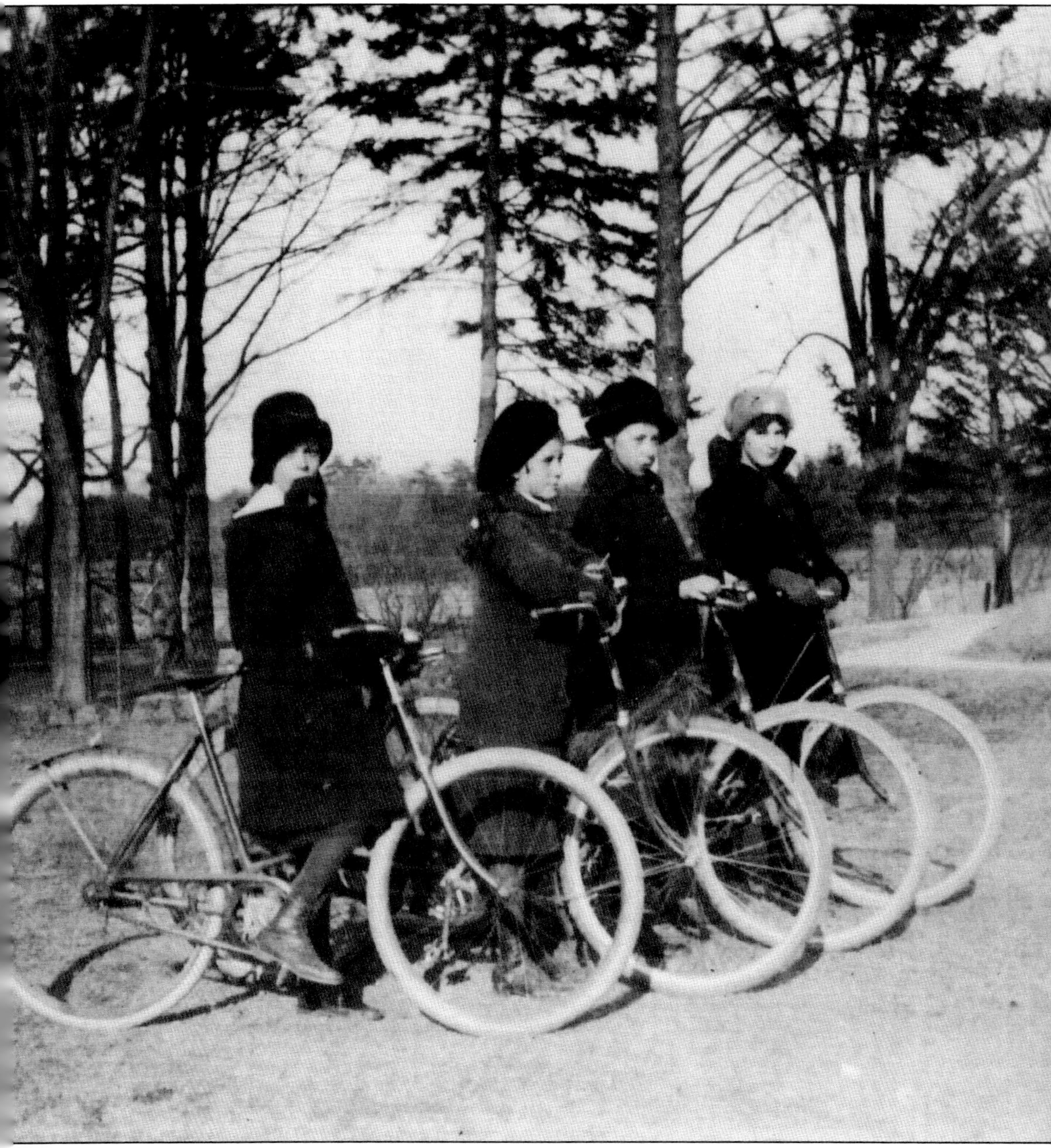

In this photograph, Dorothy Lincoln, Jean Macomber, Jane Lea, and Edith Culver enjoy a bicycle ride *c.* 1914.

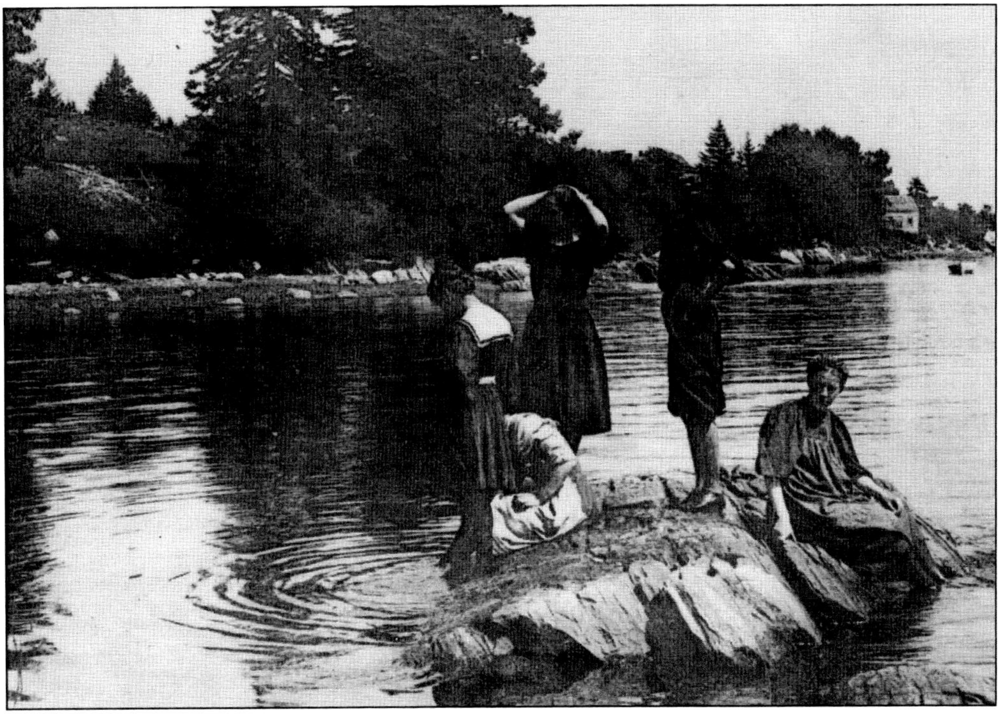

Hot summer weather brought this group of Bustins Island women to the water, as shown in this *c.* 1900 photograph.

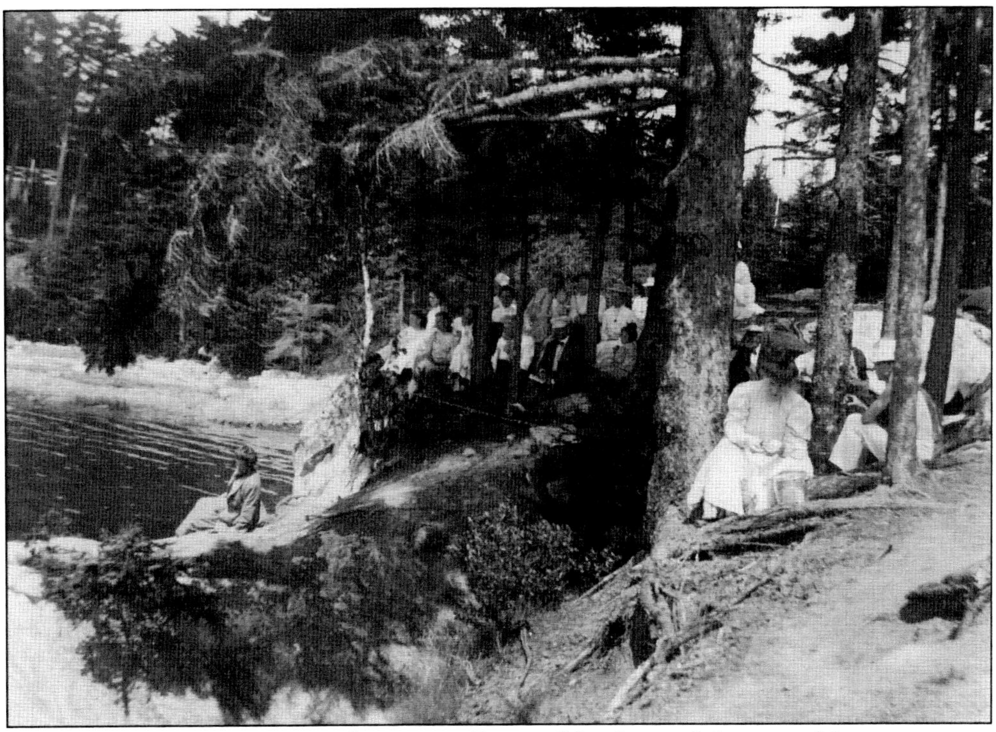

Here, a group enjoys a picnic in the grove at Bustins Island around the turn of the century.

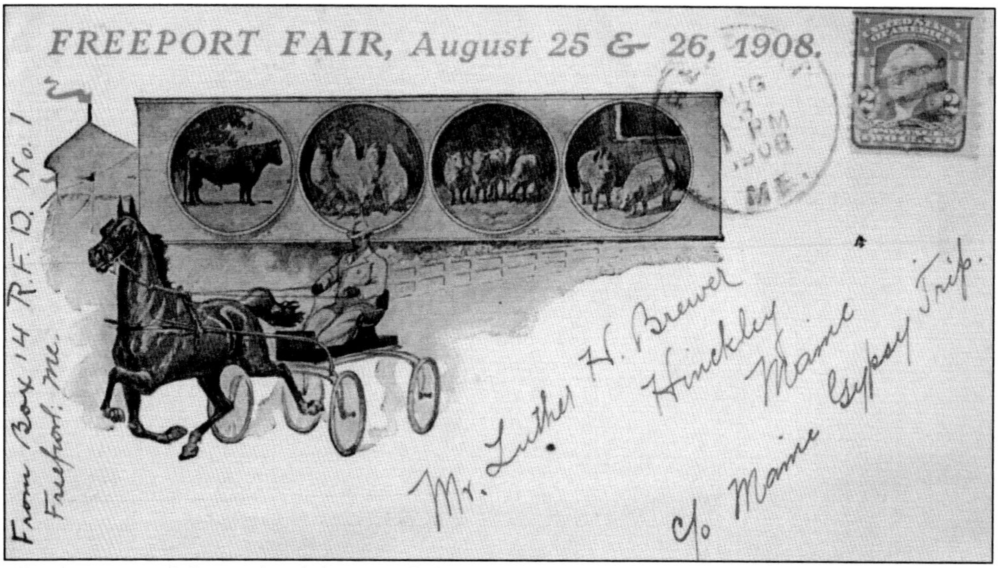

The first annual fair and exhibition of the Freeport Park Association was held in the fall of 1895. The annual fair and horse trot, held on the grounds north of the village on Pleasant Street, consisted of a display of the farm products—fruits, vegetables and live stock—as well as displays of attractive productions of household manufacture, and horse racing.

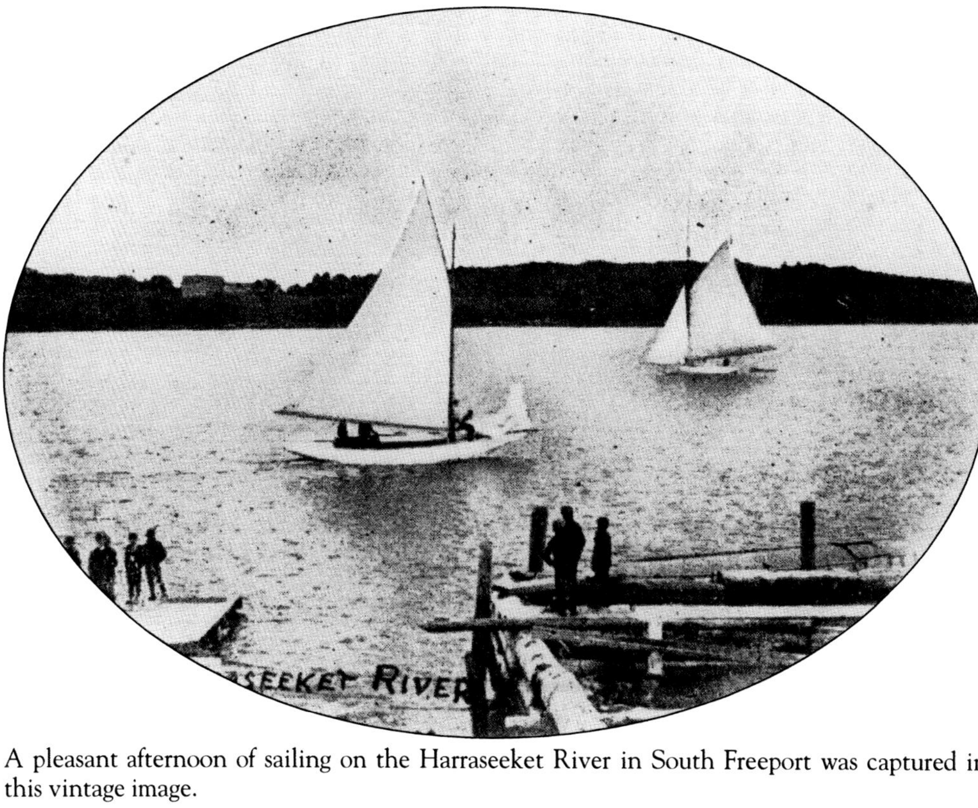

A pleasant afternoon of sailing on the Harraseeket River in South Freeport was captured in this vintage image.

Eight

Transportation

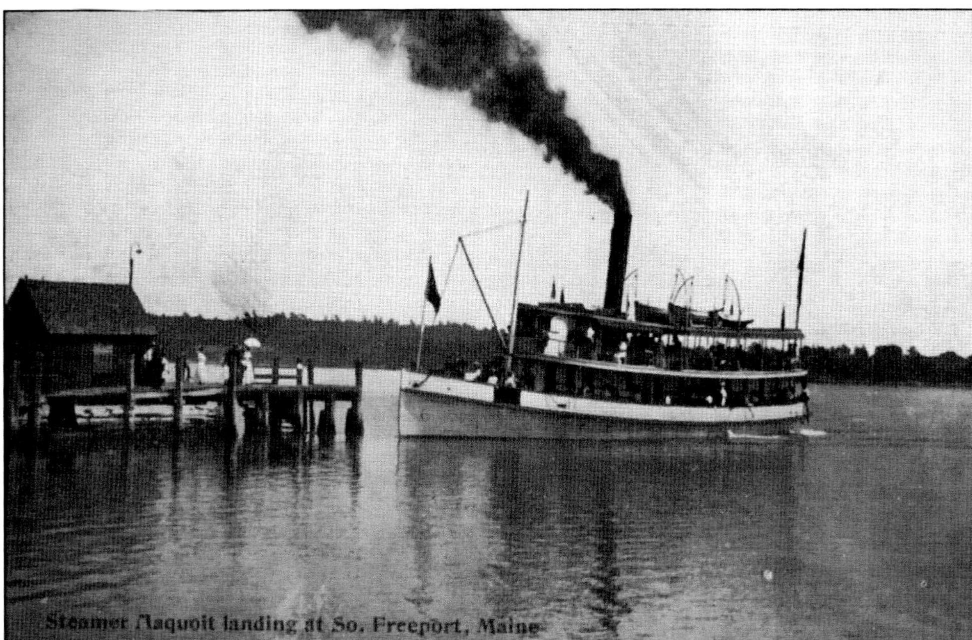

Packets and later small steamers linked the villages of Freeport with Portland and other Casco Bay communities during the nineteenth and early twentieth centuries, particularly as summer colonies began to blossom along the shore. The first coastal steamers ran in Maine in the 1820s. Captain Robert S. Soule ran a packet to Portland from Porter's Landing prior to 1842. Here, the steamer *Maquoit* lands at South Freeport.

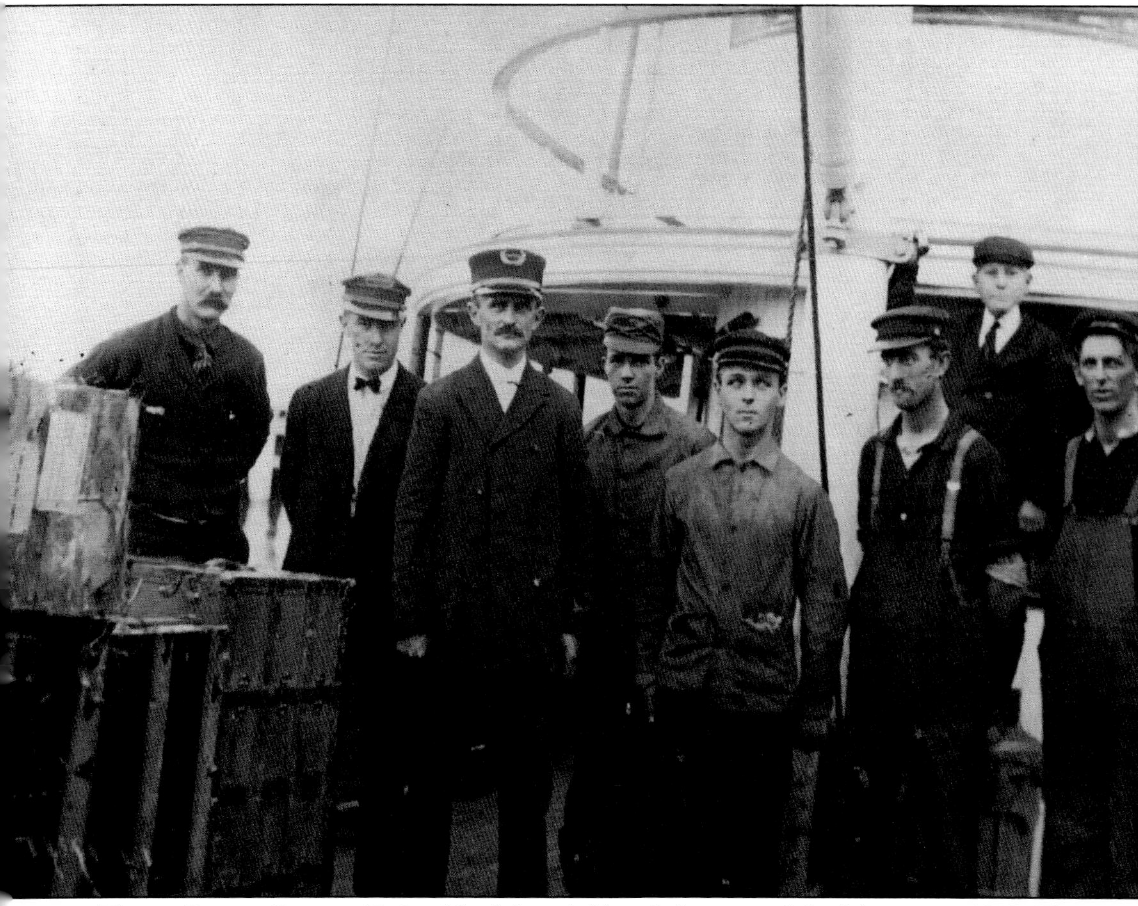

This is Captain Prescott Taylor (third from left) and the crew of the *Maquoit*, c. 1910. The *Maquoit* was built in South Bristol, Maine, and was 85 feet long and 20 feet wide.

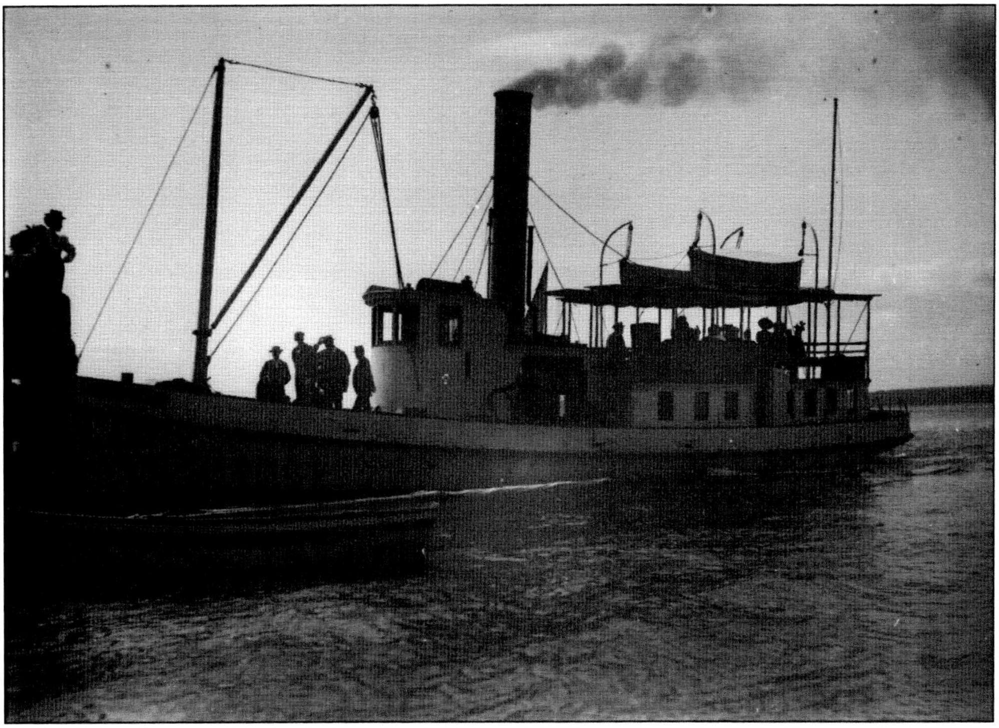

The steamer *Phantom*, shown landing at Bustins Island, was one of two steamers (the other being the *Alice*) that provided transport among the islands in Casco Bay. The *Phantom* left Porter's Landing at 6:50 am for Portland and left Portland at 3 pm for the return trip. The fare for the round trip was 60¢.

Freeport · Steamboat · Co.,

TIME TABLE FOR 1894.

COMMENCING JUNE 25.

Will leave:	A. M.	P. M.
Mere Point,	5 45	1.30
Bustins Island,	6.05	1.50
Freeport,	6.20	2.05
Wolf Point,	6.30	2.10
Chebeague,	7.00	2.40
Littlejohns,	7.05	2.45
Cousins, Island,	7.10	2.50
Falmouth,	7.35	3.10
Arrive at Portland,	8.25	3.50
RETURNING.		
Leave Portland,	A. M.	P. M.
Portland,	9.25	5.10
Falmouth,	10.00	5.40
Cousins Island,	10.25	6.10
Littlejohns,	10.30	6.15
Chebeague,	10.40	6.20
Wolf Point,	11.05	6.55
Freeport,	11.10	7.00
Bustins Island,	11.25	7.15
Arrive at Mere Point,	12 00	7.45

Will leave Freeport at 6.25 A. M. and 2 05 P. M for Bustins' Island to land passengers only.

Wednesday night and Thursday morning Boat will not run to or from Mere Point.

SUNDAY TIME TABLE.

Will leave Freeport for Great Chebeague, Littlejohn's Cousin's Peaks, and Portland at 8 30 a m. Leave Portland for Cousin's and Littlejohn's at 11.00 a. m., returning leaving Littlejohn's at 4 p. m. Leaving Portland for Freeport and above landings at 5.15. Will not make the trip in stormy weather. All Time Tables subject to change without notice.

H. B. SOULE, Manager.

MERE POINT HOUSE,

One of the most delightful Seaside resorts in Casco Bay, with country and seaside combined; good bathing, boating, fishing and pleasant drives; just the place to spend your vacation. House newly furnished and conducted in first-class manner.

Steamers to Portland and Teams to Brunswick.

Terms $4 to $7 per week.

Fish Dinners at short notice.

MRS. E. J. STETSON.

Take Steamer Phantom

FOR

MELROSE HOUSE,

LITTLEJOHN'S ISLAND.

If you want to spend a pleasant vacation or a day's outing you will find this a most delightful place.

SPECIAL FISH DINNERS

Served on Saturdays.

Mine Host, Captain Amos Cummings will always be found on deck and glad to see old friends and make new ones.

The Freeport Steamboat Company timetable for summer 1894 shows the *Phantom* running from Mere Point in Brunswick to Bustins Island, Freeport (Porter's Landing), Wolfe Point, Chebeague, Littlejohn and Cousins Island, Falmouth, Portland, and return.

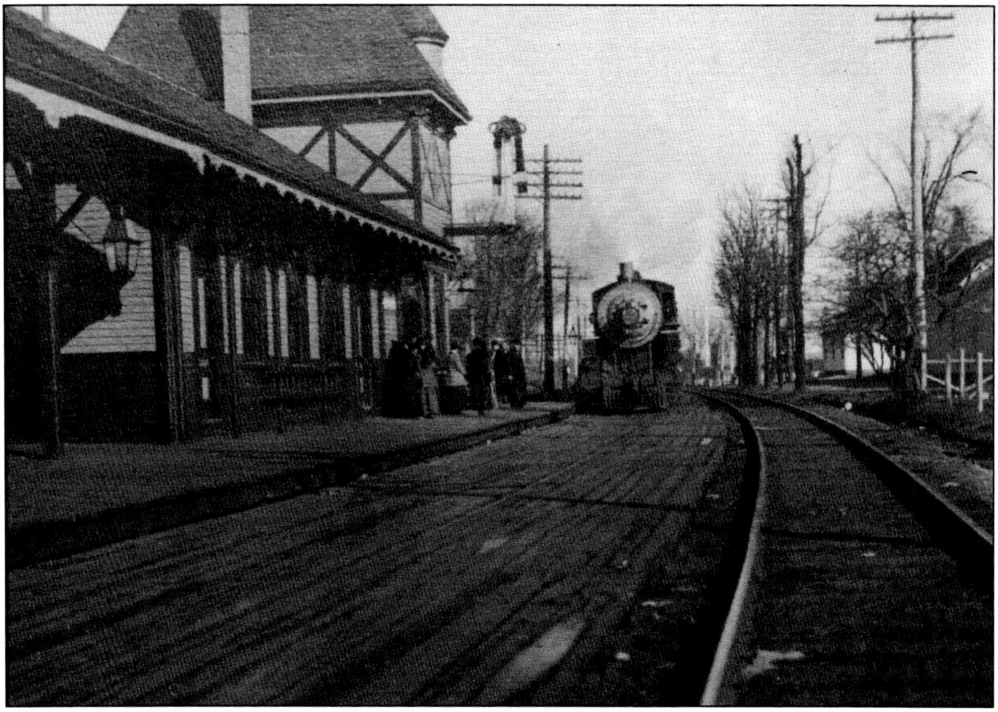

The Kennebec and Portland Railroad (later absorbed by the Maine Central) was extended from Yarmouth to Brunswick via Freeport in 1849. The railroad vitalized Freeport Center linking it to places in Maine and beyond. A 1904 report of rail exports from Freeport included shipments of hay, apples, lumber, shingles, shoes, and Christmas trees. Here, the train is pulling into the first station built near Bow Street. This station burned in 1910.

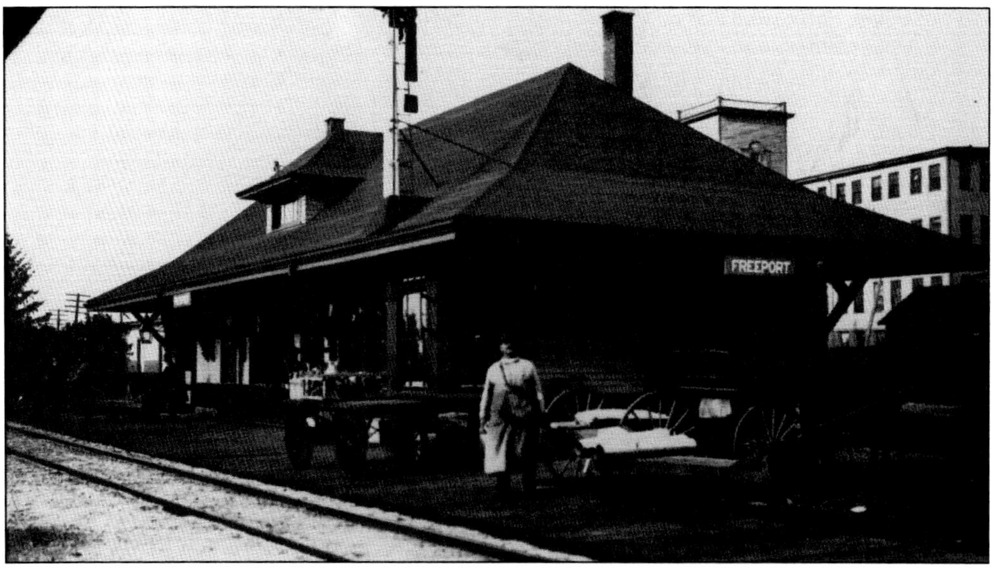

The second Freeport train station, shown in this *c.* 1920 photograph, was built in 1911 and served Freeport until passenger service was discontinued in 1960. In 1964 it was bought by the Boothbay Railway Museum and moved to the museum grounds in Boothbay Harbor. The shoe factory with its tower built by E.B. Mallet is in the background.

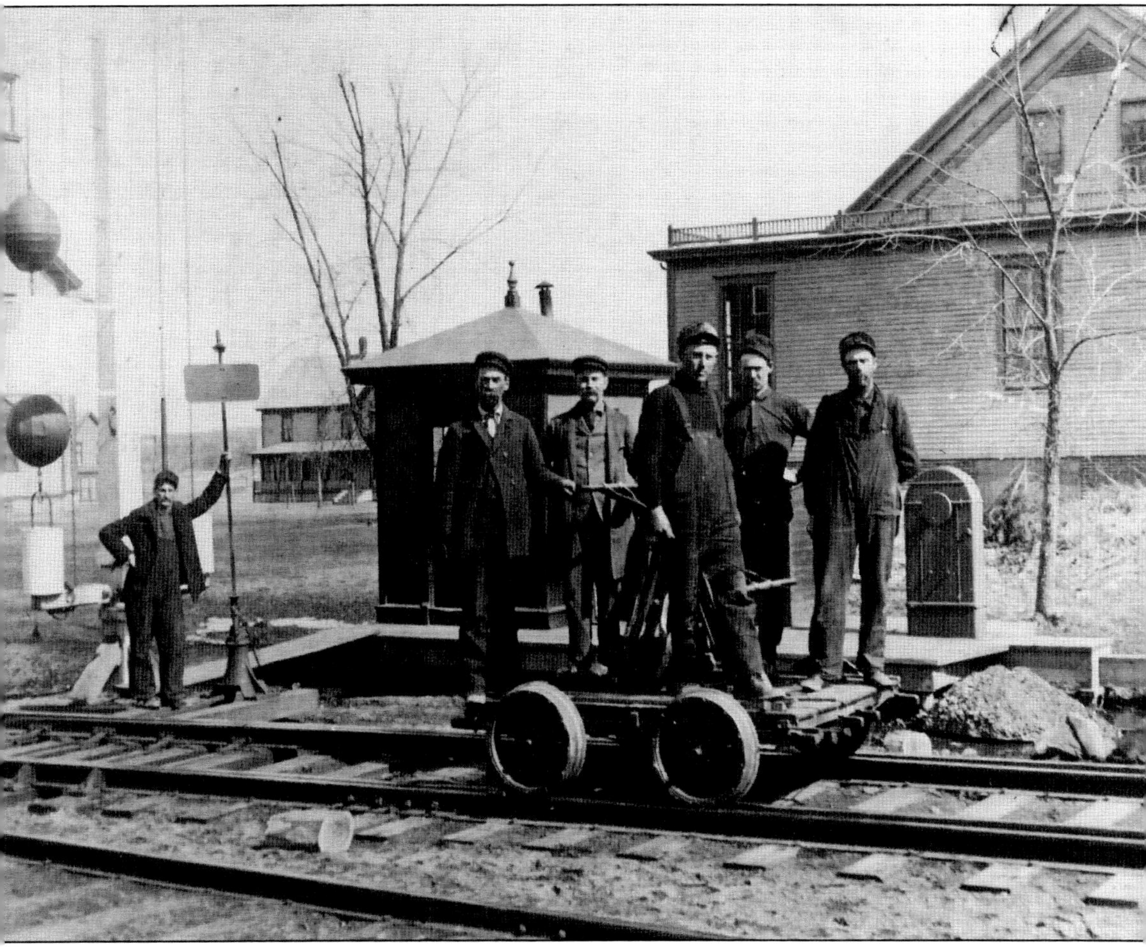

The section crew poses on a handcar near the Bow Street intersection beside the track signals. Members of the crew, from left to right, are as follows: Al Powers, Augustus DeRosier, Ed Curtis, Frank Pettengill, Joe Doucette, and Oscar Brewer.

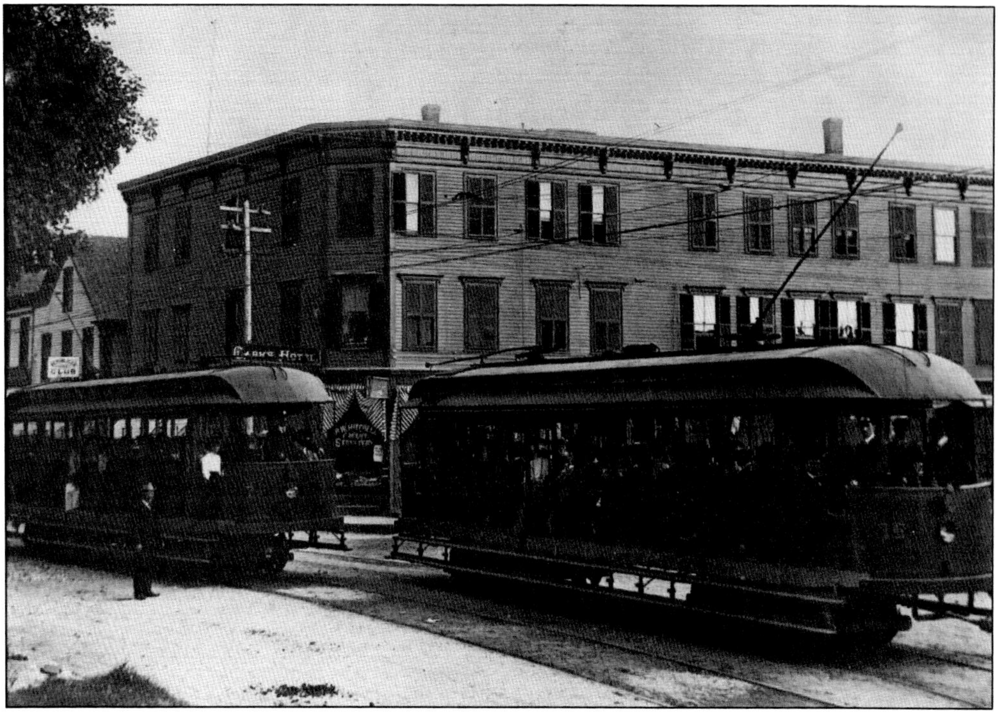

Electric railway lines began to proliferate in Maine in the late nineteenth and early twentieth centuries. In 1902, Amos Gerald, "The Electric Railway King," brought the electric railway to Freeport, providing another link to the outside world. Here two trolleys pass through Freeport Square in front of Clark's Hotel.

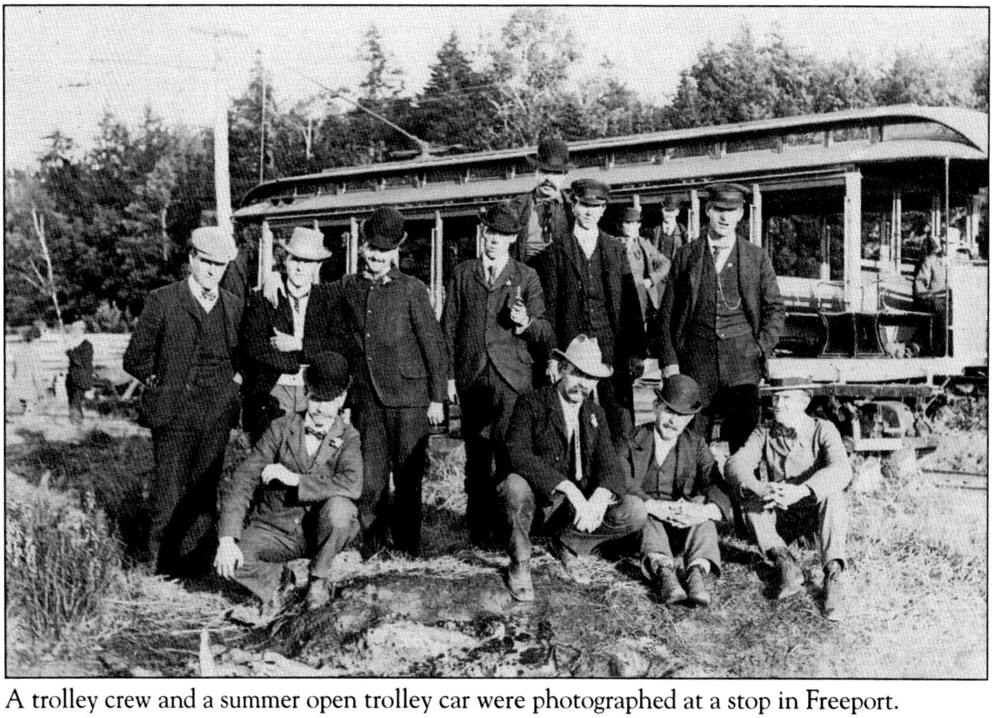

A trolley crew and a summer open trolley car were photographed at a stop in Freeport.

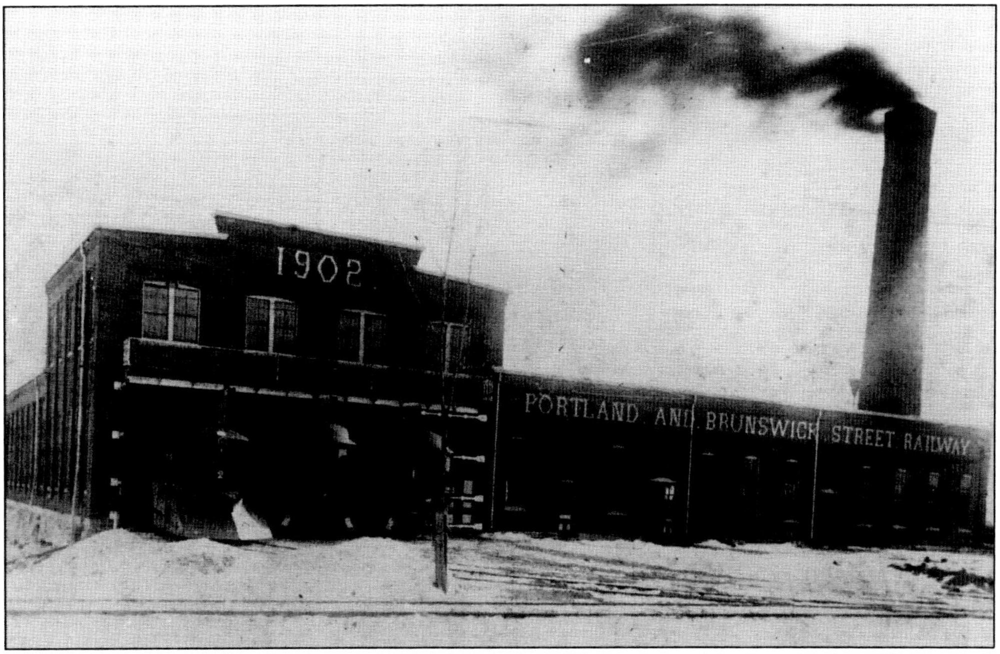

This power house and car barn was built by Amos Gerald's company, The Portland and Brunswick Street Railway. By 1939 when automobiles had become common, the building became the Car Barn Garage. It later housed the Freeport Municipal offices, before being replaced by a new building in 1994.

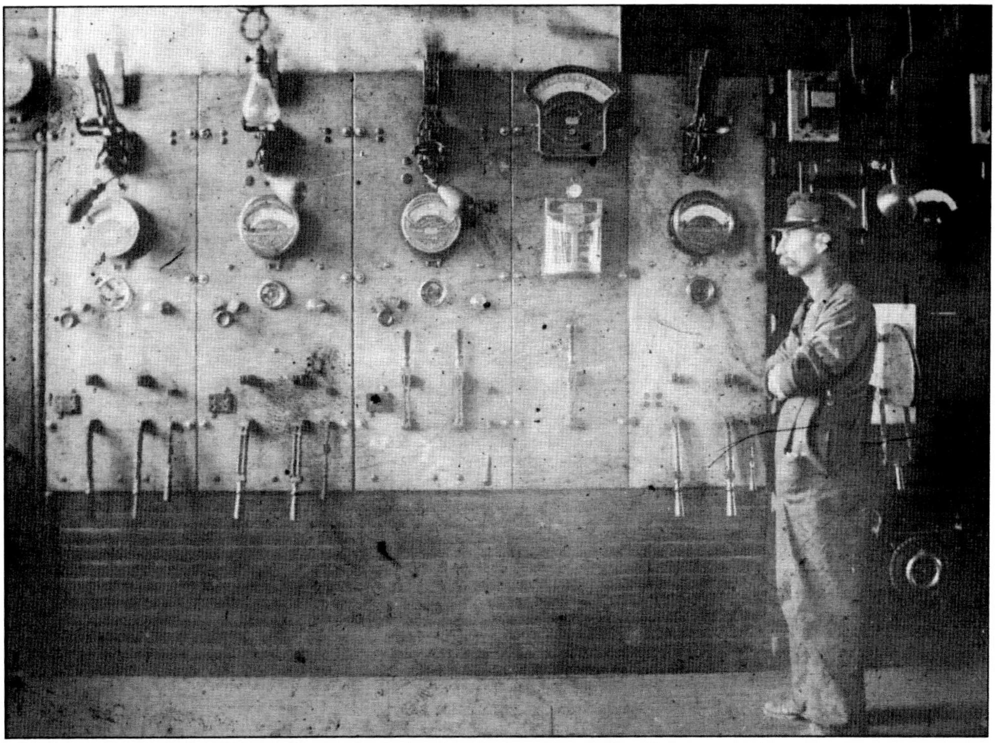

Here, engineer John Stowell watches the gauges in the old trolley power house.

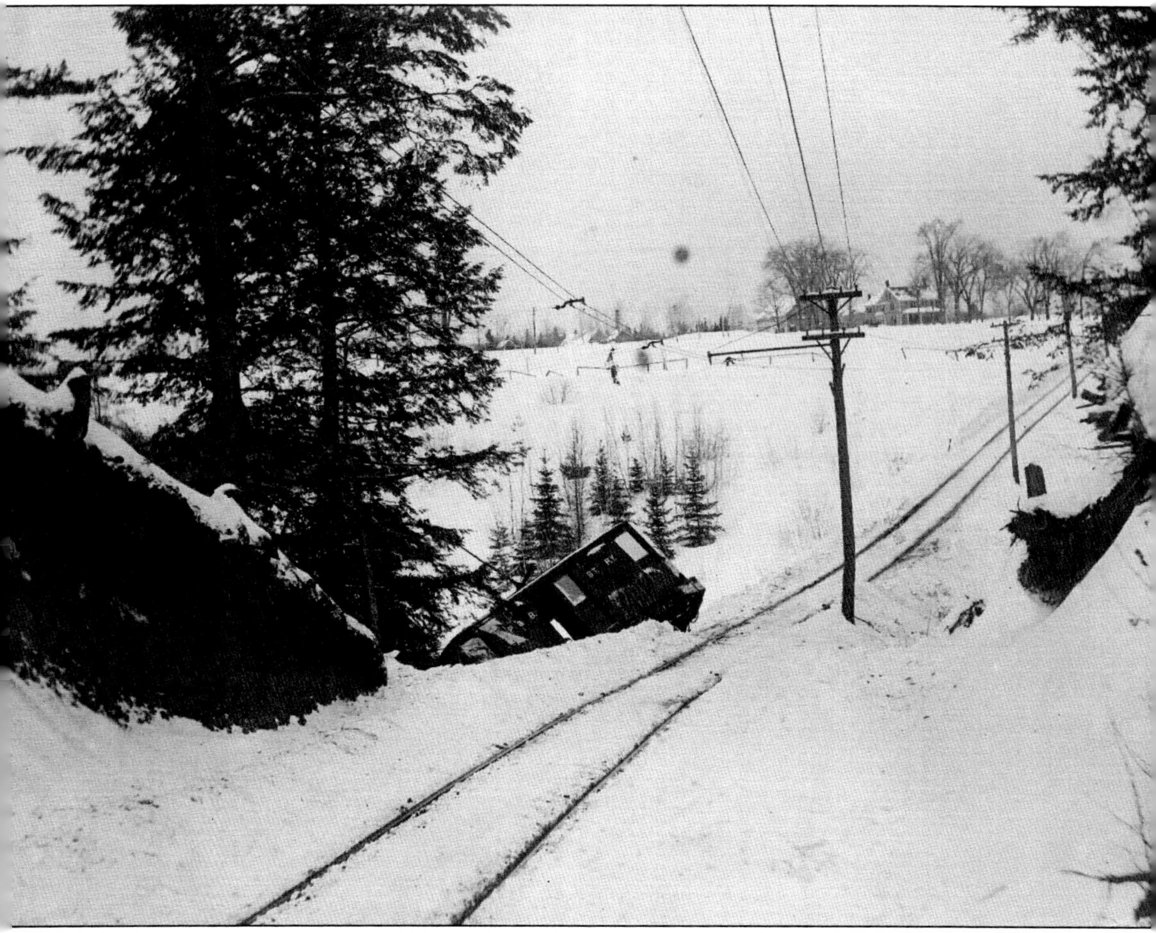

Trolleys, like cars today, could be defeated by ice and snow. This trolley lies in a drift having fallen off the track on the hill below Route 1. E.B. Mallet's house is in the background at the corner of Hunter Road.

Nine

Then and Now

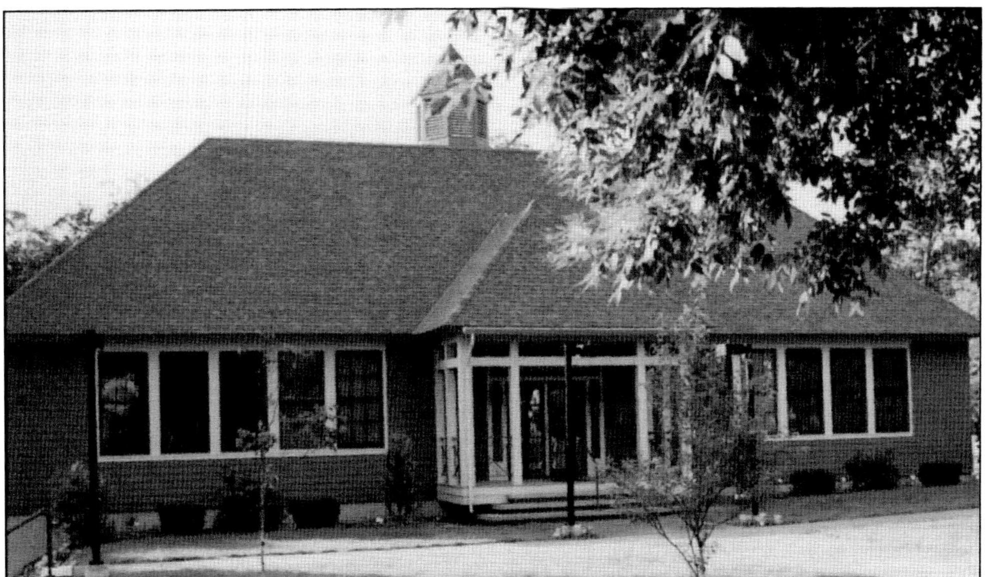

Present-day Freeport has retained many of its historic structures by finding new uses for them. The Freeport Town Hall now occupies the former Grove Street School built in 1894 on land sold to the town. By 1929, when the school could no longer accommodate the growing student population, the building was cut lengthwise and a central section was added to provide additional classroom space. Grove Street School closed its doors in 1983 and opened as the town hall in 1988.

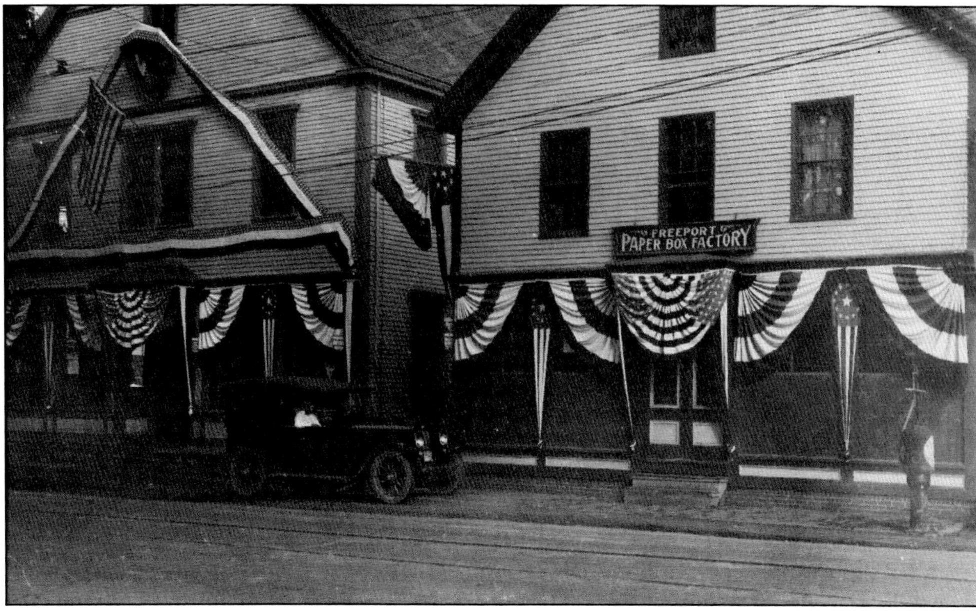

The building on the right, decorated for the centennial celebration in 1920, is the Knights of Pythias Hall on Main Street, built in 1888. The building, at one time home of the Freeport Grange, always used the first floor for commercial space. Today it is the home of Cole-Haan and its appearance has changed little over the years.

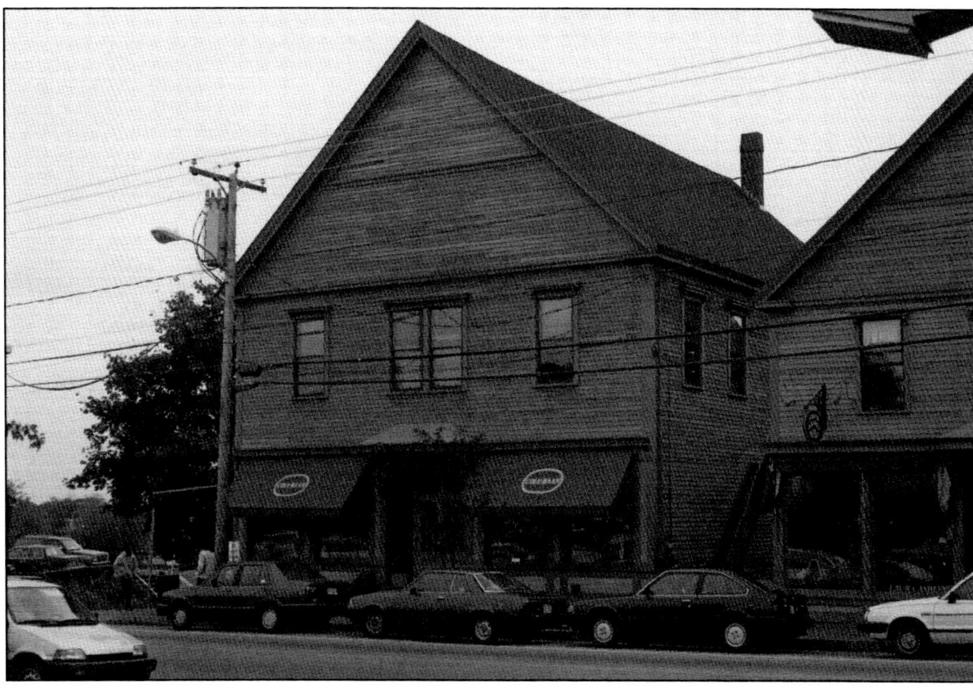

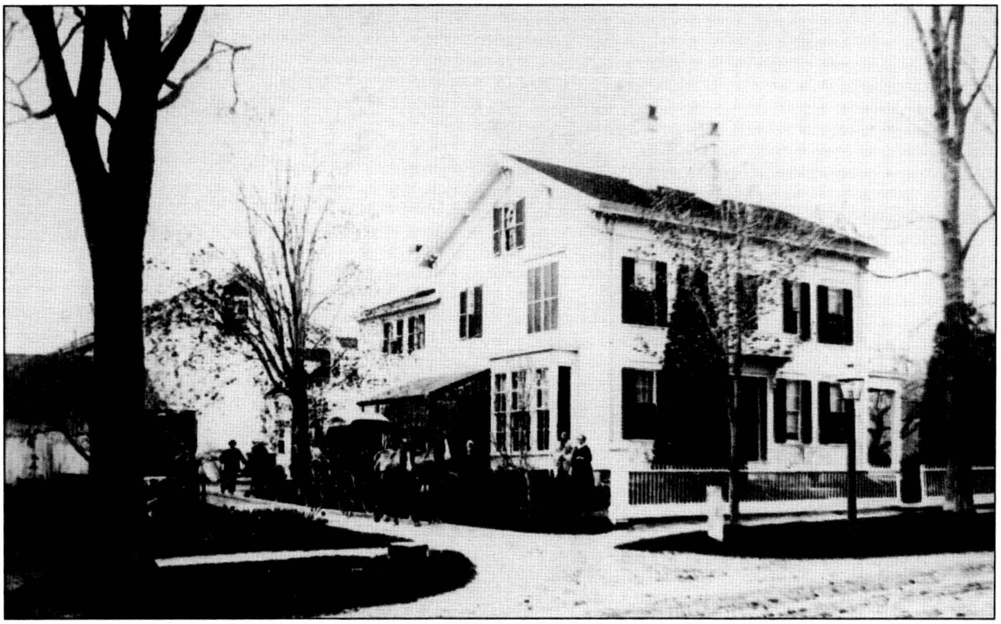

Citizens in Freeport were angry when the McDonald's Corporation bought the Gore house on the corner of Mallett Drive and Main Streets in 1983. The dwelling, a mixture of Greek Revival and Italianate architecture, was built c.1850 by William Gore, a prominent Freeport merchant. The McDonald's Corporation eventually compromised, and the building was renovated to retain much of its original character, a restaurant without the typical golden arches. The historical and architectural compatibility of the new with the old is shown in these two photographs.

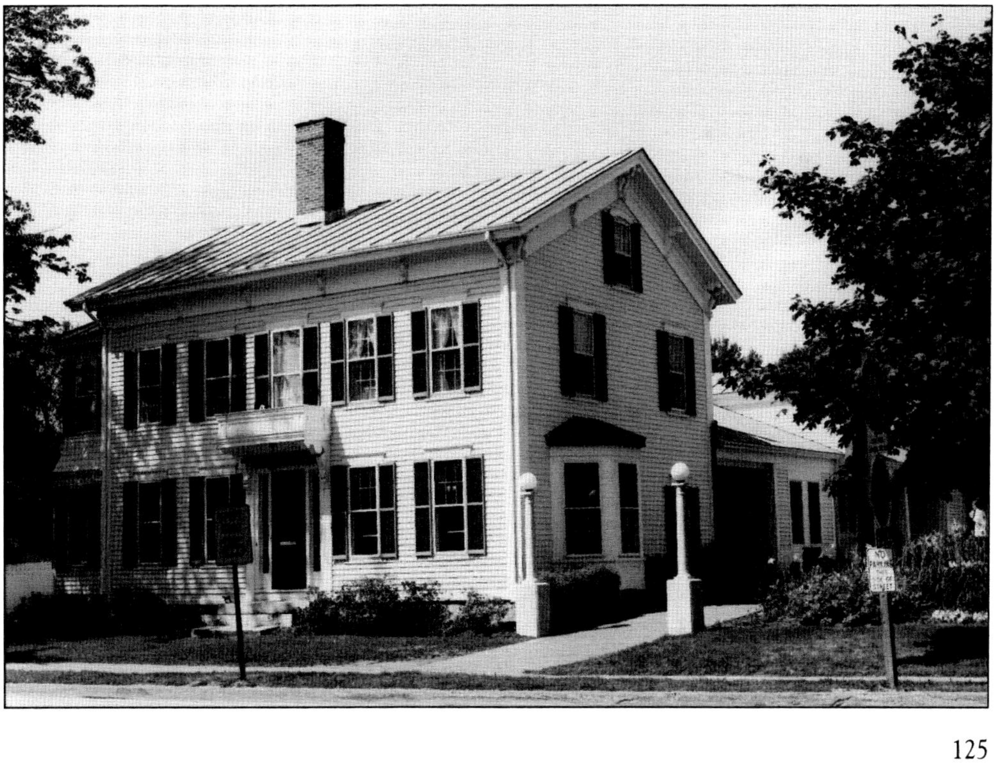

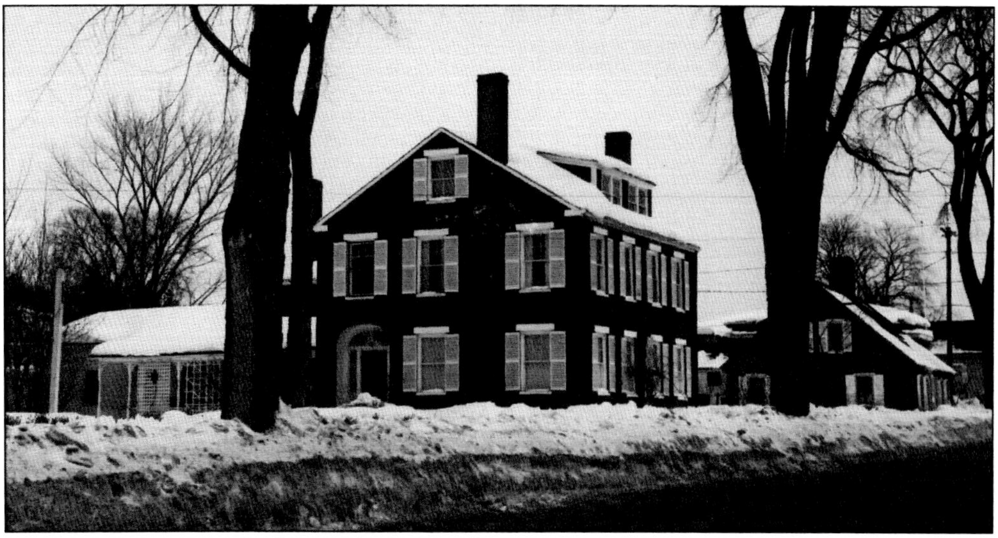

Harrington House was built in 1830 by Enoch Harrington, a Freeport merchant and trader, for his bride Eliza. This handsome transitional Greek Revival building, constructed with locally made brick, was once part of a 14-acre site with extensive gardens and orchards. After Eliza died in 1900, it became the home of Levi and Nettie Patterson and during this period the second floor and attic rooms were rented out to shoe factory workers. The third owner was artist Helen Randall, who used the ell as her studio and lived in the house when the above photograph was taken. After she died in 1976, the house became the property of the Freeport Historical Society and extensive renovations took place. Today, Harrington House (shown below) is the home of the society's offices, museum, archives, and the Harrington House Museum Store. With its beautiful brick facade and gardens, the house is an oasis in what is now a busy commercial district.

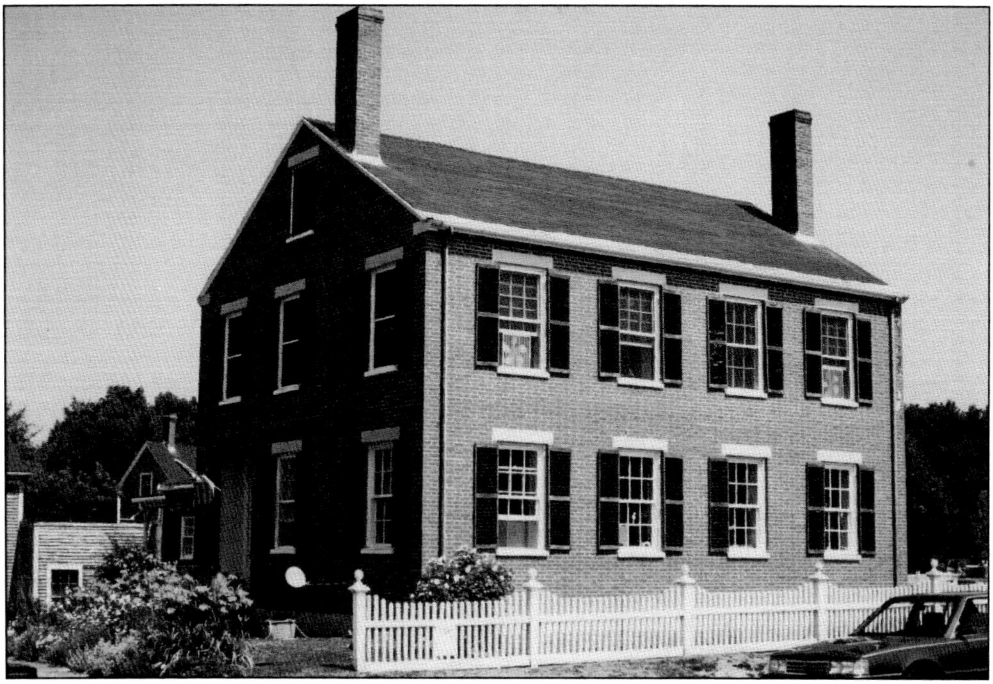

Acknowledgments

A number of individuals have been generous with photographs, time, and help. We are indebted to those individuals who have given their extensive photograph collections to the Freeport Historical Society so that the photographs may be preserved and protected for future generations. That list includes the late Clifford "Mel" Collins, E.P. Skillin, Mildred Stowell Coffin, Ray Lydston, Raymond Thomas, Paul Powers, as well as many others. We also wish to acknowledge the late Win Stowell for his care of the Freeport Historical Society archives and photographs. Other photographs borrowed for use in this book have come from anonymous sources, the Maine Historic Preservation Commission, Sam and Kathy Smith, Dennis Welsh, and the Bustins Island Historical Society.

Our loyal volunteers Nicole Carter, Gail Griffin, Thelma Sommers, Carla Skiffington, and Stella Stowell are acknowledged for their help in identifying and dating the photographs included in this book. The director of the Freeport Historical Society, Anne G. Ball, saw this book as a possibility. Hannah Ostrye, assistant to the director, was project coordinator and together with Sally W. Rand, Patricia Anderson, Connie Santomenna, and Shana Goodall brought this book to completion.

Bibliography

Part of the pleasure in adding to the chronicle of Freeport's history is acknowledging the written work of the past. The only published history is *Three Centuries of Freeport, Maine* by Florence G. Thurston and Harmon S. Cross, published in 1940. Other important works, many in unpublished manuscript form, are:

Anderson, Patricia, ed. *Main Street Walking Tours*. Freeport: Freeport Historical Society, 1993 and 1994.

Bangor (Maine) Industrial Journal. March 18, 1887 and May 6, 1887, articles on Freeport industry.

Dunning, Thurlow. *Genealogical Records of Freeport Families*.

Freeport Historical Society Sesquicentennial Committee. *Freeport Yesterdays*. Freeport, Maine: Freeport Historical Society, 1970.

Harraseeket Historic District. National Register of Historic Places nomination, 1974.

Haskell, Owen. *Church Spires and Ships' Masts, South Freeport*. 1970.

Jacobson, Bruce; Joel Eastman; and Anne Bridges. *Tides of Change*. Freeport: Freeport Historical Society, 1985.

Lowe, Vicki; Sally W. Rand; and Mary Eliza Wengren. *Architectural Survey of Freeport, Maine*. Augusta, Maine: Maine Historic Preservation Commission, 1977.

Main Street Historic District. National Register of Historic Places nomination, 1977.

Richardson, George B. *History of Bustins Island, Casco Bay 1660–1960*. Bustins Island (Freeport), Maine, 1960.

Six Town Times. Transcribed by Carolyn Kitchin for the Freeport Historical Society.

Talbot, Louisa. *South Freeport Notes*. c. 1970.

Vertical files from Freeport Historical Society archives.

White, Marian M. *Freeport Bicentennial Celebration, Harbor Village Walk*. 1989.

Wiley, Sarah, ed. *Freeport Bicentennial Commemorative Journal*. Freeport, Maine: Village Press, 1989.